CROSSING CLASS
THE INVISIBLE WALL

WISING UP ANTHOLOGIES

ILLNESS & GRACE: TERROR & TRANSFORMATION

FAMILIES: *The Frontline of Pluralism*

LOVE AFTER 70

DOUBLE LIVES, REINVENTION & THOSE WE LEAVE BEHIND

VIEW FROM THE BED: VIEW FROM THE BEDSIDE

SHIFTING BALANCE SHEETS:
Women's Stories of Naturalized Citizenship & Cultural Attachment

COMPLEX ALLEGIANCES:
Constellations of Immigration, Citizenship, & Belonging

DARING TO REPAIR: *What Is It, Who Does It & Why?*

CONNECTED: *What Remains As We All Change*

CREATIVITY & CONSTRAINT

SIBLINGS: *Our First Macrocosm*

THE KINDNESS OF STRANGERS

SURPRISED BY JOY

CROSSING CLASS
THE INVISIBLE WALL

Charles D. Brockett & Heather Tosteson
Editors

Wising Up Press

Wising Up Press
P.O. Box 2122
Decatur, GA 30031-2122
www.universaltable.org

Catalogue-in-Publication data is on file with the Library of Congress.
LCCN: 2018955382

Wising Up ISBN: 978-1-7324514-1-4

DEDICATION

To the gymnasts of class—
those who climb,
those who tumble,
those who do the heavy lifting
with an open heart

CONTENTS

III. CROSSING: ACTS OF IMAGINATION

IV. ADVOCACY: WHAT WE FIGHT FOR

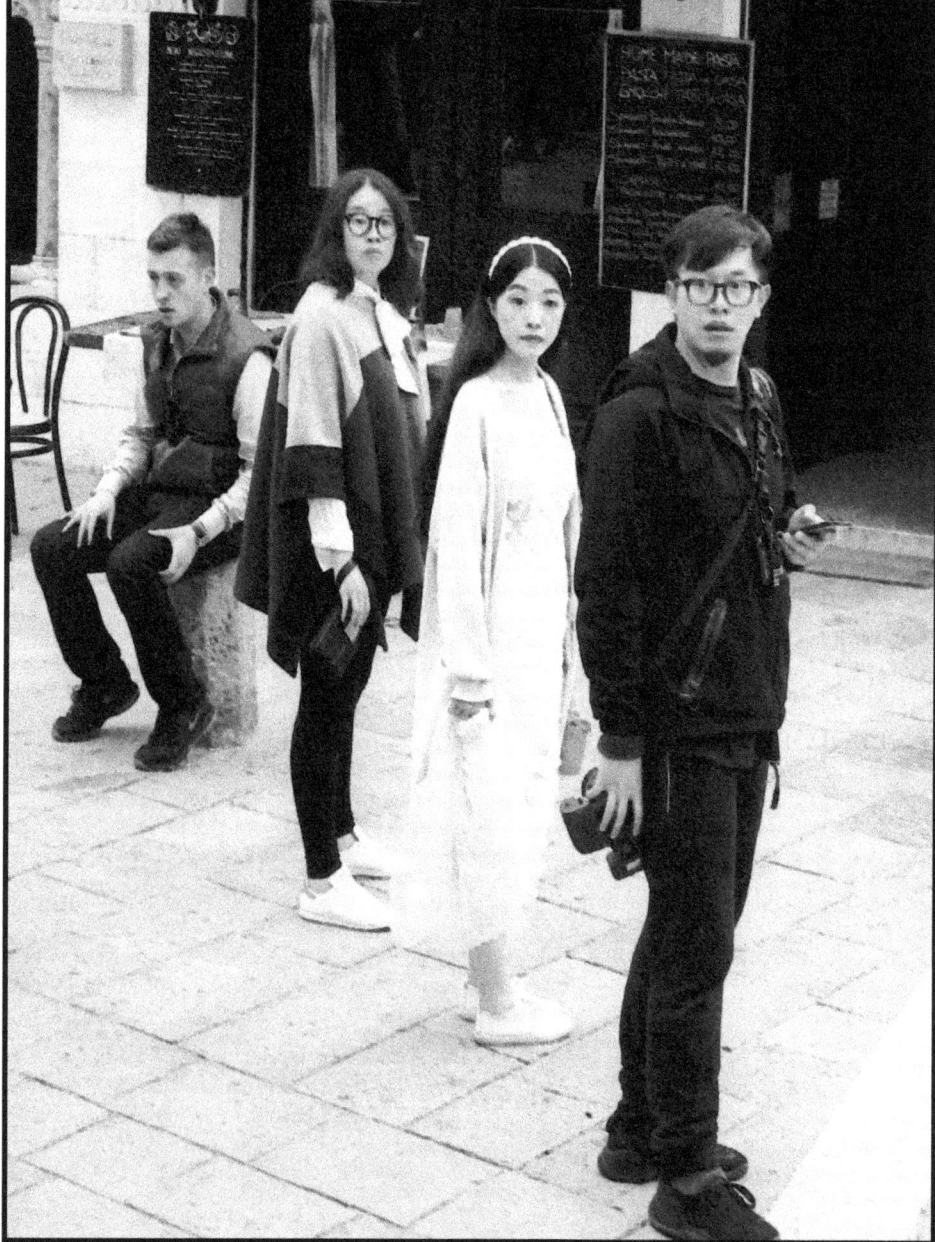

HEATHER TOSTESON

INTRODUCTION

CROSSING CLASS: THE INVISIBLE WALL

For our press, dedicated to Finding the We in Them, the Us in You, class is the biggest elephant in the room. We keep wanting to talk about it and have tried unsuccessfully several times to create an anthology exploring the subject, but the interest wasn't there. However, this year was different. Numerous writers responded. How we are all shaped, individually and as a country, by class and by other potent, often polarizing, categorizations as well, may be a question that is more alive to us now than at other less socially tumultuous times.

A remarkable number of Americans, around 70% in some surveys, consider themselves middle class, although perhaps only 50% would actually meet the economic criteria. This identification with the middle class reflects a strong belief that the United States is a meritocracy, that with hard work we can all get ahead. This remains true despite the rapidly increasing inequality of income and wealth in our country and a rate of social mobility that is actually less than that in many other developed countries (see Appendix on social mobility and inequality). In contrast, 60% of Britons identify as working class when only 25% of them are actually engaged in manual labor and express doubt about the possibility of social mobility even when they have experienced it themselves.

But what we have asked people to think about and write about is not class in the abstract, rather the felt experience of it, which is, whether imagined or real, always personal and narrative.

This is the call we ran for this anthology.

CROSSING CLASS: THE INVISIBLE WALL
CLASS: It's the great unspeakable in a society dedicated to the proposition

that all people are created equal, with inalienable rights to life, liberty, and the pursuit of happiness, and that believes in the redistributive power of personal ambition, hard work, self-intention and self-definition. It might be the most powerful and intractable of social divisions, its effects potent even within culture, race, or gender. Whether we buy in consciously or not, we are all subject to the shaping power of class.

But what exactly does it mean to be shaped by class? How does this shaping affect what we long for, strive for, believe is possible—not just for us but for those around us and the world at large? We are interested in what happens to our understanding of class, of our society and of ourselves, when we cross class boundaries upwards or downwards, willingly or unwillingly, through education, employment, marriage, divorce, friendships and other meaningful relationships, immigration or emigration, illness, economic or political upheaval. How does our experience of class mobility, wanted or unwanted, change our understanding of ourselves, our social relationships, our sense of social agency, our sense of our society? How does it change our understanding of the possibilities and challenges of living out E Pluribus Unum?

We hope you read the stories, memoirs, and poetry here with these questions resonating in mind, resonating with your own personal experience too. As we have read and selected the pieces that make up this book, I've found different scenes from my own life flashing up as well, in both agreement and counterpoise. I've decided to focus on them here because it feels to me the most trustworthy way to ground my own thoughts on class.

✕ ✕ ✕

"Every time we come here, I feel I am betraying my people," my sixteen-year-old son said, looking out at the large white sprawling country club in Chestnut Hill where we had come to have dinner with my father and his second family.

"You are," I told him. "I'm glad you realize it."

I said this as a striving artist, a working single mom. When we had moved to the Boston area the year before, it was because I was offered a job that would support us and get us out of Mexico where my own poor judgment had sent us. Proximity to my father, who had become more wealth and status-oriented as he aged, and whose children from his second marriage, the same age as my son, had been raised with a very different level of material wealth and a very different sense of entitlement, was actually a concern to me, not an enticement. I wanted to protect my son from the values this large white building, with its history of restricting its membership to white Christian men, represented. These were certainly not the values I had been raised with, nor the values I lived by, nor the ones I was raising my son to respect. I was relieved to see my son could protect himself.

I had purposefully chosen to live in Watertown, a working community with a high immigrant population, primarily Armenian, partly because of its fantastic fruit and vegetable markets and its complex multicultural vibe, but mostly because it had a high school with an independent school imbedded in it and an enlightened policy to assure its students graduated. They would create an individualized course of study for any student in danger of dropping out. My son, very bright but dyslexic, was increasingly frustrated with school, and I welcomed that assurance.

Within a year, we had invoked that dropout clause, allowing my son to take college level art and writing classes at local universities and to have his other classes through the independent school. He also worked as a host at a pizza parlor in Harvard Square on weekends, a job he got with the help of two resourceful young Armenians he met through his evening art classes, aspiring artists in their twenties, who had been on their own since the age of fifteen. They fostered his drive for self-sufficiency. They taught him how to dress, all the expectations of the job. They taught him how artists pay their rent.

So when my son talked about "my people," these two young men were part of his personal class structure. So was the young African-American cook at the restaurant who confided in him that he would like to be a host, but that he knew that was never going to happen.

"Why does he think that?" my son asked me. "I keep telling him, if I can do it, why can't you?" He would brood on this at night when he came back from work. "I bet his family's income is no different from ours," he said. "So, it's not money. I don't think its that he's black either. There are black waiters there."

He looked around our flat, all the pillows we used for sitting, the raw boards and bricks we still used as bookcases, the used novels and poetry books from my doctoral program that he was reading his way through for the pleasure of it. "These *create* something," he said. "You don't notice it, but there is this set of shared references you're kind of born into. I mean you learn them, but not consciously, so if someone says something, you know what it means, you're in a kind of club. You don't have to go to school to get it, you can get it from home, but it gives you possibilities. People make assumptions based on it. That's what he's missing—that sense of possibility."

We don't really recognize class, its force, its raw reality, unless or until we ourselves try to cross it. Then it can feel like slamming into a glass ceiling or being enveloped in a cloud of hungry no-see-ems. *Very very real.* Humblingly so. *Infuriatingly* so. Irrefutably so if you knew what *I* know.

✗   ✗   ✗

My wife thinks I have an obsession with social class. So I guess I have an obsession with social class. It probably stems from feeling like an outcast.
James Gray

When I step back and think of the different events in my early life when I first became aware of class, especially as a child, rather than a wall, what comes back to me is a sense of vertigo, of being in the grip of baffling unseen forces. Forces that had everything to do with belonging, with the dynamics of exclusion and inclusion, above all with a deep, desperate confusion at the constantly changing terms that set these forces in motion.

I didn't grow up with a sense of social inferiority, just of outsiderness, due in large part to the frequent moves of my professionally ambitious parents. Their class status, as physicians and academics, was independent of any of the places they set their children down to live for the duration of their internships or post-docs. But we, going to public schools, encountered all kinds of social stratification that we had no names for. It was my keen awareness of the discomfort of that outsiderness that determined my relationship *to* those stratifications. I knew what it felt like to be left out. I knew what it felt like not to know why.

In England, where I started school, I was sent to the local grammar school (equivalent to a public school in the States). My older sister was sent to a public school (a private school in the States) so she wouldn't be demoted for not knowing how to calculate in pounds, shillings and pence. Two events that year baffled me. The first was why my very own family roared with laughter at the Christmas pageant when I, a proud, mothering angel, sang, "I will rock you," to a little baby Jesus. The reason? I had picked up a 'low' Cambridge accent, sounding like a guttersnipe in the chorus of *Oliver*. Where once I had felt proud, for I was finally talking like everyone around me, I now felt scourged by shame.

The second incident was more confusing for me and began the intertwining of race and class that has been part of my experience of both. I had two friends at school and invited them both to my seventh birthday party. But my depressed and over-worked mother insisted I disinvite one of the girls. She had said one. "But they both wanted to come," I told her. I was, of course, *most* afraid of my mother, so went back to school the next day and obediently disinvited one of the girls.

Soon I was called in the headmistress's office. She wanted to know why I had excluded this little girl. I explained that my mother made me because I could only have one guest and I chose to disinvite the second because that was where I made my mistake. I can still feel the quality of the headmistress's attention, my shame, my sense of being caught between my two most powerful fears—my mother's anger, my teacher's disapproval. Now, looking back, I realize the reason she queried me so closely was that the second girl was the child of a black U.S. GI and an Englishwoman—something that had had no relevance in my mother's objection but certainly added to the other little girl's pain.

"It was *unkind*," the headmistress said at last, dismissing me. That word, *unkind*, had decisive shaping power for me, because it so contradicted my own motivation. In my desire to include I had excluded in a way (I could tell this by the quality of the headmistress's attention) that was important and bad but that I still didn't understand, therefore couldn't avoid in the future—something far more important than using first and second as a selection criteria.

⚒   ⚒   ⚒

The enfolding of race and class became even more confusing when we moved to the south when I was in sixth grade. Our first year we lived in Durham, North Carolina, in an old mansion scheduled for demolition, two blocks up from a large tobacco factory surrounded by mill housing. We had to show up in person to register at the public elementary school because they needed to verify the color of our skin. The social division in this classroom was between the mill children and the children of academics who lived in nearby suburbs. The mill children did not like the children of academics, particularly if those children lived in decaying mansions they had to pass on their way to and from school. I still remember cowering in my room as an aggressive older girl, fourteen to my eleven, stood on my lawn with a group of her friends and called me, among other things, a teacher's pet. It's true, my teacher *had* held her after class to give me a running start.

Our real challenge came the following year when our parents moved us out to a newly built house in the countryside between Durham and Chapel Hill. This was in the early 1960s, the height of the civil rights movement. Our parents told us that we believed in integration and that we were forbidden to enter any segregated store or restaurant. My brother, two years younger, very outspoken, and clueless, got on our bus the first day and promptly announced loudly to all the poor white farmers' children being bussed with us into Chapel Hill that we were *integrationists*. Other than my friend in England, I had personally never known or played with a child who was black. We didn't have a television, so we had no images, no social context for this word *integrationist* except the importance our parents gave it. It certainly meant something different to the boys on the bus, who promptly beat my brother up and taunted us all for being "goddamn nigger lovers."

This indeed become part of our identity. The daily torment we endured inspired my younger sister to write her first and only book, *The Bus*. For years just the sight of a yellow school bus on a country road at dawn would make me nauseated. But the self-satisfaction of those young bullies determined where, when push came to shove, I stood. *Against* them. It had everything to do with the color of *their* skin, *their* accents, *their* fields, and *their* farmhouses. The significance of the gifted classes at school was that *they* weren't in them.

But those classes were filled with another danger. Southern girls. The disdain of those prim girls, the well-bred children of southern academics, with their white bobby socks, their unscratched legs, their hair that stayed in place, their *I swanee's* and *y'all's* was equally puzzling, if less physically threatening. They didn't dislike me as a white or a northerner or a smart kid, just as someone they hadn't known from first grade who was also so socially untutored that she didn't know no one goes to seventh grade without a bra.

It didn't help that my parents, cocooned in their own professions, tormented by their fracturing marriage, were as oblivious to our social pain as they were to our social aspirations. Indeed they added to the confusion. My father's long-time affair with our au pair had recently been discovered, and my mother, once she returned from the mental hospital, had a habit of drinking and repeating, "I fixed her teeth. *I fixed her teeth.*" When she wasn't saying, "He slept with the *maid*." This was something we couldn't explain to anyone at all because we had no words to describe what she was to us. She was Lillian, she came from Denmark, and she had cared for us like a mother for years. We felt we had lost our anchor.

This level of social confusion may have explained why I, the following summer, with the help of my friend Eric, channeling the furious aggression of those white farmer boys and the disdain of those white Southern girls, tied up a dim self-satisfied little girl, and put her in the hold when she told us, "You have to do what I tell you. This is my boat and my daddy's yacht club." I can't remember now whether she was a Pulitzer, Rockefeller, or Morgan. Every year, we children from the local marine biology lab were sent to the Bar Harbor Yacht Club for sailing classes while our parents worked. Chauffeurs brought children in from the mansions in Bar Harbor. We lab rats were far better at sailing and won the races when we skippered, but they, it was true, owned the boats and shelved the trophies. Dumb, Eric and I kept muttering as we tied square knots around her ankles, bowlines around her wrists. Dumb, dumb, dumb. She couldn't recite the thirty-two points of the compass. She couldn't read the wind. She couldn't set a course, control a jibe. She hadn't read the Narnia books or *Jane Eyre* or *The Island of the Blue Dolphins* or, worse, *Animals Without Backbones*. She didn't know about active transport or how to seine for eels. All she knew was how to squeal. Dumb, dumb, dumb, we said to each other as we tacked back to our mooring. Even now, honestly, I'm not sure I can share her pain.

)(( )(( )((

This feeling of being between worlds continued to confuse—and refine—my class consciousness. When I went to Sarah Lawrence, I arrived with my suitcase knotted together with old clothesline. It had come apart unexpectedly at the airport and my siblings and I had been quite proud of the ingenuity of our emergency repair. But that sense of resourcefulness dissolved as I lugged my bag by a chauffeur standing at attention by a black limousine parked at the door to my dorm. The next year, I married—so spent my last two years in college walking the four or five blocks between my Yonkers apartment building and the campus musing on stories my nextdoor neighbor regaled me with, wondering how they fit with my Shakespeare or Eighteenth Century Novel course. She told me about how the FBI wouldn't let her see the dead body of her boyfriend, an extortionist for the mob; the way her ex-husband had tried to strangle her with a venetian cord. My writing teacher, Grace

Paley, had suggested we find ideas for our stories in the *National Enquirer*, but I didn't think they would have published stories like this. My neighbor wasn't making anything up, nor did she see anything unusual in what she was sharing. Both worlds—the chauffeured and the black market one—felt equally bizarre to me. I didn't understand how the parts fit, what made them run. But they seemed equally important to me, if you wanted to know about life. My neighbor, going to community college, seeing her daughters only on the weekends, was the more ambitious. She obviously saw me as woefully ignorant—and she was right. I also lacked something crucial, something she never questioned, a sense that I fit, that the values that determined my choices were transparent, ubiquitous, common-sense.

✕　✕　✕

My sense of disorientation was not a sense of inferiority. Neither did it lead to a sense of helplessness, especially in the area where there was coherence, academics. But it did mean that any world but that, and the criteria upon which it was built, always felt a little arbitrary and surreal. But to deny the power people gave to these systems and the power these systems gave to them felt perilous as well. It felt very important to try and imagine what these systems, these worlds might *feel* like from the inside. Perhaps that is why, later in my life, I became very interested in cross-cultural and cross-disciplinary work, in particular what made us adept and resilient in these situations. Why I have also loved stories, the *worlds* of stories. Because like those imagined worlds, class is a *system*, all the parts giving and taking meaning from each other.

To understand any system, it is crucial to see where the core value of the system lies. To cross systems, it is also necessary to have a relatively independent inner value system, both compass and spine, in order to stay oriented and hold your own. The values that have helped me cross class without disorientation have stayed remarkably similar over time. I return to this phrase of my son's, *my* people. Not my class, my country, my *people*. That's where I too find a coherence that crosses classes and also unites them.

I have a taste for *good* people. And for the good *in* people.

For those on whom life isn't wasted—who experience it as fascinating, mysterious, intrinsically valuable.

Who know the sound of one hand clapping.

Who like to make, not break, to give *and* take.

Who know that *how* we do what we do matters equally with what we do.

For whom being true isn't a choice but a vital necessity.

Who understand from experience that in our differences, fully acknowledged, lie our similarities.

That is why I have no difficulty putting all the people I care about in the same room assured they will find something of value in each other.

)(   )(   )(

The stress laid on upward social mobility in the United States has tended to obscure the fact that there can be more than one kind of mobility and more than one direction in which it can go. There can be ethical mobility as well as financial, and it can go down as well as up.

Margaret Halsey

A just society is a society that if you knew everything about it, you'd be willing to enter it in a random place.

John Rawls

One of the most damaging dimensions of all the systems we make, particularly social systems, is their capacity to *devalue*. To be human is to categorize and to categorize is to valorize. But no social system is reliable unless it can openly acknowledge the cost of its *de*valuations as fully as it can the benefits of its valorizations.

On one of my rare visits to the university where my husband used to teach, we went to a banquet where we were seated at a table with a Spanish-speaking contingent because of his academic specialty. In the course of the conversation, the wife of one of the deans, a woman of Cuban extraction, was complaining about how people lumped all Latins together. She resented being mistaken for a common immigrant, a peasant from Mexico or Guatemala for example. "Those are simple people," she said. "Why would people expect me to have anything in common with them? No one here, of course, is expected to have friends who are illiterate." She looked around the table, made an eloquent shrug, laughed.

I sat there, ready to retort, then imagined what my friend Alicia's response might be. An equally elegant shrug of her own much much smaller and wiry frame, a small smile. A gentle reminder to me that this woman had her own fears or she wouldn't speak this way. In honor of Alicia, I said nothing. In honor of Alicia, I burned.

What I love about Alicia, who comes to my shoulder, is her self-confidence and her generosity. I first met her because she knocked on my door one morning early in my half-year stay in Antigua, Guatemala. She offered to clean for me as she had for the previous owner and for someone who lived across the street. I don't usually want anyone to clean for me, but there was something about her that fascinated me. Alicia can't read because she went to work in the coffee fields when she was five. But her son now teaches Spanish to Peace Corps volunteers. She has moved her family from a house made of sticks and thatch to a large concrete house they built by hand. She has fed us and taken us up the sheer mountain she climbed daily with a baby on her back to bring her husband Cosme his lunch while he worked his maize fields. She has a wonderfully clear voice, so I quickly made her my Spanish teacher and cultural guide. She introduced me to the many saints borne through the city during Passion Week. She unquestioningly accompanied me on various quixotic artistic quests, welcomed me back unquestioningly every time I returned to Antigua over the years. It makes me wonder, in a good way, what she sees in me. I know I will never be able to match her calm faith and indomitable energy. I wish I could. Since I can't, I find myself, often, channeling her.

What I feel for Alicia is profound respect. For what she has accomplished, for what there is inside her that made her the way she is. It hurts me to imagine that those qualities could be invisible to anyone else, not for her sake but for theirs. Alicia is assured of her own value. I believe she always has been. I don't think there is anyone in the world, or any system, that can take that away from her.

X   X   X

John Rawls, the political philosopher, talks about a just system as one where we are willing to enter at random. To do so, there must be what I call *existential* equality between all the members of the system. Value that can't be received or given, but can be recognized, indeed must be. This existential equality is the essence of the I-Thou relationship, of the Golden Rule, but has pragmatic value as well. No truly stable relationship can exist without it, neither can a just system. One where we are truly willing to take each other's places.

I don't know how easy it is to put this belief into practice. As I am writing, one situation keeps echoing in my mind. When we published our *View from the Bed: View from the Bedside* anthology, we decided to have some discussion groups based on the content. I created a Bedside group and a Bed group. Both groups were made up almost exclusively of African-American friends and professional acquaintances, but there was a real class difference between the two groups. One group were primarily Muslim women I had met through another listening project on religious journeys, all of whom had been involved in increasing health awareness in their community. The other group were health professionals, physicians and psychologists I knew and worked with in public health. My intuition was that the conversations would be freer if we kept the groups distinct, but it turned out that in the interest of time and scheduling, I would need to combine them. One of the physicians offered us a meeting space in her luxurious high-rise in downtown Atlanta. I drove my Muslim friends in from my modest suburb, worrying how we were going to bridge the differences in education and professional experience.

But once we had oohed over the dramatic view and seated ourselves, the physician spoke as the caretaker of her husband, who, afflicted with frontal lobe dementia, was only able to speak in his sleep. Another woman described the difficult decisions that accompanied her own husband's long struggle with diabetes, amputation, and then dementia. Soon everyone was sharing their experience with illness as well as with the health system. The physician and psychologist, who analyzed the health system primarily through the experience of race, found some of their own suppositions being modified because race was not a frame which the other women used in these situations.

Thinking back on that time, I am struck by how my own protective worries, however well-intentioned, if they had been allowed to play out, would have reduced all of our opportunities for new ways of understanding, reduced our common store of wisdom. I was so afraid that the haute style of my black professional friends would prevent them from experiencing the wisdom of my Muslim friends that *I* lost sight of what united all of us. We were all, sooner or later, black or white, rich or poor, male or female, doctors and caretakers and patients, going to know what it looked like from the bed. We all wanted someone to care.

)X(   )X(   )X(

I have been describing how staying with the *story* of how we came to understand the *experience* of class provides us with new ways of looking at the many concepts included in that term *and* at the concepts that have helped us negotiate those experiences of class. For example, understanding that for me class is most about the dynamic of exclusion and inclusion helps me understand when, why and how I question it.

Another way to look at class is value, that place where existential and relative value confound each other, and where imagination plays a dramatic role in establishing, maintaining or destroying value. The idea of existential equality has also been very important to me in understanding my responses to the experience of class.

Perhaps that is why for the past year I can't get Keith Payne's *The Broken Ladder: How Inequality Affects the Way We Think, Live, and Die* out of my mind. Payne is an experimental social psychologist who writes about inequality from both an academic's perspective and also as someone who grew up tobacco-picking poor in Kentucky. His interest in the topic is visceral. He wants to understand how he and his brother turned out so differently.

What keeps echoing for me are the astonishingly linear relationships between inequality and all sorts of social, psychological and physical measures. The more unequal a society is, the less social mobility there is. But this linear relation to inequality is also found in life expectancy and in health status. This difference exists at every step in the social ladder, which means it is independent of basic need. What is at issue here is *relative* inequality. Enough is never enough if someone else has more. That's what I keep thinking about. It's about coveting. It's about feeling devalued in relation to someone. Most importantly, how we *interpret*, how we *imagine*, our relative standing can set off a cascade that is psychological as well as physical and has very real social consequences. If we feel one down, we begin to take bigger risks, we look for the fastest way through and up, we look for ways to blunt our frustration, we begin to feel there are intentional dark forces at work. But the distortions exist on the other side as well. If we are successful, we give ourselves personal credit for our successes, see them as due to intrinsic factors, and are much more unwilling to let everyone have a voice in the redistribution of goods. We tend to hoard, to exclude, to club together to protect what we earned. These reactions increase inequality. The perception of ourselves as unequal, in either direction, is an entropic force. For this reason, it is probably good that so many Americans define themselves as middle class, whatever evidence there may be to the contrary; it keeps us from seeing ourselves as the helpless victims of class.

What stays with me is importance of imagination in all this. We can be primed to see ourselves as the masters of our destiny. If we are asked what we did to earn our success, we will tell a story of individual effort. We will understand our world that way, and make choices with broader social implications based on that understanding. If, on the other hand, we are asked how many people helped us on our way up, what role social structures, what material benefits, and what role luck played, we will identify a very different set of contributors to success, ones that unite us with others. The stories we tell ourselves and each other about how the world works have pervasive consequences.

Our daily lives are filled with small, ambiguous gestures, multivalent words, half thoughts, multiple fleeting intentions, cross purposes—in other words, a roiling stew; but the implicit stories we draw from these sensations have linearity, assumptions of causality, predictive power. If we feel we are unequal, at whatever level on the social ladder, we begin to weave together act and consequence in ways that make that inequality more real. But what if we make those stories explicit, what if we share them? Through the listeners' responses, *their* experience, we may find our sense of what is possible, what is inevitable shifts. "Why can't you?" my son asked the cook in the pizza restaurant.

Ж　Ж　Ж

This sharing may be particularly important when we look at our own lives. We tell qualitatively different kinds of stories when we're talking about our "real" life and when we're imagining a story that reflects our inner landscape. You can hear that difference in tone between the memoirs in this collection and the fiction. The difference has to do with whether we have control of the outcome. There is often an edge to memoirs on crossing class, social mobility, an empathy and an anger that don't know quite where to alight, how to resolve. *Is* it the system, *is* it fate, *is* it our character or actions or the actions of others? *Was* any other outcome truly possible? Our stories express our ideas of justice—our lives as lived often may not.

The divisions in this anthology felt organic and had to do with these differences of how we experience and process class. The first section, Living Class—Riding the Waves, is primarily memoir, people trying in middle age or later in life to understand how their own experiences of class mobility have shaped them. There is an energy here that comes from being directly involved in the experience, from the conversation the author is having with life in the raw, and also a meditative, provisional quality that comes from that experience of bafflement and indeterminacy that is part of our "real" lives.

The second section, Locating Ourselves, is poetry and ranges from the elegiac to the wry. It is about that momentary insight that anchors us, however briefly, in some new understanding of our own relationship with class.

The third section, Crossing—Acts of Imagination, is composed of stories where people explore the impact of class from various points of view and social positions. These are interesting because they draw on our desire to transcend class as much as they do our desire to cross it. The authors identify with the less powerful, but they do so by choice. That awareness of choice influences both tone and outcome. We have the luxury, in fiction, of creating worlds that reflect the world that could and should be. In stories we can introduce those other qualities and valuations that organize our world differently from class, the ones that define *our* people—and we can give *our* people enough power to change their situations.

In the last section, Advocacy—What We Fight For, we find both stories and memoirs that seem to share a stance that is both heartening and limiting. It brings up the tension between individual choice and social determination that infuses all understandings of class. This desire to right imbalances, protect the less powerful is admirable, but when does it reduce the complexity of experience, the range of personal choice, impose an understanding of class and the effects of class that may not be true to the person we are trying to protect?

We encourage you to read all these memoirs, stories, and poems in a way that freely engages both your imagination and your direct experience of life. Where do your experiences match up with those of a particular writer, where would you have acted differently, interpreted differently? Where do you feel someone is smoothing out the edges of the experience of class, where do you feel they are exaggerating the insults? Where were you able to identify with a character or an author in a way that was new to you? What other values would you bring into play to help people choose the most validating way to act? Where do you want them to come out? What would feel like a good ending to you? Is it realistic? We also invite you to think about what is largely missing from this collection—stories of downward mobility as a lived experience. In all these stories there is an implicit assumption that up is best.

Is it always? And, more importantly, is it realistic?

There are no definitive answers to any of these questions, there are only invitations to engagement, points where we may identify and where we may refuse to identify. But all these responses are important and worthy of exploration.

We can only really understand the impact of our social schema by making them directly accountable to the quality those schema will give our real, *lived* lives if we were to be randomly assigned to any position in them. Stories, both imagined and true, are an excellent way, perhaps the best way of doing this testing. Especially if we spend as much time listening as we do telling.

What does a story, a world, that reflects that kind of wisdom, that kind of possibility look like?

What does it have to include to make room for you—and your neighbor?

REFERENCES

Patrick Butler, "Most Britons regard themselves as working class, survey finds," *The Guardian*, June 29, 2016.

Emma Martin, "70% of Americans consider themselves middle class—but only 50% are," *CNBC*, June 30, 2017.

Frank Newport, "Americans' Identification as Middle Class Edges Back Up," *Gallup*, Dec. 15, 2016.

Keith Payne, *The Broken Ladder: How Inequality Affects the Way We Think, Live, and Die*. New York: Viking, 2017.

"Socioeconomic Mobility in the United States," *Wikipedia*.

I. LIVING CLASS—RIDING THE WAVES

DONALD R. VOGEL

A SENSE OF PLACE

This is the story of someone with family in a trailer park, who was a chaperone for socialite Brooke Astor; who shoveled shit and shook hands with a Rockefeller. It begins in Brentwood, Long Island, where I spent the first eleven years of my life and where the Latin gang, MS-13, now murders teenagers with impunity. My father was a plumber, mom a housewife until she eventually had to work to help support four kids—my sister, me, and two younger brothers—especially after my parents' later divorce. One prominent memory of those years was my kindergarten teacher, Miss Luard, who was black. I remember my mom being adamant about wanting all her kids to have her as a teacher because she was great with children. That didn't happen before we moved to Bay Shore, a mostly black community on the Island's south shore, where I shoveled shit.

My father, the plumber, was the son of one. Little did he know that his bookish first son, me, wouldn't take to the family business. I remember his pride giving me my first cup of coffee on our first job together, and I needed it because I hated waking so early on Saturdays and Sundays. That was for a simple leak under a kitchen sink. Over time the work also included long days fixing boilers in unheated homes or skulking through dark crawl spaces like recruits through an obstacle course. Obstinate as I was, I began to feel working with dad was a form of punishment for me being more academically inclined. The final job I would ever do with him was a mid-winter night when our cesspool overflowed. I sometimes wonder if my disinterest in the family business added to the shame for my father who had to fix something that shouldn't happen in the home of someone counted among the plumbing fraternity.

The job was a losing battle all around, from dad breaking the downstairs toilet with his snake, a long tool slid down a drain to drill through clogs, to the ineffectiveness of his pouring gallons of acid into the flood of excrement that was our cesspool. The problem lay between the house and that destination. We had to dig a hole just outside our home to remove the fecal matter blocking outflow. There was nothing noble to say about pride in craftmanship when he handed me the shovel and said, "dig." I am proud to say that I didn't get ill as I created steaming piles in the winter air, but if there was a life lesson to be learned it is only from the hindsight of someone who now commutes daily from Trump country to the homes of New York City's landed gentry: shit is the guaranteed product of everyone, rich or poor, with the only difference being those of us who lose the olfactory sense of it.

We eventually moved again, this time to Centereach, Long Island, a white working-class town. There I received my first yearbook in seventh grade memorializing the students who were more popular, prettier, or athletic. Most of them were blonde, with chiseled features, wearing the coolest styles of the time. I'm not sure if I was just plain oblivious to social divisions until then or that my previous experiences in Brentwood and Bay Shore were lessons in assimilation—I was familiar with Stevie Wonder and Earth, Wind, and Fire well before I heard Led Zeppelin—but Centereach was where I discovered the sin of envy. My place in the social hierarchy was among the nerds, that broad class of individuals called braniacs, spastics, and socially retarded, before terms such as autistic or Asperger's were invented for some of our group. My participation in that diaspora was the gateway to rebellion and drugs when I got to high school.

An aversion to authority is also one of my fatal flaws, perhaps stemming from my resentment of my father for waking me during cold, pre-dawn hours to go plumbing. So, the high school burn-out culture, with its anti-jock stance, was a natural niche. I found a certain camaraderie passing a joint around a room, sometimes circling a fire in the woods someplace, a poor imitation of peace pipe ceremonies. It also fostered my obliviousness to the social interaction occurring without me, and how life was never as simple as us long hairs and them muscle brains. I was admittedly always baffled by athletes and cheerleaders who crossed class divisions by joining in a few tokes before first period. Worse yet, some of my stoner buddies committed the sin of hanging out with them as well.

When I joined the Navy after graduation, boot camp was the great equalizer where economic and racial divides were bridged via mutual physical and mental suffering. Everything was about breaking down individuality to build a cohesive unit because teamwork kept a ship afloat. That theory didn't prevent segmentation when we got to our commands where blacks gravitated to the radio room, whites to combat information center, and the upper crust to the officer's wardroom. The educationally challenged became boatswain's mates; "deck apes" who chipped paint and loaded storerooms. However, even these subcultures were melting pots, mixing agrarians with urbanites, united in shared skills. I was an operations specialist (basically radar, navigation, and anti-air warfare) who didn't know he had a "New Yawk" accent until it was mocked by a guy from the Kentucky hills. This was a slack-jawed rube whose drawl was thick as shit, wore coke bottle glasses, and had an Adam's apple that would poke you in the eye if you didn't duck.

From my perspective, I was a writer who happened to be a sailor. I had joined only to get the money my divorced parents hadn't saved for college. During those four years, I'd seen half the world, smoked a lot of Hawaiian dope, and bedded disreputable women. In Japan I saw the horror of the nuclear age at a museum in Nagasaki, was greeted by "Nukes go home" signs in Australia and learned that even the Filipino sex trade was stratified: streetwalkers were shunned because they were diseased while the bar girls received penicillin shots on base. Burned into my brain is the image of Filipino children with twisted limbs who begged for pesos. Rumor had it that poor families broke the limbs of their children as infants, so they garnered more sympathy when begging. Worse yet, there was a sewage canal named "shit river" by American sailors into which some of these kids dove at the splash of a coin. Some of our chief petty officers showed us that, for a few laughs, washers and screws had the same effect. I'm ashamed to admit that I took a turn at that.

All of this was just in my first two years of enlistment. Somewhere I awoke from the haze of pot smoke, beer and naivete to feeling estranged from everyone and everything. From home I received messages of family strife, as my mother had re-married and the Brady Bunch never materialized. She corralled a mailman, staying on the same rung of the social ladder, but transforming into the evil stepmother. Meanwhile, as one who had issues with authority, I hated the chain of command that was the spine of military life. Between the dissolution of family and not wanting to accept the Navy milieu, I suffered an identity crisis. I didn't sleep well and almost beat the crap out of a leading petty officer when the weight of it all burst. I needed to talk to someone without a beer or a joint between us. The only counselor available on ship was the chaplain, and the one we had was a fiery Baptist, a stark contrast to the typical Navy chaplain, usually a higher church guy who drank with the rest of the officers.

I went to see him one day when I was swabbing his passageway. Officers had their own staterooms while the enlisted men, like me, were crammed into one room, fifty-bed compartments. He answered when I knocked, after I made sure no one saw me. The chaplain was a tall lanky southerner with light drawl and bushy mustache who was considerate and thoughtful as I told him my issues. However, instead of some practical advice, learned wisdom, or even psychobabble, I got Jesus as the answer to everything. Eighteen and naïve, I prayed the sinner's prayer with him, looked up and said, "is that it?" His response was that it was the first step on a long journey. For my final two years in the Navy, I spent one year straddling the fence between being who I was, the sailor, and who I was supposed to be, the Christian. I then got serious about religion, attending Bible studies, quitting drinking, and hanging with the shipboard fellowship. I learned all about the importance of being separate from the world, as God had advised Israel.

Christian or not, I still clung to the belief that I was a writer, scribbling in a journal what I felt was wisdom to change the world, when that's what the Bible should have been to me. After my discharge, I enrolled in Houghton College, a Wesleyan School—a "no drinky, no dancey," daily chapel institution—not to get a solid Christian education, but because, in the mid-1980s it was one of the few places in New York State that had a creative writing major. Writer and Christian aside, I was a working-class guy who was, as an entering freshman, the same age as college seniors. My military benefits allowed me to afford this small private school with upper crust kids who had experienced little of the world beyond their small town, right-side-of-the-tracks upbringing. To me, they were the naïve ones. At least that's what arrogance had me believe.

Ironically, it was a course at Houghton that lead me back to worldly ways, but not as I was in the Navy or high school. Sociology was a challenge to the foundational beliefs I had begun to hold sacred. It said that reality is socially defined. One anecdote I most remembered was a story the professor shared about a tribe of pygmies in Africa whose physical attributes and depth perception of the world were influenced by living in the thick rainforest for thousands of years. The story goes that missionaries took one of the tribesman out of the bush and showed him a herd of water buffalo a few miles away. They asked him what he saw, and he said "flies." When they drove him right up to the herd they told him they were buffalo. He corrected them saying "no, they're magic flies." I began to feel that I too saw flies where water buffaloes should be. While I was delighted to find that there was wisdom beyond what many considered the Word of God, I also read works by writers like Karl Marx as part of the course work, who infamously said, "religion . . . is the opium of the people."

It also became hard for me to accept parts of the Bible such as in 1 Timothy 6 where Paul admonishes believing slaves to be obedient to their believing masters, because they are brothers in Christ. How are they brothers when they are another's property? Passages like that and others have served to justify some horrible acts and institutions in this world. Hell, God telling Adam in Genesis to subdue the earth is the root of so much environmental degradation. I learned there are reasons for terms like "higher church" and it had less to do with the classification of denominations than it did with the classes of the people who attend them. Over the years, I became what some called "backslidden," but I never fully abandoned the Faith. I just had other sacred cows competing for attention.

When I graduated college, I was a twenty-six year-old who came back to a house that wasn't the home he left. First was the new family, fractured: my mother had driven out the oldest of three step-children, my sister too, but showered favor on me and my remaining two brothers over two younger step-kids. Next was the world outside. I had moved on from the stoner crowd I had graduated with and needed to build a different life and find a career. There was a two-year period in which I worked at a local supermarket, meeting new people and dating cashiers. Meanwhile, we moved from Centereach to a brand-new house in a lower-class neighborhood called Shirley. It was a town populated by predominantly welfare-reliant households, in which the gentrification that took place in its fraternal twin on the west side of a parkway, the demarcation between rich and poor, never transpired. I left when I landed my first job in fundraising.

Fundraising is the ultimate classroom for learning about the haves and have-nots. It is a legitimate career that no one grows up wanting to be, like others who aspire to be a doctor or cop. Though it is much more, the short description for the field is professional begging. I fell into it because I wanted to write for a living. One day I went to work for a nonprofit as a newsletter writer when someone dropped a Request for Proposal (RFP) on my desk and said, "if we don't write this grant, we're all unemployed." So, I wrote for a living, literally. It was that and not some remnant altruism from my Christian days that inspired me to engage and stay in the philanthropic sector. I'm at it more than twenty-five years now and I hope that some form of wanting to do good trumps naked ambition or necessity.

Fundraising is also not the highest paying field, so the search for higher salary or positions took me from storefront nonprofits to elite cultural, educational, and activist institutions. For much of the time I wrote grants, caring little about the people and faces involved on the money side. To me, that was the purview of my bosses, until my "aha" moment at the New York Botanical Garden. I worked there for four years, around the time I got married. The Garden is one of the myriad cultural institutions in New York City started by robber barons such as John D. Rockefeller and J. P. Morgan at or before the turn of the twentieth century. When I worked there, its fundraising galas were attended by nouveau riche corporate titans who made millions off Viagra, or descendants of said barons who, if they got their faces stretched back any further, would've been in danger of swallowing themselves.

Brooke Astor might have been one of those, but she was in her nineties when I met her, an age at which surgeries have long lost their effectiveness. I was clueless as to who she was. It was my first year at the Garden and my first Conservatory Ball. Events were all hands-on deck for those of us in development, the fundraising department. Each of us were given assignments: lower level staff manning tables and upper level shadowing the well-off. I was assigned to escort Ms. Astor because I was the last person in the department who could drive a golf cart for her. The Garden's president was to be her escort at the ball, but I was to first give her a tour of the grounds. I picked her up, and we spent a half hour touring with her using "how" to preface everything she said: "Oh, HOW beautiful," "HOW lovely," "HOW quaint." Her accent was nasal with British overtones.

I got home late that night and my wife was already in bed. She woke when I joined her and asked how it went. I rolled onto my side and mumbled, "I had to drive around some old woman named Brooke Astor." She sat up and said, "Brooke Astor! You met Brooke Astor!" When I said "yeah, so?" she said, "You've heard of Astor Place, the Waldorf-*Astoria*, haven't you?" It took a second but then I said, "Oh, those Astors?" Even though I had been writing successful grants for a few years, that was really my first lesson in philanthropy and the fact that I needed to know who was who if I planned on going further in fundraising. A few months later, when we re-opened the Peggy Rockefeller Rose Garden after a long renovation, I made sure I knew who David Rockefeller was when I shook his hand. I remember his eyes tearing at the whole affair as his wife, after whom the garden was named, had just passed away after a long illness.

I think of my father when I remember both scions of wealth, not only because of that infamous day of excrement, contrasted with my hanging with the wealthy. No, what's striking now is that both Rockefeller and Astor lived to be a century or more, most likely because their respective fortunes allowed them to live a lifestyle healthier than a plumber for whom shit, as well as asbestos-covered pipes and shimmying through dirty crawl spaces was a daily fact of life. He died of chronic leukemia at sixty-two. Come to think of it, my grandfather, a plumber as well, was about the same age as dad when he died of a brain tumor. I'm fifty-five now and wonder if I'm doomed to genetics or if my college degree, which led to a different career path, is my salvation.

Either way, this is about legacies: plumbers' and philanthropists'. The latter can pass on the benefits of wealth which, genetics aside, allows their progeny to avoid many of the pitfalls of working class, Social Darwinism, outside of greed. (For that, look no further than how Brooke Astor's own son treated her in her declining years.) On my father's side of the family, he had one sister with three kids. She and my cousins moved to New Mexico when I was twelve or thirteen and, outside of contacting my aunt when my father died in 1999, we had not been in touch with them for decades. I recently met one of those cousins at my mother's trailer in Pennsylvania. She was staying at my sister's trailer a few doors down. My cousin told us stories of how her family was so poor that they lived in an Airstream camper in the desert, eating only what they could catch. Today, she is the only other member of our extended family, besides me, who has a degree, and is building a 5,000-square foot home in the desert where she once lived.

As I mentioned, my sister lives in a trailer two doors from my mother while my youngest brother and his wife live with mom. This is a situation of partly my mother's creation, having always bailed out the two of them whenever they've lost jobs or homes, which is quite frequently. My brother is a drunk, and my sister is generally unstable with any number of mental deficiencies diagnosed as an excuse for any one of her various failures. Perhaps failure is genetic. My mother had a sister and a brother. One time my aunt on that side paid me in marijuana for babysitting my two nephews: one who became a drug dealer, and another who did time after stealing cars for the mob. My uncle, a thrice-married chubby chaser, divorced his first wife, the mother of my other two cousins, because she was dating a convicted child molester.

I am fiercely proud of having avoided the pitfalls of my family. I attended a private college because my military benefits paid for 95% of it, with little debt when I graduated. Married with one son, I live in a working/middle class community and, as mentioned, I have worked in fundraising for more than twenty-five years. Sometimes, on those inevitable bad days at work, when I come home from a long-delayed train commute (normally two hours), and something in the house is broken, and my wife says, "your brother called asking for money," I wonder if everything in my world is broken. This is not out of envy of the upper crust people from whom I regularly ask money, but more out of envy of the "normals" in my immediate community, whose homes are regularly updated palaces and whose stories always seem to involve the extended family singing joyful carols around the piano at Christmas.

I think my envy of the normal may also be because my son, my only child, is diagnosed in the autistic spectrum. Thankfully, he is higher functioning (his challenges are more social). I have found, and written about, how even this dictates what strata of society one dwells in. Ours isn't the typical athletics-centered, bro-culture that defines our town, but is among the special education and special needs families, with their own *schadenfreude* infused hierarchy. This involves gossip that sometimes centers on the family whose child has more publicly embarrassing quirks than those of the parents present in the conversation. Still, given a choice, I would take this milieu over that of another family in my community that connects with other families that have lost a young child to cancer. Nobody, no matter what stratum of society, should find their acquaintances in that way.

My community is conservative, consisting of an Irish/Italian-Catholic, working class ethic. This conflicts with the values at the place where I currently work in New York City, a progressive nonprofit committed to eliminating race and gender bias. This is nothing special as one can cross the same spectrum by taking the subway a few stops. What it means for me is that I must watch what I say to whom, especially in our currently volatile political moment where the only common ground is a seething at those who don't fall within our tribe. Mostly, it means that at home I'm a cultural elitist, preferring jazz concerts at the Blue Note and the Vanguard over tailgating parties for athletic events. Yet I'm not highbrow enough to not feel inadequate among cosmopolitan colleagues who discuss vacations canoeing the Mekong Delta in Vietnam, when I'm just back from kayaking some local waterhole.

It would be arrogant of me to pontificate lessons to be learned in all of this because it is just me and my life. Like anyone else, envy and wisdom have their place among the myriad sins and virtues that define anyone of us. I might try to focus on the flaws of the monied people I meet daily, saying how poorer folks are richer in values than the superficial people who live on the Upper Eastside, but that would make me no better than the people in the special needs crowd who share a wink or a nudge about neighbors with more seriously challenged kids than their own. I could mine the wisdom of sociology or the Bible, but how many people have heard of Émile Durkheim and what, if any, faith-based tradition is not founded on some text written by a pre-historic, patriarchal, tribal culture rapidly losing relevance nowadays.

I've gone from shit to *schadenfreude* and I find myself grateful for what I have, less than many but much more than myriad others. I can imagine a chorus of "duh" if I shared that death is the great equalizer, with the rich having more to lose than the poor. Oh, and time is the only currency we must be prudent with but can't save. Duh, there too. Sex is something else that puts us on common ground. I dare anyone, no matter what social strata or gender identity, to do "gonzo station," more than 30+ straight days at sea (I once did sixty), and not find that sex is grammatical: any person, place, or thing. All that aside, here's a few thoughts: be grounded, but don't stagnate; know where you're from and never go back; *carpe diem* is nice in theory but a bitch to practice if you're not among the privileged. Try seizing the day or anything else on a crowded and dark subway without getting arrested.

David Rockefeller, whose hand I shook almost a quarter century back, died just a few years ago. In the late aughts he was the patriarch Bill Gates and Warren Buffet enlisted to bring old money together with Silicon Valley billionaires to sign what has come to be called the Giving Pledge. It was an effort to get all signatories, many of them whose net worth equaled that of small countries, to commit much of that vast wealth to charity before they died. I read that he was quite successful in bridging the old and new Gilded Ages. But that is not what I'll remember about Mr. Rockefeller. It's what I saw in his eyes that day I shook his hand in the garden named after his deceased wife of fifty-six years. I wonder how much of his wealth he would have given to have her back. He was no different than me, except that nothing is ever likely to be named after anyone in my family. Thank God for that.

JOHN LAUE

THE BEAUTIFUL PEOPLE

Kiawe trees reach to the sea,
long gnarled limbs bleached white,
some half-buried in white sand,

some extending crooked roots where
waves wash up the slanted beach
that we've retired to after swimming.

We've claimed this plot of sand,
feel secure in this 25 foot stretch
held by sheltering tree arms.

The four of us sit quietly
wait for another lovely sunset,
waves hissing almost to our feet.

A few bathers wade by slowly
avoiding limbs that border our small space,
but none try to join us.

Sand crabs pop in and out of holes
and sometimes stare at us
with small black dots of eyes.

Suddenly from a few feet back
five people march up,
three men in colorful, expensive shirts,

one smoking a large cigar,
two women beautiful as Vogue models
but who seem approachable.

The women look from left to right,
greet us with warm eyes.
I think, I'd like to know them.

The man with the cigar poses
while another snaps a picture
then turns his camera toward us.

He looks again at our ashen skin,
ill-fitting suits, frowns, lowers his camera,
says, I thought you were someone else!

We're almost close enough to touch
but the gap between us
stretches wide as the horizon.

PATRICIA SMITH RANZONI

CULTURAL GUIDE
OR
WHY DOESN'T THE HUMANITIES COUNCIL
FUND A DOCUMENTARY BEFORE THOSE
WHO KNOW ARE GONE

1887, <u>A Romance of Mount Desert</u>
. . . thus do Capital and Labor exert themselves in peaceful co-operation, for the comfort and pleasure of the most noble and exacting potentate, the summer visitor . . . do not Peace and Plenty smilingly reign, and Content sit jocund on the housetop? Truly should the grateful native rear, on the highest peak . . . a monument to his benefactor. . . .

1997, <u>Bangor Daily News</u>
In the days when social distinction demanded being named to Mrs. Vanderbilt's list of "The 400" . . . local residents were forbidden from becoming members of the island social clubs . . . people knew their place. There were two separate societies: the very wealthy and those who worked for them . . . when the sun sank below the trees, the young danced to bands hired from New York and Boston.

1997, "Social Studies," Joshua Clover
. . . in fact, they aren't waitresses/at all but witnesses.

The servantry here then. The way you were lined up on the carpet,
disciplined to hear over and over the laws of keeping place. Rule one:
never speak.

If they ask anything say just enough to be polite but not
to encourage more. Do not ask anything not related to their meal.
If you see them outside the hotel, do not make eye contact. Avoid being
where they are cross the street if required. Here's where you

are allowed. Here but not here or here. Never never of course
think to dance on the porch remember that audacious Brewer girl
                                                who got fired
not even for that but for accepting an invitation from one of them
                                                to go out
somewhere where no one need see. From the city, that one was, how could
she be expected to agree to our ways or whys.

So she polishes herself and her glassware and silver for inspection,
having served her time in Side Hall studying on maids and butlers
and chauffeurs. Scissors buds from the rose garden for the tables in her
station as instructed. Masters *consommé, au jus, julienne, parfait,*
serve to the left clear from the right. How to fold choice napkins class-
ically and where everything belongs at each place framing the service
plates with the celadon sailing scenes. How to crumb with grace the
crumbs of class, prepare fingerbowls for privileged hands. When.
When. How to wait. The art of it. And she knows her part and keeps
it gratefully for the chance to show how good she is and earn a couple
hundred toward her high school class ring, yearbook, cheerleading
blouse and sneakers. Tuition. Only once these summers allowing
herself a purchase every penny banked working her way for these winters
only once this frayed book this cobalt *Mrs. Browning* (*Complete*)
From The Twelfth London Edition 1882 this gold-gilded volume first
gold anything she's *owned* only once from this sale for seventy-five cents
these words this way that she can buy For to dream of a sweetness
is sweet/as to know only once when this companion from Swarthmore
teaching her guests' boy boating yes her very own weeklong, monthlong,
summerlong, yearly, *guests* this deep-seeming fellow she's never seen
the likes of, only once when he keeps asking her about Maine and the
University and what she plans to study until the hostess reprimands her,
only this once does she imagine taking a twirl on that grand veranda
to that Philadelphia music she calls it. The orchestra always striking up
while she is still cleaning up from their dinner parties where she gets so
deft with her own system of menumarks she dazzles those Greek chefs
with how she can order and present most elegantly with master busboys
an entire banquet and get it right who selected what. Her vaseless runner
of freshlaced greens and glads the longest spray for the longest table she's

ever seen. Serve to the left, clear from the right, one arm always clamped
across her back when not in use, unobtrusive as a ballerina ghost, *there
but not there.* Every night she sees them collect straight from days
on the water and whatever else they do, glazed in their high summer dress
lush as she guesses Mrs. Rockefeller's gardens must be.

Once after shining her silver and goblets until they could be held up
to the light and only gleam, her toppers each replaced, damask smoothed,
placesettings composed for breakfast, she catches herself glimpsing
through the great glass to the porch. She sees how they are with each other,
how they float and pose. Enchanted, she drifts nearer the archway not
realizing where she's gone. There, this tall sun-in-his-hair boy in Madras
she's heard it's called, sees her and for whatever reason or no reason
at all, glides back to the dining room's edge in a step imprinted still
and smiles hello.

> *It could have been an opera! Their companies aghast*
> *they cluster and swallow their shock.*
> *He only knows he caught something*
> *reminding him of fieldpeople he's watched in the meadow*
> *on the way to his summer rooms perhaps the arc*
> *her practiced arms make loving as partners those massive*
> *oval trays over her shoulder like pitchforks*
> *balancing with hay the grandest dance in the county*
> *and he thinks he'll damned well speak to her if he wants to.*
>   *He reminds her of a brand new book she hasn't yet read*
> *and wants to and 4th of July picnics at the shore*
> *and something she can't quite decipher*
> *but it doesn't matter she doesn't know it yet.*
> *The harbornight air appears to befriend them without their intention,*
> *a hush settling across the scene when*
> *they take one another for a waltz. She's never danced*
> *his way nor he hers—they know neither how to hold each other*
> *nor how to let go—*
> *their pluck in the very fact of it a terrible lucky swirl.*
>   *She follows him from her world toward his*
> *until something shudders and falls. Something centuries old*

and fought and paid for.
Something his people and hers have guarded their whole
histories and there it is on the floor, shattered.
Horrified, she flies back to her room in the dorm
over the rickety maintenance shed only the dried salt paths
from the corners of her eyes to the pillow to testify
how she would die before sleep to be right now please God
back on the farm.
Seeing their people's disdain look what she has done
they are themselves mortified. Nothing,
they insist, it was nothing and please
they'll never disgrace this place again and they don't.
        Dancenights after,
she cleans up even faster than before, trying not to show
she expects anything but wishing beyond wish to fix it,
let them know she's beyond sorry she crossed the line,
be permitted to save a pittance of face, earn back
her own sense of worth but they will have none of it.
There is no allowance for this
without trespassing again.
And she has nothing left she can afford to spend.
        For the summer people it is as if it never happened
only better. It happened and didn't count.
        For the balance of that season, when she has to be
where they are, they are more accomplished than ever
at showing she is not. Never to look at her again,
to her they become a people with no eyes
except whenever she seeks to see if what she's seen is true,
it's her own eyes dissolving in a blur her
hands nothing but air until she will never, after that summer,
go where they are again, deafened forever
to the what did you expect from her own.
        As for the young man, he never knew
what she'd given him
in trust.
No one would ever know he'd left a poem
in her apron pocket, and to the end of her life

she would labor to work it off
and would not say what he'd done
but to himself.

Decades later, in features called "Growing Up In Maine"
they'll say how perfect those summers they'd come for were back then.
How everyone you met on the street was family or friend.

County cultural directories organized with best intentions
by the lately settled making history here, uneducated in the system
before them, name Carnegies, Fords, Rockefellers, Morgans, Vanderbilts,
Biddles, Astors (she could tell you where they sat what they ate) solely
on the basis of their wealth and *magnificent summer "cottages" serve*
to the left clear from the right one arm always behind her back
when not in use throw her back in place just as if it isn't
the beginning of the twenty-first century and there is no collective memory
or vocabulary yet to name, *name* the worldclass peoples
who've labored here and *their* richness
the way Judge Silsby's "Looking Backward" does in the *Ellsworth American.*
Not even a token *live together in mutual respect*
while those who know *know* what's out of the box and those who act
as if our story here opens and concludes with what *they* see and study
dance over the surface of hard old fact
not aware what chests they've broken open

repeating how Maine's artists, many
with global reputations, live quietly in communities that honor them
by respecting their privacy

> *artists who every day*
> *dip into the lives*
> *of her exposed people*
> *without shame.*

A far off good-hearted fund
will grant a sum in excess of a half million to address why
long-time locals under a certain income level

seldom turn out for their shows.

Transient scholars will pull off drive-by poems of anthologized literary merit
shooting poor people, as if a poor man in a T-shirt and no stairs for his door
and a poor woman in a bathrobe in the afternoon and their poor chubby
                                                                children
playing with hubcaps and their poor ashamed teenage daughter
and their poor protective dog knowing danger when she smells it
are the ones to be afraid of . . . *So that's*
how it is out there in Maine. Be careful out there
one gives himself away
on the community radio station.

MAIDA BERENBLATT

LOOKING AT UPPER CLASS

As my lifespan becomes longer, memories grow dim but the photographs remain clear. The earliest photo in my album is of my mom standing beside my carriage, wearing a fur coat, reflecting good times. Her black hat has several feathers on the side and I see black gloves covering her hands. I am sitting in my carriage, wearing a jacket, pants, hat and mittens, all in white. The photo is in black and white, but the leaves and trees in the picture spell late fall or early winter. The next photo shows Mom and me in a sparse bedroom with one window on the side of a single bed and a crib; we were essentially homeless while Dad was in a sanatorium recovering from tuberculosis. We were staying for the two years he was away in the house owned by two of his sisters—he had been the youngest of fifteen siblings. Turning the page finds another photo, this one of Mom and me sitting on a swing in front of a cute little house, followed by a photo of Dad and me on a chaise at the beach on a bright, sunny day. Things must have gotten better. That was the rhythm, the twists and the turns in my life's journey.

The following photo reveals my younger sister sitting next to me on the front steps of a different house. It was not clear what house or to whom it belonged. That photo was taken before we moved from Pawtucket, Rhode Island to Boston, Massachusetts then to Claremont, New Hampshire. No one ever explained why or when the moves were to come. Was I too young or the family silent? Actually, no one ever explained anything; I watched the boxes come and then go and heard the words "pack now." There was constant tension and conflict. Sometimes, loud angry fights and at other times, long periods of silence.

One year later there was another big move. We were back in Boston with a new baby brother and an absent younger sister. This time we were in a house living three floors up; I had to climb a lot of steps to get upstairs. The stairs had a creaking, squeaky sound if I stepped in the middle. I tried to step on the sides, both left and right, to figure out where it would be less noisy. I couldn't. I finally gave up and didn't care. It was a very old house; the wind would whistle through the cracked window frames—even raindrops made their way inside. The house made groaning sounds and I was told it was "settling in." From what, I wondered.

The neighborhood was scattered with only a handful of old houses, all odd-shaped and in different states of needing repair. But it was a safe place and I could play outside until the sun went down. An old couple lived on the second floor of our house and they hardly went out, day or night. On Sundays a man came to them with many packages, bags that looked to hold groceries. The family on the first floor had a big, black dog that barked a lot and very loudly. When I walked home from school I didn't know where he would be. It was my first thought when I approached my house: where was the black dog and would he jump on me?

I walked to elementary school and came home each day for lunch, time I shared with my mother; we listened to the daytime soaps on the radio, especially *Helen Trent* who always had trouble with her life—not so different from today. There were always dramas to be told only now there are images on television to connect to the tragedies. There was a healthy, kosher lunch ready for me: vegetable soup, a cheese sandwich, and milk. On good days there was a cookie beside the milk.

During that time, it was only my baby brother and me in this very old house. We moved twice after that, remaining in the Boston area. My little sister, gone from the family for eight years, had been hospitalized nearby for a rare disease of paralysis of the muscles and skin. Children were not allowed to visit there; being a child myself, I was not allowed see her. One day, a stranger—my sister—came home. She was very short, thin, and kind of bent over. I had started high school by then and didn't have room in my life for her—what was I going to do with her? She had no social skills and I wasn't willing to try to help her to adapt, even though my mother asked me to, many times. I couldn't make up for what was lost in the long period she spent in the hospital. This new sister held no interest for me.

Finally, by the middle of high school, things were better again. Turning another page, I find the photo taken of my parents and me celebrating my 16th birthday at the famous *Latin Quarter* in downtown Boston, a photo the club went on to use as an advertisement on their matchbook covers. I could hardly believe I was actually there and witnessed Sammy Davis Jr. sing and dance—one of the rat pack who frequented Sam Walters' hot nightclub. I felt incredibly special to be celebrated in such a fashion. This must have been what it felt like to be a movie star.

Keeping a familiar pace, within two years, the next move was to Long Island, New York; my freshman year at Emerson College, majoring in theater, disrupted. I was so unhappy—they took me away from my life, my friends, my dreams of a career in theater. The sunny days were over once again. Dad was unemployed, sitting in a corner chair, staring out the window, and Mom had a briefcase filled with books and papers, teaching Math and English in a junior high school. She was under so much stress she one day arrived at school wearing only a slip, having to keep her coat on in the classroom the whole day.

I was clueless as to the reasons for all the changes—the moving about my entire life. One year we were celebrating life in style, the next we struggled in despair, not knowing what would happen next, not knowing what world I was living in. No one offered any explanation, and now I realize, I never asked.

I escaped, finding my own world of fantasy, where everything and everyone was beautiful, rich, and happy. I went to the movies, a lot. My girlfriend Edwina's father was the manager in a movie theater. I was Grace Kelly in *High Society*, Audrey Hepburn as a princess in *Roman Holiday* and beautiful Elizabeth Taylor as *Cleopatra* in faraway Egypt. I imitated their phrases in my conversations and mimicked their styles in my fashion. But the most important observation to me was "the show must go on" which became my mantra. I put myself in a Hollywood mindset and I didn't move from there for a very long time.

My bedroom walls were decorated with celebrities from the movie world. When one of them divorced or died, I moved their photographs around. I learned about two different worlds: one in which there was white linen on the tables and on the beds, fresh flowers in vases, and music in the rooms for parties and dining. I saw pool parties, ballroom dances, and fancy cars that would glide along the Hollywood hills in California. I thought all problems in life could be resolved just as I'd learned within the two-hour film. And then, there was my real life, my ever-changing merry-go-round, without any music.

I was infatuated with the privileges of the unbelievable choices these celebrities had in the world because of their financial position, and the opportunities of the special, upper-class lifestyle. I never knew to look behind the scenes, wanting to keep the fantasy alive to cover my own bleak life, my awareness of my class level, even from myself.

I found my way into a college again, working days in retail and nights waitressing and hostessing to pay tuition. I see now the picture of myself, dressed up and wearing heels, seating an elderly gentleman at his table while working as a hostess in the Garden City Hotel. Even though I worked in the service industry, the Hollywood address in my mind remained unchanged, the glittering of the stars staying with me.

While there are no pictures documenting the day, tucked into the album I come across the horserace sheets from Belmont Park, bringing back the memory of being there with my father. Then, I knew: the money was connected to winning and losing—our family's good times and bad. It was something I hadn't realized before. It was the reason behind my family's history of moving. My dad was a gambler. Now, finally, it all made sense.

Dad's loyalty, also known as addiction, to his gambling activities did not diminish by a fraction until his debt to his bookie increased to the point that his life was at risk. A man came to the door demanding he pay up; a deal was made by my mother and my father's family to pay off the debt providing he leave New York and return to Boston, permanently. He left. We stayed behind, along with the consequences of our class.

I asked myself how could I, or anyone, make sense of all the changes endured throughout our family's lifetime? I hadn't seen this problem— gambling, addiction—in my movies; but of course, it was there, waiting for me to recognize it. I had only accepted the colorful and whimsical presentation on the screen without question or reflection of reality. At least within my circle of friends, I wasn't the only one.

From living through my earlier life experiences, it seemed to me that at the core of the equation to happiness was money. The upper class always had money, allowing them to enjoy life's privileges. Their lives definitely looked good—better than mine. But, I wondered, how much is enough money to be safe and secure, and to avoid the threat of continuing to live on the cusp of the lower class? I was driven to move beyond the class I knew, earning not one but two college degrees and elevating myself into the professional world. This began to afford me better things like nicer clothing, theater tickets on Broadway, even a vacation—a cruise! I felt like I was doing something the upper class would do.

I was focused on the upper class, observed, even researched them, obsessively, noting the multitude of things they acquired and possessed: houses, cars, boats, airplanes, jewelry, art, designer clothing, domestic help, even their spouses and children. Still, they seemed to seek more. I watched the wealthy as they fell into the pit of mega-wealth, media coverage, and saw how their position, in my judgment, distanced their view of normalcy. I began to understand the disorder of "more," the possession of more translating into power, perhaps blanketing a deep layer of insecurity. I saw the upper class exhibit unimaginable behaviors, especially the careless manipulation and humiliation of others to gain this power, to gain more pleasure in every possible way, in the attempt to fill a bottomless pit.

I began to feel somewhat disenchanted. As an adult, I began to understand so much more than I did as a child. The prize, the promise of fame, power, and even adoration, can be as false and make-believe as any movie. No longer a little girl, starry-eyed in a darkened theater, as a grown woman working in the field of psychology I could see how the marathon race to acquire the power to get "more" works—how the hypoxia that occurs in the competitive push to be on top deprives brain cells of oxygen, causing good judgement to disappear while impulsive behaviors threaten to ruin the prize. I see, too, that there are exceptions; many in the top financial hierarchy fund advancements in science, medicine, and aerospace, or provide resources for hungry nations.

What I was beginning to understand from my observances was that you can only sit in one chair in one room in one house at one time.

It wasn't without a struggle that I had climbed my way out of the class of my childhood, nor was it a straight path. During college, at my parents' insistence, I was married. Maybe ironically, the only picture remaining in this album is one of me, alone, the bride in her wedding gown, beneath a canopy. My mother made this wedding a very fancy, over-the-top event. Was it all possible because my father had been winning? Before my thirtieth year, I had three children and became divorced. In the time the union lasted, I visited middle class: drove a sports car, had a nurse in the house when the babies came so I could continue to go to work. I still wanted more. After my divorce, I remained in the working class, paid the mortgage, finished my master's degree; I saved for my children's college, hoping an education would put them on a path to prosperity. I still kept my mental address in Hollywood, watching celebrities and those who were moving higher into the wealthier classes.

I had come to learn that to change one's mindset based on emotion, rather than on cognition, is indeed a challenge that can take a lifetime. The emotional memories that were positive in my life so far had all circled around good times, winning times, while the drastic rollercoaster changes, the bad times, the losing times, were directly related to the same thing: money. The good news is that I have had a full lifetime to examine this equation: being in the upper class and having enough money brings happiness and good times. This was the belief system I held, motivating me throughout all of the successes I'd worked toward and achieved in my lifetime. These actions resulted in bringing me money; I was able to buy expensive, fancy things which, for a time, brought me the happiness I was after.

However, the other good news is that having never left my mental Hollywood state also disproved my original equation. Thank you, Hollywood: producers, directors, actors and actresses, costume designers and set directors, for your glamorous lifestyles educated me in the ways I most needed. While I learned from observing that one could work to achieve their goals, leading to the financial wealth that could seemingly buy many things, I began to see, too, that underneath, it didn't necessarily buy lasting happiness, good health, or loving relationships. I took a second look, seeing that all of what was promised wasn't always delivered. The lifestyles I saw on the big screen, on television, in magazines weren't often true. Thank you, too, leaders, politicians, and financiers for providing lessons in character, or the lack there of, for my emotional growth, for I have come to see that life is simply not about the money but rather what you do with your wealth and the integrity of your character. It's about choices and kindness toward other people, no matter the differences in class. What I have grown to discover is that some of the most memorable and happy times in my life have had nothing to do with wealth.

I look at a faded color picture of my daughter's birthday party, held in our backyard, balloons hanging from trees, children playing games, a simple cake glowing with candles. We were not in a financial position to do more, and yet, it was enough: there was, without a doubt, happiness. Good times despite a lack of wealth. These events, holidays, even a surprise visit from an old friend or lending a helping hand to someone in need despite your own circumstances, these are the ribbons in life's memorable bouquet.

I ask, what is enough? It appears not to be money, power, possessions, or position of authority. Does anyone have enough, and how do you know when *you* have enough? Even a sybarite, in their dedication to luxurious living, must continue to work at their lifestyle, keeping in step to maintain their status in order not to lose their place in line.

Part of what was enough for me was to stop moving, stop relocating. In order to escape the endless chaos, disruptions and uncertainties that came with bouncing from state to state, home to home as in my childhood, I stayed put on Long Island, having my children and career in one place. Part of what was enough for me was to create my own class, one of exclusive fantasy. I placed upon my bedroom door a metallic star; next to my front door, I hung a mirror with the saying, "You are a Star." *This* degree of stardom, despite excessive wealth not coming along with it, became enough.

As I continue turning the pages in the album of my life, I am reminded that there is another piece of my story that was enough, one that is still nearly unbelievable to me. Along with my daughter, Alena Joy, I wrote a book, *Make an Appointment with Yourself; Simple Steps to Positive Self-Esteem*. It was published by Health Communications, Inc. and was featured on the *Oprah* show. It was incredibly exciting to be an *Oprah* guest and to be treated so royally, from the limousine and hotel suite to meeting my warm, engaging hostess. I look now at the photograph of the two of us, Oprah's arm around me. It is true that I was a "star" for those fifteen minutes and that was just enough for me. The book went on to have several printings, and I was a guest on radio and other television shows.

Next to the photo of my moment in the spotlight, a picture of my daughter and my healthy new grandson. More than enough, this was perfect. Dreams can come true!

I am reminded too, that my adult life wasn't always ideal, as the horrors of cancer and drug addiction within my immediate family were battles to be overcome. Keeping the Hollywood address in my mind magically worked to help me get through those bad times. As the saying goes, "the show must go on," and that theme propelled me to cope with the chaos of moving through my life's journey.

On the remaining album pages, I prepare to add new memories: pictures from my brother's wedding—he and his third wife—being added to the album today, my sister missing from these recent photos so much like she was missing in my early life. Happily, her physical limitations did not prevent her from moving on successfully with her life, a scientist working in satellite communications along with her husband. Traveling to this event, held last weekend in a small town in Vermont, I was in a well-appointed limousine. I had never ridden in such luxury, the driver telling me the car cost over $200,000. Wow! I was in Hollywood! I sat up front with the driver, a mature gentleman, on our long, late night journey. We made conversation about the financial market, he telling me he's not in the market, preferring to earn money the old-fashioned way—by working for it—but his brother is a senior broker with an international company. While his brother is travelling and boating on weekends, this man is driving; he's been doing so for twenty-seven years, but now owns the limo company, employing thirty drivers. Once again, the question presents itself: what is enough?

Like the cloudy ring of a cataract around the objects in my view, I perceived wealth to be the golden path to happiness; my perspective and evaluation are now totally different. It is not simply about the amount of money but, rather, how it is used and to what purpose.

I never had to live my life homeless on the street, though where I was going to live was, early on in life, a perpetual question. I may never have joined the upper class, often staying somewhere in the middle, but in retrospect, I feel virtually class-less. I may not be far from where I started, having travelled from lower class and having visited middle class, all by watching how the upper class lived, but it's an interesting place to be, now, to fully realize that it's the intense drive in the search for money, for power, and for fame that most people strive in order to feel valuable, especially when even "everything" isn't enough; the search so elusive and fluid. What *is* sustainable is to honor the integrity of who you are and how you relate to other people in your world. Upper class, middle class, and lower class all have a common denominator, that of human beings' commitment to humanity in order to create a world in which we can all live in harmony. And that . . . is class-less.

PATTY SOMLO

THIS EXPLAINS EVERYTHING

Before that summer, I considered my family poor. Or at least by the time I entered my last two years of high school, I pictured my family someplace close to the bottom rungs of the economic ladder. One reason was that we lacked certain things, like nice furniture that matched. Another was that if I wanted the same shoes or name-brand dress the popular girls at school all had, my mother would claim we couldn't afford it.

In addition to seeming poor, we were also military people, which meant that we lived on Air Force bases most of the time. At Scott Air Force Base, Illinois, stuck in the middle of vast, flat farmland occasionally interrupted by small towns, we lived in a small drab apartment. On the island of Oahu, our home at Hickam Air Force Base was half of a duplex. In Germany, at Rhein Main Air Force Base, we spent two years in a second-floor apartment, furnished with military-issue green and gray beds, tables and chairs.

Even though my father was a career Air Force officer, I felt as if we lived like a lower-ranking sergeant's family. At that point, and for several years after, my impressions about wealth and class came from sizing up what my family had next to that of my friends.

As if I didn't feel poor enough, I foolishly decided to attend an expensive private university that I would later learn we couldn't really afford. Situated in a toney Washington, D.C. neighborhood, American University (AU) was in walking distance of several cherry tree-lined streets, framed by elegant old homes that housed the embassies of foreign governments. Almost everyone I knew at American came from a family we would now dub *the one percent*. There was Joe, whose dad was president of Revlon; Andrea, whose father headed up Columbia Pictures; and David, whose father owned the Philadelphia 76ers basketball team. My AU friends spent winter breaks in the Caribbean and summers at mountain camps, before returning to their fancy high-end houses in exclusive suburbs outside of Philadelphia, Boston, Chicago and New York.

The sparse wardrobe I'd carefully put together using money earned from an after-school and weekend job typing letters in a realtor's office barely filled the narrow closet allotted to me in my Anderson Hall dorm room. Friends hauled each season's clothes back home to make room for the upcoming season's collection. Where I'd felt poor before college, I now considered myself downright destitute.

Summer jobs were hard to come by in Mount Holly, the small Southern New Jersey town where I spent my last two years of high school and returned to the summer after my freshman year at American. That year, my father was serving in Vietnam, commanding an Air Evacuation Squadron.

Mt. Holly was too far away from the cities of Philadelphia and New York to be considered a suburb. Unlike most rural places today, in the summer of 1968, the town still managed to be a place where a person could earn a decent living. A portion of the residents were military, with dads stationed at nearby McGuire Air Force Base or Fort Dix, the neighboring army installation. A shopping mall had opened a half-hour away in Cherry Hill the year before, but local businesses, including clothing and shoe stores, restaurants and even a movie theater, thrived on Main Street, in Mt. Holly's historic downtown. Family farms, and an occasional factory, appeared alongside the two-lane roads outside of town. No one I knew in Mt. Holly came close to being wealthy like the kids at American. But we considered the people living in the large old houses lining Main Street—doctors, the funeral home director and the owner of a large car dealership—well-off.

When I returned home that June, I heard that staff were being hired for a summer program for migrant farmworkers' children. I applied right away but learned I was too late. All of the positions had been filled.

In order to get a job anyplace else, I would need to lie, pretending I wasn't planning to return to college in the fall. So that's what I did, and immediately got hired to work in a local factory that manufactured small radio parts.

Up until then, my only official job had been at the realtor's office. I knew nothing about the dreary, mind-numbing tasks people without skills and education were forced to do for forty hours every week. Having accepted the factory job, I was about to find out.

We sat in a dimly lit room on high chairs, facing an equally tall table. Like me, the rest of the workers in this part of the factory were female, or *girls*, as we were then called, even though some of the women were in their forties and fifties. At the beginning of the day, each worker was given a sharpened steel square, one smooth shiny edge of which could easily have sliced off a finger. A man came around periodically and dropped off piles of tiny resistors in front of each woman, and stacks of empty rectangular cardboard cards, with a series of slits cut into two narrow columns. He also gave us rubber bands and sheets listing orders.

The entire job consisted of using the steel tool to scrape an infinitesimal amount of paint from the thin metal needle of the resistor. Color had splattered there when paint was applied by a machine to the thicker plastic part. After that, the cleaned resistors needed to be slipped into slots in the cardboard. The final task was to gather up and count enough filled cardboard containers to match an order, rubber-band them together with the order on top, and set them in a pile on the side, to be picked up by another man circulating around the tables pushing a cart.

That was all. Eight excruciatingly slow hours. Sixty minutes that crawled. What felt like the longest days of my life.

The women talked and laughed through every single one of those hours. Jokes were crude, more like what I would have expected from a group of guys at a bar. A good student who loved to read and write, I excelled in English. It pained me to hear these women, most of whom probably hadn't graduated from high school, brutalize verb tenses and simple grammar.

I packed a lunch every day but felt too ill to eat. Before leaving the house in the morning, I cried. I couldn't imagine how I would make it until September.

But two weeks after I'd started, I got a call. One of the women hired to work in the migrant program had turned down the job. Might I still be interested, the kind woman on the phone inquired.

Run by the county, the program had been started to give children of migrant farmworkers a safe place to go during the day, while their parents were working. Without such a program, most parents would take their kids out to the fields with them. Since the children were yanked from school whenever their parents had to move on to a different state as they followed the crops, nearly all were academically behind. In addition to safety and some fun, the program aimed to help the children with reading and math, so when they returned to school in the fall, they might be able to keep up.

There were two separate programs, one for Spanish-speaking children and the other for native English speakers. I had been hired to work with the

English-speaking kids.

In the orientation meeting before my first day, I learned that the children in the program fell into two groups. The first group consisted of African American children, mostly from the South. The second group was white, predominantly from Appalachia.

The first half of the summer I started work every morning just after dawn. My day began with a ride out past town in a white van driven by an older woman named Marge to dirt and gravel roads that ran alongside farms. Every morning, we stopped at rundown, haphazard, wood-sided houses to pick up children before their parents headed out to pick the crops.

The second half of the summer I didn't arrive at work until the afternoon. Each day's activities ended just before dusk. That's when I would climb into the passenger seat of the van driven by Marge and ride back out past the fields, to take the children home.

In addition to school-age children who participated in a variety of activities, including swimming lessons and all sorts of games, the program had a nursery. A crew of mostly older women and one nurse took care of the babies. There were many lessons for me about class and poverty that summer, but the first centered around one of the babies.

This particular baby girl, Tanya, was suffering from malnutrition when she came into the program. The nurse who diagnosed the baby assumed the child's mother didn't have enough money to feed her properly. The truth turned out to be more complicated.

Marge related the story to me one morning, as she steered the van out of town.

"The mother is illiterate," she began. "Can't read a word."

I thought about this fact for a moment, trying to figure out why an inability to read would lead to a baby's malnutrition. Then Marge enlightened me.

"The mother thought there might be some instructions on the baby food jars that she needed to know, in order to prepare them. Since she couldn't read, the mom thought it best not to give the child baby food. So, she fed her things that didn't need to be cooked, like candy."

While this was my first eye-opening glimpse into the many unexpected tentacles of poverty, the children I worked with that summer taught me something almost every day—about race, class, segregation and opportunity. A pudgy eight-year old with large eyes, a super-sweet smile and dark brown skin named James would happily hold my hand like the child he was when we walked down the street and then shock me by whispering suggestive phrases he must have heard at home, about what he planned to do to me sexually. Sometimes when I was sitting in a circle with the kids reading a story, James, or one of the other young African-American kids, would run their fingers through my hair, marveling at how different a white woman's hair felt from theirs.

Of all that summer's lessons, though, none burned into my psyche the way what I learned from the Barger family did. Originally from Appalachia, the five Barger children ranged in age from five to eleven. Every one of them had the palest skin. The two youngest, Jesse and Clive, had jet black hair that fell in thick bangs over their eyes. The older three's hair was sandy brown, bordering on red.

It must have been Marge who shared something about the kids that surprised me. Several of the children had been deemed by more than one school they attended to be *retarded*. (This was the catch-all phrase in the late-sixties for a range of learning disabilities and challenges.) I was surprised to hear this, because I found the Barger children to be quite bright. They were fast learners and eager to try new things.

What did stand out about the children, and several counselors thought this might have been what got them placed into special education classes, was their speech. All of them were hard to understand. When the children spoke, they failed to form the letters completely. Their mouths didn't quite get around words, as if they were talking with food stuffed in there. The way they mispronounced words forced me to ask them to repeat what they were saying, in order that I might understand.

Late in the second half of the summer, the cause of the Barger children's speech problem finally revealed itself to me. As on every other day, Marge and I piled the children into the van for the long ride out of town, my favorite part of the day. I loved gliding along the narrow country roads, past tall corn stalks and squat tomato plants, the fields taking on a pale rosy glow.

I had been to the Bargers' house several times before, or at least sat in the passenger seat while Marge pulled up in front. Each time we'd been to the house, Mr. Barger hadn't been around. Since most of the parents worked long hours, from sunup to sundown, his absence didn't seem especially odd.

On this particular night, Marge carefully steered the van down the long dirt road, doing her best to avoid ruts and large rocks, to a house that must have been white once but was now a pale gray-brown, missing shingles, with plastic covering windows in place of glass. Marge stopped the van, and I opened the door to let the Barger children out. Then I noticed a man, standing in the bare dirt yard.

"Daddy," one of the two Barger girls shouted and ran toward him.

I stepped out and leaned against the van, while the other kids ran to the man I assumed to be their father and greeted him. I watched as he bent down and patted several of the kids on the head, before they hurried past him and headed into the house.

He was tall, around six feet, and thin, dressed in a short-sleeved undershirt with a V-neck. The once-white undershirt was caked with reddish-brown dirt. There was a wide rip on the lower left side, which had been tucked in, while the right side hung loosely out.

He had on a pair of dark gray pants that looked like they might once have been part of a work uniform. The cuffs rode a bit high above laced brown boots. Around his neck, he'd haphazardly tied a navy-blue cotton scarf.

He walked toward me, just as Marge was getting out of the van.

"You must be Mr. Barger," I said, and reached out my hand. "I'm Patty, one of the counselors."

He reached his right hand out to shake mine. I couldn't help but notice that his hand was as dirty as his shirt, the area underneath his jagged fingernails nearly black.

I raised my head then and studied his face. He had large eyes, like those of his youngest children, in a long, narrow face. But instead of being dark like Jesse's eyes, Mr. Barger's were pale blue, the shade of alpine lake water.

His cheekbones were high, the skin on his face deeply tanned and wrinkled. It might have been the fact that he spent so much time out in the sun, but Mr. Barger appeared much too old to have children as young as he did. If I hadn't known otherwise, I would have assumed him to be the children's grandfather.

At that moment, he said something, but I didn't understand.

"Pardon me?" I asked.

He repeated what he'd said and this time I managed to get it. He'd said, "Nice to meet you." Then he thanked me for helping his children.

I smiled and told him that I found the children very bright and well-mannered, which they were. But the entire time, I couldn't get over how he talked. He spoke exactly the way the kids did.

And then his lips slid into a wide grin.

I had to bite my lip to keep from shouting, *Oh, my God. This explains everything.* Because when Mr. Barger grinned, I saw that he had almost no front teeth. The lack of teeth caused him to speak the way he did. And the children, I now realized, had probably learned to talk by listening and mimicking him.

Jesse, my favorite of the Barger children, ran out of the house past his dad, and grabbed my hand.

"You wanta see the baby pigs?" he asked.

"Sure," I said.

He seemed eager to show me, so I didn't want to decline, though I really had no interest in pigs and feared I'd be holding up Marge, who probably wanted to get going.

Jesse pulled me through the dusty yard, around ragged old pieces of bleached wood and rusted metal. The space looked more like a garbage dump than a yard. He ran as we went and I started jogging to keep up.

The pen was fenced and dotted with lumps of dark brown mud. Jesse pulled me along, until we stood on the right side.

"See?" he said, pointing down.

There lay a big gray mama, with at least six tiny gray-white piglets suckling.

"They're cute," I said, and Jesse smiled.

"You ever see baby pigs before?"

"No, I never have."

At that point, Jesse must have decided to give me a tour. He pulled me along, past the pigpen, to a large garden plot. I had to admit, in that otherwise dreary place, the garden was lush and lovely.

Using his index finger, Jesse began pointing out plants, starting with the tomatoes, moving on to the lettuce and green beans, and ending with the strawberries and corn. He then led me behind the house, where the only thing to see was the family's wash, hanging on the line.

By the time we'd come around the other side of the house to the front, it was starting to get dark.

"I think we need to leave now," I told Jesse. "But thanks so much for showing me around."

As I headed for the van, I noticed Mrs. Barger standing there, her arms wrapped around a large brown paper bag. Though I'd seen her many times before, I now felt the need to study her. She was tall, like her husband, and slender, though appeared to be at least two decades younger than her husband. Her blondish-brown hair was wispy and long, pulled into a low ponytail in back, but with stray strands coming out. Like her husband, she had lovely blue eyes. When she smiled, I could see she had a full set of teeth in front.

When I reached her, she thrust the bag toward me.

"Here. Some good fresh food."

I held out my arms. As she transferred the bag to me, I peered inside. I could see ripe red tomatoes and some greens. The bag was filled to overflowing.

"Oh, I can't take all this," I said, trying to get her to take the bag back. "We'll never be able to eat it."

In response, Mrs. Barger wrapped her arms tightly around her waist.

)(   )(   )(

I don't know what happened to any of the children I got to know that long-ago summer. Neither would I learn whether their being in that summer program helped or changed them. My hope, of course, is that it did make a positive difference in their lives.

In the same way, I can't pinpoint exactly what impact that summer had on my life, except to say that in the ten-plus years I spent as a journalist, and now as a creative writer, I have been continually drawn to tell the stories of people who struggle.

As much as I would like to claim that coming face to face with real poverty in the summer of 1968 caused me to be grateful for everything I had, I have to admit that wasn't the case. A week after meeting Mr. Barger, I returned to American University, where I would share a small square dorm room in Anderson Hall with my best friend, Alice Shalom, the rest of the year. Of all the well-off kids I knew at school, Alice was one of the richest. Being in close proximity to a glamorous lifestyle I never could have imagined before, I found myself sucked back in to wanting what Alice had—closets-full of gorgeous designer clothes from Lord & Taylor and Saks Fifth Avenue, a boyfriend who drove a brand-new silver Jaguar sports car, and an enormous house in Great Neck, New York, that her parents were making do with, while an even larger and more luxurious estate was being built, smack on the water in Kings Point. Whatever lessons I'd learned from Tanya, James and the Bargers faded, when I was in the company of people who had so much.

As it turned out, just as my experience with the poor was short-lived, my hobnobbing with the one percent didn't last. Almost since I started at American, my mother had constantly badgered me about the money she was spending on my education. It got so bad, I asked my roommates to screen the calls. If my mother was on the phone, Nina or Gloria, my freshman-year dorm-mates, would inform her that I wasn't around.

By my junior year, I couldn't bear the fights any longer. At the end of one of those seemingly endless arguments, I shouted to my mother that she could keep her money. I wasn't going back to American again.

Following that fight, I refused to take another dime from my mother. That's when I learned another important lesson about poverty and wealth in America. I, like most Americans, would remain in the economic class to which I was born.

I struggled to finish college, working low-wage jobs as a supermarket checker and waitress. Eventually, while supporting myself with a part-time office job, I would make my way through graduate school, earning a masters degree in the midst of a deep recession, when jobs I'd hoped to get were scarce.

Like my mother, I've never owned a set of living room furniture that matched. As much as I can still drool over designer outfits at Nordstrom, I restrict my buying to lower-priced imitations, and only when they're on sale.

Once a month, I volunteer to feed the homeless, many of whom avoid the toasted bagels that require vigorous chewing, because they're missing teeth. And I understand that poverty is rarely a choice, but, instead, happens to be the only pathway through life that too many people are given.

LOWELL JAEGER

CARNY

The horses we minded reverently,
lifting them down with both arms
from where they'd been strapped in the truck
on padded racks to cushion the miles
between shows. Had to worry extra hard
not to drop them for fear we'd chip the paint
or worse, break a leg. Had to progress
in a particular order when fastening each horse
on the pole to which it belonged, building
the "jenny"—as the boss called it—from the bottom

upward, hanging the struts and rafters
according to how they'd been numbered,
taking care to put a wrench on each fitting
where it might have rattled its nuts loose.
Raising the canvas on its ropes to the central shaft,
draping it neatly, evenly. Last, screwing
all the colored lights in place, replacing the bad ones.
Then stepping back to admire the musical-mechanical
marvel, while the most-trusted among us eased the clutch
to give it a test go.
         Yes, we lacked hygiene,
but we scrubbed what we could with wet towels
while standing clustered in the muddy splash
beneath an outdoor fairground spigot, though
at times the water had been shut down, anticipating
our arrival, small town hospitality refusing us
even that.

SUSAN G. DUNCAN

SCHWINN

think myself back
to three-quarter fingers
wrapped around handlebars
pink snapping tassels
patty-cake patter
get going go faster
blister-hot blacktop
glitter and chrome
saddle shoes pumping
faster and faster
keep going
keep going
to the end of the block
to the end of the street
where stiles cross barbed fences
keep cows from our picnics
keep blacks from our picnics
keep moving get moving
my best friend Betsy
has homework she shows me
3 nuns plus 5 nuns
make 8 and she crayons
so neat and keeps in the lines
but I keep on going and
I have a crush
on Betsy's big brother
Jimmy next door
beats up on his sister

Mama's best friend's
met only 2 Protestants
Mama she said she
never knew a Jew

Summers seem shorter now.
Fences seem higher.
Betsy got married,
moved to Saint Louis.
To no one's surprise, Jimmy's in prison.
His dad's still drinking, can't seem to stop it.
And I just kept going.

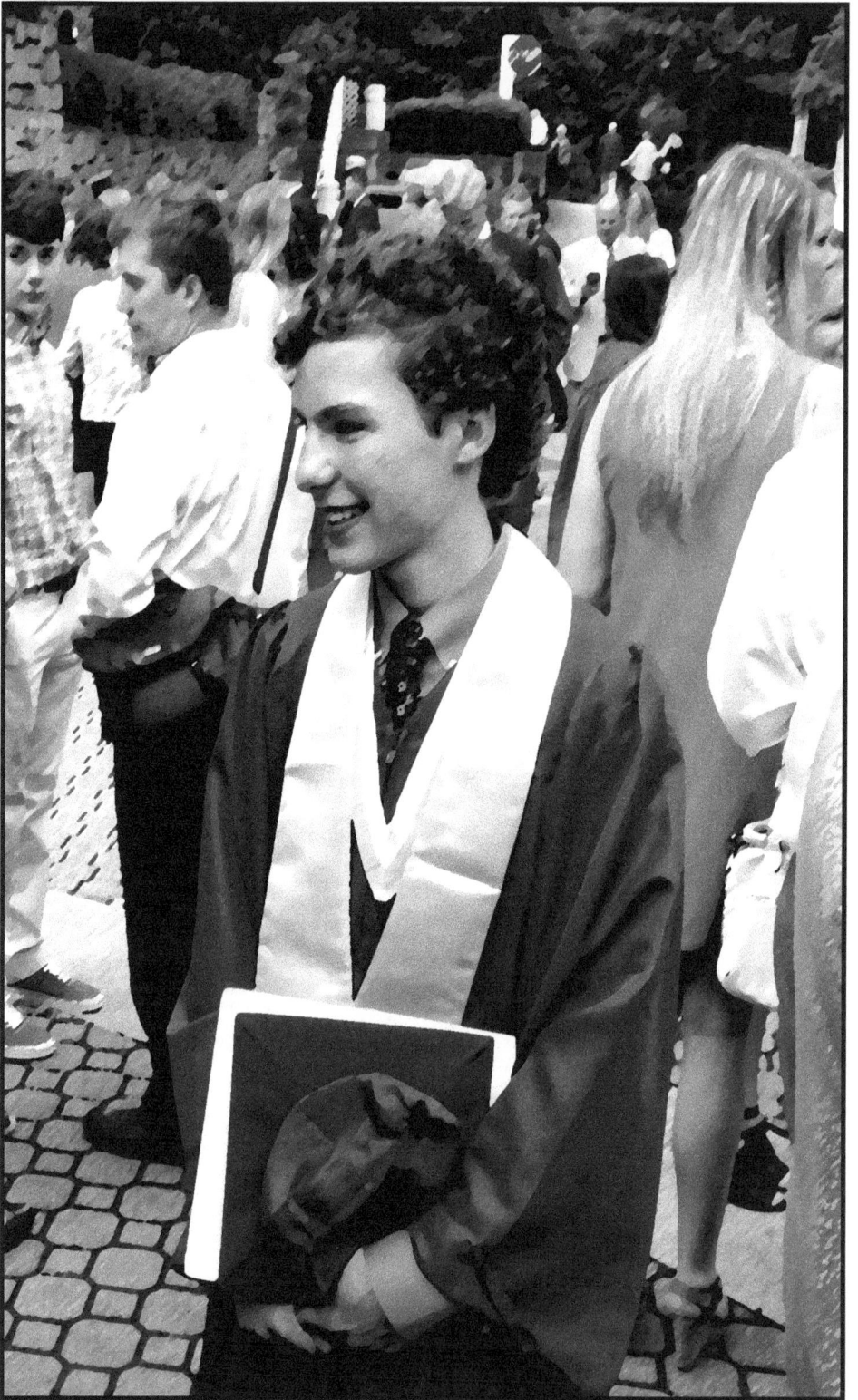

MARK PAWLAK

CLASS ACTS

Act I
Wearing overalls on weekdays, painting somebody else's house
to earn money? You're working class. Wearing overalls at weekends,
painting your own house to save money? You're middle class.
Lawrence Sutton

As newlyweds, Mom and Dad lived with Dad's parents. Their first child, I spent my infancy in that bungalow on Ridge Road in Cheektowaga ("Place-of-crab-apple-trees" in Erie-Seneca). I wasn't quite two years old when they relocated to the Prorok household, Mom's parents, less than a mile away just inside the Buffalo city line. The Polish-Catholic St. John Gualbert parish, to which both Pawlak and Prorok families belonged, straddled the border between the two municipalities. Within its parochial milieu, my parents met, started dating, and eventually married. Their wedding took place in the parish church; a year later, I was baptized there.

Mom was pregnant with brother Chuck when we took up residence in the larger Doat Street house. But the reason wasn't crowding, rather it was the friction between Mom and Grandma Pawlak, a demanding task-mistress. As Mom tells it, she couldn't do anything right in her mother-in-law's eyes. Mom felt belittled by her because she had never learned to cook or sew, or, for that matter, crochet, knit, hang wallpaper, or any of the myriad other skills that Babcia Pawlak deftly executed, all the while nursing her sickly husband. (My Pawlak Dziadek died young from silicosis, a consequence of his job sandblasting castings at a Buffalo foundry.)

I remember almost nothing of Ridge Road in those years, being but a babe. In contrast, I have a wealth of idyllic childhood memories from the bustling Doat Street household that was filled with Polish chatter and the smells of Babcia Prorok's cooking. Mom, the youngest of eight kids, was the last to marry, but her two eldest siblings, Charlotte and Fred were also living in that family "manse." Charlotte had moved back in shortly after her husband died and Fred took up residence after his divorce. Ever present Dziadek Prorok puttered about the house, wearing his signature sleeveless T-shirt and pants held up by suspenders, pulling out his gold-plated watch by the chain at regular interval to check the time.

My romance with train travel dates from then. Dziadek was retired from the New York Central Railroad, but his sons, my Uncles Ted and Joe, still worked in the switching yard, and Uncle Fred was the night foreman. On more than one occasion, I got to sit on an engineer's lap and "help" drive his diesel switching-engine in the rail yard.

I must have been about four when we picked up and moved into public housing. Mom was pregnant with my youngest brother Greg. Our growing family needed more room and Dad wanted his own place—an apartment if he couldn't yet afford to buy a house. The Langfield Housing Development on Buffalo's east side, where we relocated, was one of several in the city that accommodated returning war veterans and their booming families. It was a large sprawling complex, four to five blocks on a side, consisting of more than two hundred, mostly two-story, brick row houses, each with six or more family units.

My parents struggled financially in those early years with three young boys to feed and clothe. We never went hungry but we did eat a lot of peanut-butter-and-jelly sandwiches made with spongy Wonder Bread. We were fed Chef Boyardee Spaghetti and Meatballs, Beefaroni, and Ravioli canned dinners; plus, Sloppy Joes—a ground beef extender—ladled over slices of bread. At the end of the month, when money was stretched thin until Dad's next payday, Mom often served a platter of kieshka, a Polish "delicacy" consisting of pig's intestine stuffed with spiced rice and ground meat. (I discovered that liberal applications of catsup made it palatable.) As for clothes, my brothers and I each had store-bought, Sunday-go-to-church clothes, but for daily wear, I was often dressed in hand-me-downs from Mom's nephew David, the son of Great Uncle Henry the pharmacist—good quality hand-me-downs, which I, in turn, passed on to my brother Chuck.

Although Dad had never finished high school, he was nevertheless bright, a self-learner, and manually gifted. As the only boy in a family run by his mother and two sisters, he learned to cook, sew, knit, crochet, hang wallpaper, do minor repairs, etc. He could take apart, rebuild, or fix any mechanical device. He had taught himself cabinetry and had a basement workshop fitted out with Sears & Roebuck table saw, jointer-plane, and lathe. (I inherited and still use them.)

He worked as a grease monkey in a friend's garage as a young man before the Second World War; then, parlayed that experience into a stateside assignment as an airplane mechanic when he enlisted in the Army Air Corps. He was working as a welder at Harrison Radiator when he married Mom two years after his discharge. That job, and his next, flushing tanks to purify drinking water at the Buffalo Water Works, were both shift-work at a barely-living-wage.

Throughout much of my childhood, Dad often worked two eight-hour shifts, back-to-back, making quick visits home between them for dinner, or to put us kids to bed, or to discipline us with the palm of his hand when Mom reported we'd misbehaved. If an extra shift wasn't offered, he moonlighted, first at his friend's garage, pumping gas, then as an itinerant radio and TV repairman—another skill he taught himself—working out of the trunk of his car, where he kept two specially designed fold-out suitcases, one for tools, the other filled with vacuum tubes.

All the while, Dad was putting away money toward a down-payment on a house. I was in fifth grade when he was finally able to buy a modest three-bedroom bungalow on Weston Street, a "handyman's dream." That first year in our new digs, he spent his days off and all his summer vacation, applying an electric rotary sander to its badly weathered shingles, stripping them down to bare wood before repainting—because he couldn't afford to replace them. Fixed in my memory is the image of him standing high up on an extension ladder in the hot sun, his forehead beaded with sweat, a red bandanna covering his nose and mouth against paint flakes and sawdust.

Although we were no longer public housing tenants, we hadn't moved far. Our former project row-house at 6 Hempstead Court was just four blocks away; and behind our backyard fence stood the wood-frame row-houses of another section of the same projects. Weston Street was the line of demarcation between public and private housing; a high wooden fence—actually, a succession of high wooden fences, one per house lot—ran its entire length. The only breech in this palisade was an alley halfway down the street that cut through to the projects behind.

After we moved, I continued to attend Immaculate Heart of Mary Elementary School on the far side of the projects, a fifteen-minute walk from our Weston Street home. I always took the short-cut through the alley, then followed a diagonal path through the projects, passing our old apartment on my way. With my brother Chuck as companion, I made this journey to and from school four times each weekday until I completed eighth grade. (Immaculate Heart had no cafeteria, so we went home for lunch.)

Friendships with classmates from my old neighborhood didn't end, but those bonds grew weaker over time. With the encouragement of my parents, as much as for my own convenience, I made new friends among the kids on Weston Street. Their fathers were, for the most part, blue-collar workers like my own—like fathers on the other side of the fence, too; but in my parents' eyes, they stood apart from those public housing breadwinners because of their aspirations and motivation to better themselves. It was these values my parents hoped I would absorb through association with Weston Street kids.

My parents made it clear that being homeowners, we were now "better off" than those who lived on the other side of the fence. The bedroom I had to myself as eldest son was pointed to as evidence of our elevated status—back in the projects I had had to share a room with my two brothers. This and related lessons were sometimes delivered as lectures, other times as reprimands. I could count on a severe scolding if my mother caught me clambering up the back fence to peer over and call out to school friends on the other side. Upward mobility, I learned, was all about keeping eyes focused forward; never looking back at where you had come from.

X X X

Act II
Parents exert an overwhelming effect upon their children by their words, their deeds, their omissions and their concealments, but children simultaneously conduct their own education, absorbing everything that crosses their field of perception.
Luc Sante, *The Factory of Facts*

Shortly after we moved, I acquired my first paper route. I later added Weston Street to my route, but at the start, ironically, my customers all lived in the projects. Early each morning, seven days a week for the next four years, I shouldered my bag of *Buffalo Courier Express* newspapers and crossed to the other side of the fence.

In summer, I cracked opened one standard issue screen door after another, each painted the same forest green, and tossed a paper inside, quickly closing it before the paper landed. In fall and winter, screen doors taken down, I folded the paper in thirds and pushed it through the uniform-size mail slots in the heavy wooden front doors, behind which some of my classmates slept. When I finished my route, I would return home, hang my bag on its peg and take a short nap on the living room couch before rising again. If, as sometimes happened, a customer called to complain of a missing paper, I could drop one off on my way to school.

My daily route consisted of about sixty households. On Sundays, when it swelled to one hundred fifty, brother Chuck helped haul the green, wood-sided, double-decker wagon stacked precariously high with Sunday papers, thick with the weekend supplement of comics, magazine, and advertising circulars. And every Saturday afternoon, chrome-plated coin changer hooked onto my belt, receipt book under my arm, I headed off into the projects to collect payments.

This weekly ritual, conducted in the light of day instead of the pre-dawn dark, gave me a new perspective on the life that I had formerly led. Because my route encompassed most of the Langfield projects, I soon became acquainted with households and courtyard communities I hadn't previously explored. My coin-changer and receipt book were talismans, granting me safe-passage to places I never would have dared ventured when I lived there, fearing the consequences of treading a rival courtyard gang's turf.

I learned, among other things, that more than just families with kids lived in the projects. One multi-story corner building just behind my former courtyard, a building I had frequently passed by but never entered when we lived there, turned out to be honeycombed with studio apartments, each one occupied by an elderly woman—widows living off their deceased husbands' pensions or veterans' benefits, Mom told me when I shared my discovery.

The project row houses were laid out around courtyards, onto which the back door of each unit opened—six units per row house in the section where we had lived. Traffic, in and out of the houses was always by way of the back door, never the front. This arrangement made for a feeling of neighborliness, each courtyard a distinct little community.

My routine was to visit every customer in one courtyard before moving on to the next. I'd knock, call out, "Paper Boy"; the back door would open to me; and while the child who answered went to fetch its mother, or the housewife went to find her change purse, I stood in the doorway looking at a kitchen right out of my childhood.

"Collecting," as I called it, was my schooling in the socio-economics of public housing. Most customers paid up weekly; but others regularly asked me to come back another day or the next week when they hoped not to be so short of cash. A few showed me their empty change purses week after week; still others just stopped answering my knock, pretending not to be home.

On my Saturday afternoon rounds I saw clean scrubbed, neatly organized kitchens, and I saw kitchens with dirty dinner dishes left on the table and pots and pans piled in the sink. I was greeted by mothers in housedresses, sometimes with broom or dust mop in hand; and I was greeted by women dressed in slacks just back from grocery shopping or just about to go out. There was one house where a sleepy-eyed woman always answered my knock, wearing her bathrobe in mid-afternoon, and there were more than a few houses overrun with small children where the parents were never home when I called. Men seldom came to the door, but now and then I'd catch a glimpse of one through a doorway, asleep on the living room couch.

Whenever a classmate answered my knock, we would exchange pleasantries while I conducted my business; but these occasions could turn uncomfortable—or worse, embarrassing. At one house, where the bill was often weeks in arrears, lived a girl I had a crush on from school. I prayed each time I stood before her door that she wouldn't be the one to open it. It pained me to see her blush, making the excuse that her mother was out and, once again, had forgotten to leave money to pay me.

✕ ✕ ✕

Act III

Then I . . . began to notice that everyone on this side of Bushwick
Avenue was white and everyone on the other side of the el was black.
Robert Hershon

To my paper route I owe another eye-opener about lives lived in the projects. Between Weston Street and the brick courtyards of my former neighborhood, stood an expanse of wood-frame row houses, two blocks wide and more in length. These were the multi-family structures behind our backyard fence. I had no customers there, but now walked through them every day to where my route started and when traveling to and from school.

Seeing mothers hanging laundry outside on clotheslines, their preschool-age children playing in the yards, it slowly dawned on me that this section of the Langfield projects was occupied almost entirely by families of color. Mom helped this realization gel in my mind when she reprimanded me for associating with "those Colored boys" on the other side of the fence. Based on my casual observations, I also drew the conclusion that this neighborhood I walked through every day was public housing for the least well off.

Chalk it up to childhood innocence, but I never paid much attention to racial differences until we moved to Weston Street. Sure, there were "Colored" kids—the term my parents used—who attended Immaculate Heart, but very few, and there was only one Colored family living in our project courtyard. Had there been a quota? Today the Langfield projects are predominantly Black and Hispanic. (I've made return visits.)

Willie Wells and all the members of his large family were noticeably dark skinned, but otherwise I viewed him as no different from the rest of us kids. Willie was one of our gang and joined in all our activities. Together in the courtyard or in the school playground during recess, we played dodge-ball, kickball, baseball, tag, and hide-'n'-seek. And we shared the bond of passive resistance to the strict discipline imposed by the Franciscan nuns who taught us. If my mother had anything disparaging to say about Willie, his family, or Colored people in general while we were courtyard neighbors, I don't remember hearing it.

I was in fourth grade, when a second Colored family moved into the adjacent courtyard and Michael Britt joined my class at Immaculate Heart. His skin was the color of caramel and he spoke a noticeably British-inflected English—West Indian most likely. Beside his accent, Michael was different for being an only child—the rest of us all had siblings, frequently many. I was intrigued by the idea that he didn't have to share everything with brothers.

Another thing that made his family stand out was that there was no "man-of-the-house." It was just Michael and his mother. Whether she was divorced, a widow, or a single parent, I never thought to inquire. If Mom had any insight, she never offered it. Also, Mrs. Britt worked outside the home—a rarity among project mothers. She went off in the morning to her job in an office and returned home at dinner-time, making Michael a latch-key kid. Curiosity drew me to him and we quickly became best friends.

During the remaining time we lived in the projects, I spent most afternoons hanging out with Michael in his house, just the two of us. We played checkers, chess, and other board games, traded baseball cards, and read comic books together. Mom took a liking to him and actively encouraged our friendship.

All that changed when we crossed to the other side of the fence. There not a single Colored family lived—not on Weston Street, or on any of the parallel streets of single family homes in that neighborhood.

✕   ✕   ✕

Act IV
It ain't me, it ain't me, I ain't no millionaire's son, no.
Creedence Clearwater Revival

The reason I picked Kensington High School, a Buffalo public school that bordered the projects, was not the convenience of having to only walk a few blocks from my Weston Street home. It was the curriculum. I wanted to become a scientist. It was 1962. Sputnik had rocketed into orbit four years earlier. "The Race for Space" was on and my imagination was fired by it.

The diocesan high school the nuns had me slated to attend would have required me to study Latin and general science in my first year. I had no interest in becoming a biologist or even a doctor, so why learn Latin I reasoned? I wanted to study physics and become a rocket scientist like Werner von Braun. Learning German, which I could do at Kensington, made more sense to me. Also, at Kensington, I could skip over general science, a subject I had mastered on my own. There, I could start right in with biology, followed, in subsequent years, by chemistry, and physics. To my thinking, that was the ticket.

This was a decision that disappointed my mother and went contrary to the advice and expectations of the nuns at Immaculate Heart, but my father supported my choice. Unlike my Mom, who went through twelve years of Catholic schooling, graduating from Villa Maria Academy where she was a favorite of the nuns, there was no love lost between my father and those holy women. He had bridled at their harsh discipline in the St. Gualbert parish school he briefly attended as a kid. Dad relished telling the story of how, in second grade, he stopped attending and instead showed up on the doorstep of the local public school, his mother giving her grudging approval after the fact.

Kensington was an adjustment of major proportions for me, however. Lay teachers, both male and female, in professional attire, replaced the nuns wearing brown habits cinched with cord and adorned with rosary beads. There were no more catechism lessons or obligatory visits to church to celebrate feast days; history lessons included far more than just saints and heretics, popes, synods, crusades, or Holy Roman Emperors.

But these differences were minor. It was the scale of Kensington that I found overwhelming. In comparison to Immaculate Heart, the physical plant was enormous—four stories tall, taking up an entire city block to accommodate more than two thousand teenagers. The school was a microcosm of the City of Buffalo, drawing students from all neighborhoods and social classes. Thrown together were Irish, Polish, Italian and German kids; WASPs, blacks, and Jews. This mix sometimes resulted in "rumbles" breaking out on the school grounds—turf fights between rival neighborhood gangs. My cousin Louie, who was a year ahead of me at Kensington, had to travel to and from school by city bus each day from his mixed German and Italian neighborhood several miles away. Others I befriended traveled even greater distances.

At Immaculate Heart, there had been one over-crowded classroom per grade, numbering thirty or so neighborhood kids and overseen by a single nun who taught us all subjects—but not all equally well. At Kensington, the classes were smaller and the teachers were specialists in their subject—and demanding; and the hundreds of students in each grade were grouped by expected levels of achievement into vocational, general, college, and honors tracks.

Because I had earned good grades at Immaculate Heart, I found myself in the honors courses with about twenty other students. We studied biology, history, English, and algebra. I saw the same faces, one class period after another, with the exceptions of when we dispersed for instruction in the foreign language of our choice, and PE, which was segregated by gender and included boys from the other tracks.

At Kensington I was thrown in with the sons and daughters of doctors, lawyers, teachers, and businessmen. From the very start I felt out of the loop but didn't understand why. The others all seemed to already know one another. I soon found out that most of them had attended the same elementary school, where they had been grouped together as high achievers since the early grades. How different from Immaculate Heart where the nuns saw little to distinguish me from any other kid.

Another thing I discovered was that my new classmates started high school with reputations that preceded them. PS 80, the elementary school many had come from, was considered one of the best in the city. This cachet, along with individual rankings was transferred from eigth to ninth grades along with their school records. Each one's talents, interests, avocations were already known to the high school teachers before the first day of school. They were expected to stand out from the masses of other students by virtue of their better preparation and social standing. All this gave them an air of entitlement. They expected special attention from teachers and got it. I marveled at how naturally my new classmates took to being paraded onto the stage of the school auditorium during the academic awards assembly after the first marking period.

Subtle though it was, my antennae picked up the message loud and clear that I should know my place and be grateful for being grouped with these kids. I also realized that I would need to work very hard to prove myself in the eyes of my peers and teachers. Prodded by my mother, encouraged by my father, I tested myself against them and found, in one subject after another, that these children of means really weren't any smarter. By the third marking period, I was called up to the auditorium stage to stand beside them in front of the assembled faculty and students.

But I was never first, one or two others always had a higher grade point average. Some previously determined ranking seemed to be at work when the teachers tallied marks. Mom, with whom I discussed such things, chalked it up to favoritism. At Immaculate Heart, it had never crossed my mind that the neighborhood in which my family lived, or the way my father earned his living might influence how a teacher viewed me and graded the work I produced.

If I was surprised to find myself in such company, I was just as surprised to discover that I wasn't the only Immaculate Heart alumnus enrolled in the Kensington honors courses. Seated in English class several rows away I noticed Cathy Sullivan's familiar moon-face. Short in stature, squarely built, freckle-faced, with carrot-color hair, Cathy had been my Immaculate Heart classmate since third grade. But we were acquaintances, nothing more. She lived in a different project courtyard; she had had her own circle of school friends.

Those first months at Kensington, when everything was so new and intimidating, we traded nervous glances. We shared an understanding, communicated silently when our eyes met, that we two did not belong among these privileged children of the professional class. But trade glances was all we ever did. We never publicly acknowledged our bond, seldom said more than a passing "Hello," and avoided sitting too close, partly out of shyness—we were fourteen, a girl and a boy, after all. But, I think now, more than anything, we were afraid to associate lest one of us slip up, exposing us to our classmates as the interlopers we felt we were.

"Class privilege" is a term I first encountered in college, but in high school, long before I ever heard it uttered, I experienced its meaning.

MARY KAY RUMMEL

LILACS AND HARLEYS

On West Seventh along the Mississippi
sagging houses and narrow streets discharge
teens born during the war or just after.
Lilacs droop over sidewalks,
scent the edges of drive-in parking lots.

Saddle shoes crush fallen blossoms,
scarves circle our junior high faces—
bright lips and cheeks, nylon knots
on our chins, our badges of sophistication.
We eye the boys in fish tail Chevies,
watch older girls balancing trays—
root beer, burgers, deep fried onions.

In a cloud of greasy vapor, motorcycles roar
up West Seventh from the Harley Davidson shop.
My disbelieving stare trails Cookie and Rose,
their short bleached hair and leather jackets,
arms wrapped around the waists
of favorite bikers while crows in bare oaks
intone, *You can't   You can't.*

One night big Dave offers me a ride.
On his huge black Harley, my long braid flying
in that joyous wind, I cling to him
senses open like mouths shouting *Yes!*

Yes! to the long tongue of the road
lolling out before me.

Yes! to West Seventh transformed to ridge
across hills, shining Aegean below.
Yes! to a white trail up mountains
where moose dance through drifts of snow.

Yes! to the clouds blooming lavender.
Yes! to grand bazaars and cobbled streets.
No! to staying home, my mother's anger,
my brothers' fights.
My pulse like a stadium of fists
punching *Yes!*   *Yes!*   *Yes!*

Later, I walk with Kathy and Sharon
past dark, crowded bars
ankle deep in tenderness and lilacs,
the roar of Harleys in my blood

II. LOCATING OURSELVES

ANDRENA ZAWINSKI

ON THE ROAD, HIJACKED BY MEMORY

We draw our strength from the very despair in which we have been forced to live.—Cesar Chavez

Riding another lazy Sunday afternoon
along the sun-drenched blacktop stretch
coasting through California's Central Valley,
its pastures peppered by slaughterhouse steer,
its fields dense with migrants—some sporting
United Farm Worker eagles on caps, all of them
packed into growers' whitewashed school buses,
all of them off to bend and hoe, chop and prune,
pick and haul Ag Giants nuts and roots and fruits
for the Walmart Super Centers and Taco Bells.

In the car's backseat, church onion domes
crop up inside my head, their rows of candles
flickering again for all my dead:

For the Ukrainian grandfather, face reddened
from the heat of hot steel, muscles knotted
and clothes grimy, who choked to death
struggling with words in a strange tongue,
lungs dense in smoke and soot, air and water
fouled forging Pittsburgh steel for the Carnegies.

For the Slovak one who carried United Mine Worker
protest pickets to the coal bosses instead of pick and shovel
down into the pitch dark shafts of the Windber mine,
who survived a cave-in, but not being robbed
by the company store and a black lung death.

For my mother, after the assembly line night shift
at Federal Enamel inspecting pots and pans
for dimples and blisters, one hand at the small
of her aching back bent over the Amana. the other
scrambling eggs then scooting my brother and me
off to school neatly dressed with full bellies.

For my father at Pressed Steel welding railroad cars
in the McKees Rocks Bottoms, tagged Cossack
and taunted to jump and spin and kick,
who got lost in a bottle of vodka and thorazine,
another blue collar chasing a middle-class dream.

But the range here today along this California stretch
runs ragged in rain shadow and a watery-eyed sky
looming above tract homes and trailer camp estates,
flashy billboards boasting sprouting condos,
commercial real estate for Nestles' Purina works,
another Chrysler-Jeep dealership, new strip mall
saddling up to wheat and oats and alfalfa,
the Delta's humpback hills carpeted green in spring—
everything predictable, unlike this day trip, hijacked
by memory to detour along a bumpy backroad,
my own breath now so heavy-laden,
my every muscle aching.

WHAT THEY TOLD US, WHAT WE BELIEVED
...No meaning but what we find here.
No purpose but what we make.—Gregory Orr

This is how they told us it would be:
hard work
hard as digging up clods of earth
parched by sun,

an inheritance
to make something of nothing,
no purpose but what we make,

the natural phenomena
of hummingbird defying gravity
or the return of the eagle,

all the gloriously hard wing beats
a chorus of courage,
no meaning but what we find here.

This is what they said it would be:
the calloused hands
that shovel shale,
that stoke the furnace,

the steady work
of molten ash,
a gift of steel,

the nails chewed to the quick
with layoffs threatening
the next paycheck,

the face muffled in winter
to hide the shame of the food line,
its dehydrated cheese and powdered milk.

This is what they told us
about the jewels
that fired furnaces,
the glow of slag smelting,

the same fiery brilliance
as the filthy sunset bleeding down
upon the gray Pittsburgh skyline,

pig iron at the open hearth
a cauldron of magic
making steel.

This is what we believed,
even as we choked
on their smoke
and soot.

ADA JILL SCHNEIDER

VIEWS OF SAN FRANCISCO

My father worked
his grease-solvent-callused hands off
so I could work my way up
Telegraph Hill, panting
in *Polo* logos, hanging on
to winding iron railings, trudging
up steep banks of worn brick steps
bordered by broad-leafed
nasturtium, umbrellas of fennel, steps
painstakingly laid down more than a half-century ago
by construction crews slogging in sweat
and hungry for pay.

The higher I climbed, the harder
I labored from one plateau
to the next for a glimpse of another San Francisco vista:
the drawn-out cursive loops of the Golden Gate Bridge,
the calm blue bay imprisoning Alcatraz.
Even higher to the Coit Tower
with its Great Depression WPA wall murals
of pale factory workers, squat farm laborers, civil servants:
workers working when there was no work.
1934. My folks newly married,
bathtub in the kitchen, two-cent *Daily News*,
when *We always had bread on the table*
because, thank God, Daddy had a job.

Blue-Collar runs through my veins
like a shot of *Johnny Walker Red*
at the end of a tough week. I knew the men
who built these sights I see, smelled
their waxed-paper bologna and mustard
sandwiches, their thermoses of lukewarm coffee
made at 4 am, danced with their frozen-stiff union suits
pullied off winter clotheslines, watched them slip
a week's wages out of a small manila envelope.
My dollies slept on a 24x9x6-inch wooden toolbox
with Daddy's initials carved into it.
I look for Daddy in the Coit WPA murals.
I want to show him his medals,
these logos I wear.

PRIVILEGE

Chaos in the universe? Fate? Serendipity?
Why wasn't I born into sumptuous royalty?
To live in a veritable museum brimming
with intricate privileges of responsibility?
Where dust motes stream through stained
glass windows, and the past echoes off
terrazzo tile in expansive baronial halls.

Among the metal suits of armor, I would
line up my little brother Sid's lead soldiers,
and showcase his confident, knee-scuffed
baseball uniform, his *Louisville Slugger*,
and mint 1948 Stan Musial Rookie Card.

An elaborate ancestral oil portrait of *Dad
the Foreman,* self-assured in his carpenter's
overalls, would be framed in baroque gilt.
A small, dated brass plaque would explain
that on this extraordinary day he received
a $2 tip and treated us to ice cream cones.

Next to it, a magnificent silk, hand-woven,
15th century-type tapestry triptych of *Mom,
the Lady of the House*: on the left, in front
of the kerosene stove, stirring crepe batter;
center, wearing a Stone Marten fur draped
around her shoulders; on the right, posing
in front of her new GE washing machine.

As for me, my future might have been history,
my name and title on illuminated scrolls.
Yet, who knows? Cherubim, looking down
from hand-painted heavenly ceilings,
might find me resenting my monogrammed
life and trying to daydream my way out.

WORKING CLASS

Why does working class run through my marrow?
My father's lunchbox, his union dues.
The steel beams he carried "for a better tomorrow."
Why does working class run through my marrow?
Dad was the laborer, his boss like a pharaoh
whose coffers Dad filled. He hauled like a mule.
Why does working class run through my marrow?
My father's rough hands, his carpenter tools.

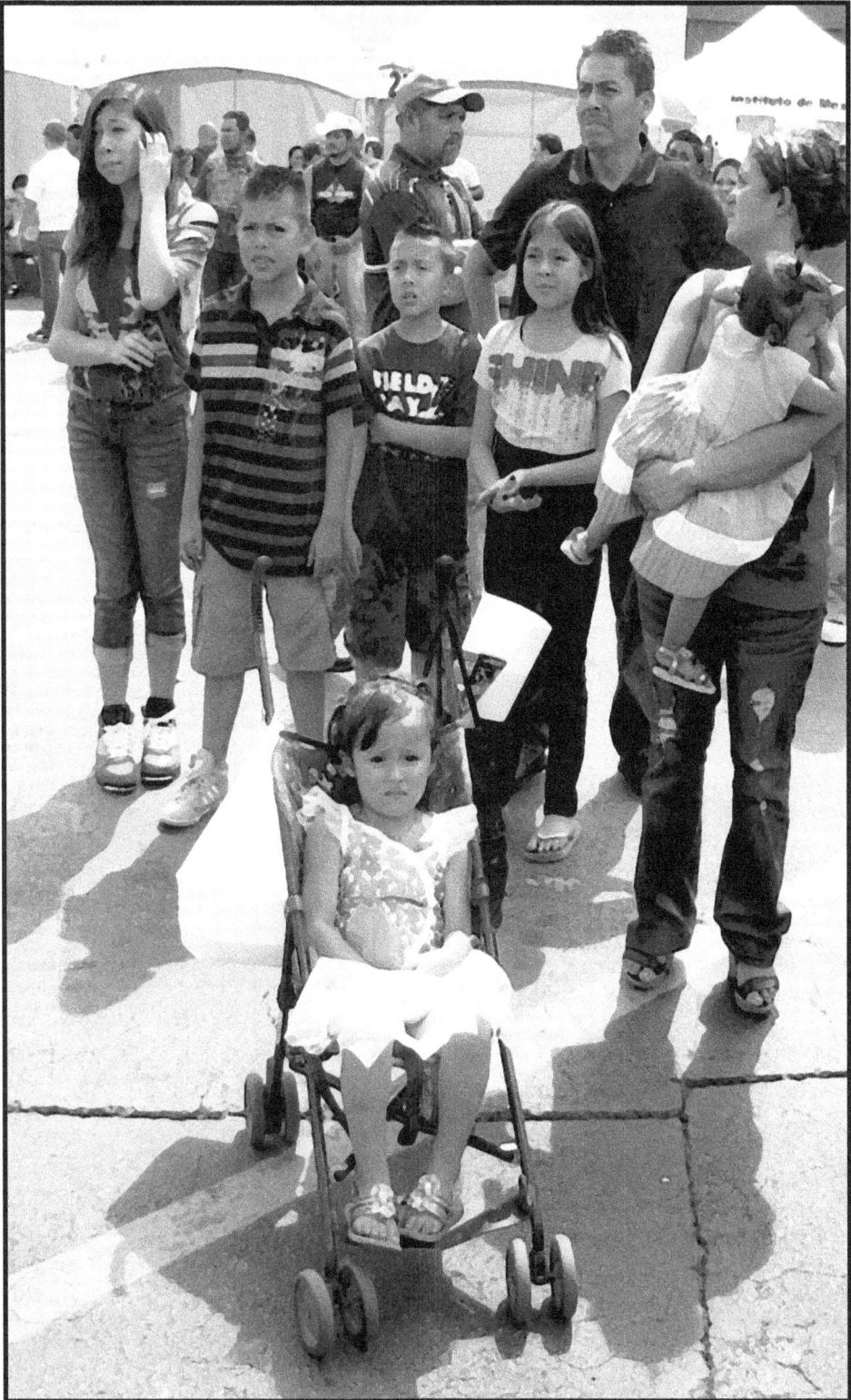

JUDITH J. KATZ

HOW I GOT HERE

When I hear slam poets spit
it makes me
want to speak
the way they speak
and say something
important
about the way
my people were treated
and how I am a person
of color
and the color is not white
because my people
were herded in cattle-
cars
and gassed in ovens
and worked in fields
until their hands bled
and they couldn't lift
their one potato a day to their mouths
and so they died.

Or fled to the sea
Packed in the holds of steam ships.
And yes
we were free when we came:
with our one dollar American
and our one bar of Hersheys.
We were free when we came:
to leave our health, wealth

and happiness behind us
Oh, yes, we were free
when we came,
in a way.

And we learned
your language and
wept our tears in private
and lived in our fifth floor
walk up, cold water flats.
And we went on.
And so will you,
safe, in the knowledge
that no one people
owns the exclusive rights
to freedom or misery.

NANCY L. MEYER

POOR RELATIONS

Even I know the rules. Pull on the pink dress
with smocking that itches my neck. Grandpa knots
his maroon wool tie instead of the frayed blue plaid.
Gramma squeezes into her dotted Swiss, digs out
the one pair of lisle stockings not darned in scars of tiny x's.
Crunch up the gravel drive in the rusty Nash Rambler
under arching maples, past gabled barn, white colonial
with its ells and slate roof.

Aunt Nina emerges from her parlor, gray hair
swooped in a bun. Luncheon on the wrap-around porch,
linens monogrammed in blue. Bouillon and blancmange.
Gramma dabs her worn handkerchief at the sweat
bee-lining her cheek. How many children
with names like Dinny and Rabbit does she have to nod
and smile about? No mention of the job Grandpa
lost at Amherst College.

Every month Gramma slits the envelope
with a paring knife, wishing the ivory vellum were not
so thick, the flourish of Nina's signature on the check
not so bold. Gramma buries the blue rectangle in her purse,
walks it up Amity Street to the red brick bank.
Her housedress sticks, home past the American Legion,
fawn-grey cannon, black hole of its muzzle.
She tromps by too-yellow forsythia, Gregg's Furniture,
scuffs the path by the smoke bush up the back steps,
dashes the pocketbook on the kitchen table.

She sucks blue ink into her fountain pen,
a slash of plain paper on the drop-down desk.
Dear Nina, Many thanks once again . . .
A pause of pen, blob of ink bursts from the nib.
She lets the stain spread.

I HEARD NETTIE SAY CLARA SWEATS LIKE A PIG

Sheets droop from mangles
like dog tongues on a hot day. Washers
whirr in rows under harsh fluorescent
Basement hallways, shadows and grime.
Sweat shines like coal
in Clara's neck folds. She irons
monogrammed sheets, pillow cases
Nettie's slips and silk panties. Hers
are sticking to her thighs. *No breath*
under this damn uniform. The other
washerwomen shake their heads, arms
steady as pendulums across their boards.
Can you believe, this old woman—more panties
than my whole family put together.

STOLEN YIDDISH

Before we decorate the Christmas tree
Baruch a toh unwinds off
mother's gentile tongue, lands on
ner shel Hanukkah.
She prays over the Menorah, teaching us
Dad's tradition.

We spin the *dreidel* together,
but tucked in bed that night
I hear them argue. *Why did you*
tell Joe what the Ford wagon cost?
she scolds, . . . *so boorish.*

Just because your people
won't discuss money . . .
he retorts. Their voices rumble
into the night.

Last week she called him
bourgeois for coming home
with yet another pair of shoes.
Mama's prince, too coddled
to put up the storm windows.
She hauls them up the ladder.

Chides me, *Rude just like*
your Father, when I interrupt.
If I brag . . . *Such chutzpah!* she flings
her stolen Yiddish at me
like a stone.
Insensitive   like THEM,
like him. Like me.

HOUSE ENVY

Architects, contractors, general
and sub. From a swallow-you-up
hole in the ground to sconces, shingles, rebar and hinges,
tinted paint, granite and tubs. Where do you want
the light switches? How about this tree? Low flush or
regular? Please sign this change order.

At last we're in. Now what?
Punch lists and heartaches. How can we
not have closet space? What about this leak?
Ninety degrees in the bedroom. Not enough light to cook by.
Get that electrician back here, please!

Friends come looking. Gray tweed
carpet, oh so practical. Red, yellow, even
turquoise. How did they dare skip beige?
With all those stairs, no aging parent could stay here.
Why is his office twice as big as hers? The artwork is
so bold. So cold. All that room for just those two?
I love the view.

I'm quick to tell them it's not perfect.
I always try to share the space. Besides,
it's all my husband's wealth. I used to
be on Food Stamps, long ago. I rarely say
I love the light curling over the kitchen floor,
the mountains from my favorite chair, bright colors

and curves, double showers, big TV.
Roll up the rugs and invite fifty
friends to dance. How lucky can I be?

And still, I envy richer friends whose cabinets
are custom-hewn and dining rooms seat twelve.
Or humbler ones with wind chimes and comfy corners
where you want to sit for hours sipping tea.
Do come in. It's just a house, that's all.

HIGGLERS*

Early in the cool of day, the women
set down heavy baskets of yam,
breadfruit, tomato and callaloo,
spread out their piece of cloth,
check the change purse snug
in a skirt pocket, call *Mawnin*
to their neighbor, if they're
on speaking terms.

They see me coming, white gal
from University housing, pony tail
streaming to my waist. Head ties,
thick patois, cave-black skin scare me off.
Only fair they should make me pay
for all of Colonialism in the price
of one star-apple.

One woman
whose mangoes are sweetest,
Rebeccah her name. Gold specks
surprise me glinting from her sepia
eyes. Her skin dark chocolate,
dusted white at elbow and heel—
too much sun, not enough time to rub in
cocoa butter. Now I start my rounds
at her cloth every day.

Chaw, you k'yan ask that much
for one scrawny cah-rot, I muster
my Jamaican accent.
She chuckles, throws in three more.

*Higglers: pronounced Igglahs—from the verb "to higgle," to haggle or to bargain

CARL "PAPA" PALMER

ASSUMPTION OF ACCENT

I know you'll like this one,
grinning into his racist joke
after hearing my southern drawl.

LOVE/HATE RELATIONSHIP

shaved head nose ring black beard
frayed jeans leather jacketed arms
crude tattooed right fist spells HATE
across knuckles eyes daring comment
from strangers in the full visitors room

wheel-chaired sleeping mother sighs
as he whisps a stray hair from her eyes
with his left hand labeled LOVE
gently touches his lips to her cheek
smiles shyly at new friends in the room

SUSAN G. DUNCAN

CORRECT

No one kindly corrects her—
the black woman on our North Woods tour—

when she spies a swan on the Harlem Meer.

The rest of us—
white, right—
knew an egret when we saw one.

III. CROSSING: ACTS OF IMAGINATION

JANE ST. CLAIR

SECRETS OF MAMA KARDASHIAN

What surprises people about the TV show, *You Guess the Price*, is that their producers do not pick the contestants randomly. Now Shirley Diemski knew this in advance. In fact, knowing how they pick contestants was part of her strategy to get on the show.

Shirley knew that the producers divide the entire audience into groups of twelve, and then they take those little groups into interview rooms. She also knew they're more likely to choose you if you're vivacious or if it's your birthday or if you're wearing an Armed Services uniform or a homemade T-shirt customized with the show's theme. With all this in mind, Shirley got a ticket for the show that fell on her birthday and wore a T-shirt made by her best friend Vera with a hand-painted portrait of the show's host. So it really was no big surprise to her when the show's host, Yip the Lip Serge, yelled, "Shirley Diemski, come on down! You're a contestant on *You Guess the Price!*"

Shirley knew to act surprised and teary-eyed, and to jump up and down as if she'd swallowed a jalapeno pepper. The truth was the only thing that surprised Shirley, who always taped every show to watch after work, was how loud Yip's voice was. He didn't need to yell like that. After all, he had a microphone.

If you're like Shirley and watch the show every day, you also find out that they use the same prizes over and over, so if you're watching the show all the time and taking notes, you get a feel for how much the usual prizes cost, including the big screen TV, the all-expense paid seven-day trip to Cancún, and the smallest American compact car.

So when Shirley went up against three other contestants to guess the price of a big screen TV, the actual retail price and not the price people really pay after they go online and check at Walmart, Shirley guessed $1200. When the highest bid was $1100, all she had to do was bid $1101.

Next Yip Serge asked Shirley if she would like to win . . . *a six-day vacation to Martha's Vineyard! Yes, Shirley, we'll fly you and your guest from Los Angeles to the Franklin Stone Manor, a fabulous resort where you'll experience the lifestyle of the rich and famous! Plus you and your guest will receive two all-day passes to the Bambi Pamper Day Spa for eight full hours of pampering, hair styling, mani-pedis and massage. This fabulous vacation is all yours if you guess the price!*

As Yip the Lip kept blasting Shirley's eardrums, she had only one thought. She was going to win this trip for herself and her daughter Brooke. She pictured them in that Bambi Pamper Day Spa, stretched out on fur-covered tables next to the likes of Barbra S and Hillary RC herself, chatting them up and sipping herbal tea with organic honey. On second thought Shirley decided the spa's tables would not be fur because nobody sharp does fur anymore. Shirley thought how Brooke would be proud of her for once, and how excited she would be when her mother presented her with this fabulous vacation. After all, Brooke could handle Martha's Vineyard. Brooke was so classy, you'd think she was BFFs with Chelsea and Ivanka—either one —Brooke was right up here with them.

The game required Shirley to rearrange the number 7363 to mirror the price of the trip. When she guessed $6753, the prize was hers. Her luck ran out after spinning a roulette wheel that eliminated her for a chance to win the grand prize showcase. It didn't matter for Shirley had won *prizes worth over $8100*, an unbelievable amount when you're only making $21,000 a year as a full-time groomer at PetSmart.

As Shirley and Vera drove from Hollywood back home to Tucson, Shirley phoned Brooke with the good news. Brooke never answered her phone. Brooke was living in New York City and so she hardly ever picked up her phone because there is so much else to do there.

"If she can't go, then you've got to take me," Vera pleaded. "I want that spa day."

"It might even be the spa where Jackie Kennedy went to lose weight," Shirley said.

"Jackie never had to lose any weight," Vera replied, swerving to avoid hitting a coyote, "because she lived on hard-boiled eggs and lettuce. I read that in her nanny's book. But come on, I need that spa more than Brooke."

"The thing is . . ." Shirley began, "The thing is . . . I've been thinking a long time about Brooke and me. About taking a road trip just Brooke and me. I got the idea from watching the Kardashians. Whenever one of the Dash girls act up, which is all the time, Kris takes her on a road trip, just the two of them, and they watch old movies on TV all night long, and they eat popcorn so it's just like an itty-bitty pajama party, and by the end of the trip, they've bonded. They're close again."

"She's such a great mom," Vera said.

"Absolutely," Shirley agreed.

"But I'd be surprised if Brooke goes on that trip," Vera said. "Oh, I'm sorry—I didn't mean that the way it came out. But it's just she's in that stage when you think your mother's beneath you. You and I went through that, remember?"

"Yeah. It was right before our bimbo stage. The bimbo stage was more fun."

"And it lasted longer. But then, we weren't like her. We never got snobbified back East like her," her friend told her.

"She didn't get snobbified, she just got upscale."

Upscale was the word Shirley used to describe Brooke, a word she learned at PetSmart. Certain brands of merchandise were cheap and ordinary, but there were a few that were upscale. Martha Stewart dog beds, for example, had fancy artist designs on them and better-quality fabrics so they were upscale.

That night Shirley lay in bed, unable to sleep and hoping Brooke would call her. "Lord, I've screwed up plenty," Shirley prayed, "especially with Paul Shloss. And I know I owe You more than You owe me. But I just wish that just this once, You'll say yes and make Brooke go to Martha's Vineyard with me."

There were no return calls all morning but at noon, Shirley got a text from Brooke. "What dates would work for you? For the Vineyard? I'll get back to you with my dates," the text read.

They decided that Shirley would fly from Los Angeles and meet Brooke at the Island's airport the third week in July. *You Guess the Price* refused to pay for Brooke's ticket from New York, even though she told them that New York to Martha's Vineyard was cheaper than a ticket from Los Angeles, the one they had originally promised. There's no talking to some people.

Brooke was standing by herself in the middle of the airport lobby. She was more beautiful than Shirley remembered. Brooke never fixed herself up with makeup, and her hair was clipped haphazardly into a messy bun, yet she was exquisite.

"Oh my God, baby, you're beautiful!" Shirley said, rushing to hug her daughter. Ever since she began living alone, Shirley often felt a hunger for human touch, and sometimes she longed for the sensuality of early motherhood when she had been so close to her baby that it had been an erotic, sensual time for her.

But Brooke pulled away before Shirley could embrace her.

"Will we have a car waiting for us or do we have to pick it up?" she asked.

"We're getting a red Mustang convertible—do you believe that? Isn't that awesome? This whole thing feels like a dream come true. I mean—there I was on *You Guess the Price* and here we are at—"

"Let's just get the car," Brooke interrupted. "I'm tired."

"Okay, tired. Got it. We can fix tired when we get to the hotel."

As Brooke stood by impatiently, Shirley got into a long, animated conversation with the car rental clerk about how she won her trip on *You Guess the Price.*

"Get out of here!" the rental clerk squealed. "I don't believe it. You won six days at Franklin Stone Manor? That's incredible. That place costs an arm and a leg."

"It's easy if you watch the show all the time," Shirley responded.

"You're being modest."

"Mom—please," Brooke said.

"Your mother's really smart," the clerk said, "and she's so funny. Let me know how the vacation goes when you get back here."

"Oh sure, honey," Shirley promised, "bye for now. Love you."

Brooke stood by, tapping her feet. Brooke was all about foot tapping, both mental and physical.

"Let's put the top down on the car!" Shirley said as they walked toward the convertible. "That is, if we can figure out how to do it. I've always wanted to drive a convertible with the top down. Oh my God, this car's perfect!"

"Let's not mess with the top. I'm tired."

"Okay. Tired. Got it. Do you want to hold the map while I drive?"

"Really, Mom, nobody uses maps anymore." Brooke pulled out her cell phone and spoke into it. "Directions to Franklin Stone Manor in Martha's Vineyard."

The phone replied in broken computer English, "Frankenstein Manor. Seventeen minutes via Barnes Road."

Shirley laughed. Brooke did not.

They lapsed into silence again. Shirley tried to fill it with nervous chatter, but she finally kept her mouth shut to avoid Brooke's correcting her again. The only sound was the strange voice of the bossy woman computer who pronounced "Vin-yard" as "Vine Yard." When Shirley missed a street, the computer scolded her by repeating, "Recalculating. Recalculating." Gee, I can't even please a goddamn robot, Shirley thought.

Franklin Stone Manor was an impressive white wooden structure that stood on stilts on the beach of the Oak Bluff section of the island. Even in the twilight Shirley could see how big the resort was: four stories high with a massive wrap-around porch. It wasn't her idea of a luxury resort. In fact, it looked like a gigantic version of her grandmother's clapboard house in Globe, Arizona, but she tried nevertheless to act enthusiastic.

"I can hardly wait to sit on that porch and watch the ocean," Shirley exclaimed as she parked the car.

"Whatever," Brooke replied.

The hotel lobby had a musty smell from standing so many years next to the sea. It was decorated with ancient rickety furniture and old paintings of clipper ships, and its carpeting was old-fashioned with a faded rose botanical design. Everything looked run-down to Shirley.

"It's not what I pictured," she confessed to Brooke. "I thought everything would be new and shiny."

"It's historic," Brooke replied with irritation. "Those are expensive eighteenth-century antiques."

"Oh. Okay. Historic. Antiques. Got it."

Three bored hotel clerks stood imprisoned behind wooden cages that looked like something out of the bank scenes in the movie, *It's a Wonderful Life*. Shirley approached an older female clerk and began to chatter.

"I'm the one from *You Guess the Price*," she said. "I can't believe I'm here. I came all the way from Tucson. This is an historic hotel, right?"

"Oh yes," the clerk replied with a smile. "It's very old. In fact, Daniel Webster stayed here."

"The one who wrote the dictionary? Oh my gosh, I'll have to watch my Ps and Qs while I'm here."

"Daniel Webster and Nathaniel Hawthorne stayed here together," the clerk told her.

"I didn't know they were gay," Shirley said. "Just think of the courage that took way back then."

"Mom, please," Brooke sighed. "I'm tired."

"Oh, okay. Tired. Got it. You said that before. We need to get up to our room."

"But I want to hear all about *You Guess the Price*," the clerk said. "I watch it all the time."

"Then you'd be a shoo-in to win because you know how much the prizes cost."

"Mom, please, I'm tired."

The clerk rang for a bus boy to carry their luggage upstairs to a large suite on the second floor. He went into the rooms with them and turned down their beds, expertly placing a rose and an imported piece of chocolate on their pillows.

"Can I bring you anything else?" he asked. "Perhaps a hot toddy?"

"No, that'll be all," Brooke said, expertly slipping him a $5 tip.

How did she know how much to give? Shirley wondered. Do they teach that stuff at that fancy girls' college I sent her to? Brooke was operating so smoothly in this world of tradition and established ways of doing things, which is nothing like the way you do things out West.

"I guess they don't have a refrigerator," Shirley said, walking around the three-room suite. "That's too bad. Sometimes you can get a doggy bag at lunch and then bingo, you have enough for dinner. But you need a fridge to do that. The show didn't give us meal vouchers, you know."

"Oh, Mom," Brooke sighed. "They have all kinds of restaurants here. We'll manage."

Shirley started to exclaim about the soft silkiness of the sheets, the humongous size of the bathtub with its squirting spouts, and the French windows with their airy dotted Swiss curtains that disguised black-out shades. Brooke just sighed. Don't talk so much, Shirley told herself. Don't talk so loud. Don't talk at all.

The next morning, they walked to Oak Bluff Boulevard, a wooden boardwalk from an historic era now lined with boutiques and small cafes. Brooke suggested they get croissants, pronouncing it "Kuh-ray-sonts" and not the way they say it in Tucson, which is "cray-saints."

They entered a small French café and sat at a tiny round wooden table not much bigger than a Thanksgiving platter. Shirley assumed that it must be some historic table. By now she had figured out if a thing in Martha's

Vineyard wasn't luxurious, it was some old expensive antique. She could sense the nearness of the ocean in the slight smell of salt in the air and the easy breezes coming through the open door of the restaurant. She had only been to the ocean once, back when she was a child. She remembered that the California ocean was green not blue, and that it had gray seaweed covering its sand, but she also remembered liking the ocean for how big it was and for its constant motion.

"I wonder if their ocean looks different than the one in California," Shirley mused.

Brooke wasn't paying attention. She was looking out the window at a group of tourists passing by. Shirley's eyes followed Brooke's gaze, and then she said, "Oh my God, that's Diane Sawyer."

"Mom, sit down. Right this instant."

Shirley did as she was told.

"Celebrities are entitled to their privacy," Brooke whispered.

Shirley nodded, still staring at Diane Sawyer passing by, and studying the line of her clothes and the cut of her hair, both of which were casual like Brooke's. Both Brooke and Diane Sawyer looked as if they were going hiking in their high-tech clothes from the REI catalog, clothes that were serious. Just then Shirley felt embarrassed. Her matching tunic and slacks, embroidered with beach balls and sunglasses and purchased in Palm Springs Pink especially for this trip from QVC on Easy Pay, looked all wrong.

"She's perfect," Shirley said. "Diane Sawyer is perfect. Wait until I tell Vera."

"Are you done gaping at her? We should go."

"I'd like to see where the Kennedys lived," Shirley said.

"Oh, Mom, it'll take hours—it's way out there on Hyannis Port. Besides, they didn't live here. They just vacationed here."

"I'd like to see it."

"I really hate your celebrity thing," Brooke said. "It's so tacky."

Shirley bit back tears, but she couldn't bite back the dam that was holding her emotions.

"I said I hate your celebrity thing," her daughter repeated.

"I heard you the first time," Shirley said in a quaking voice, as tears filled her eyes. "I may be your mother but I have feelings. I'm your mother but I'm also a person. And sometimes you go too far."

The tears rolled down Shirley's cheeks. She wiped them off with a tissue and blew her nose. Brooke seemed to soften.

"We could take the ferry boat to Hyannis Port," she said.

"Okey dokey," Shirley smiled.

It took more than an hour to make it to the Kennedy Legacy Trail, which turned out to be a disappointment in that you can't really get close to the compound of Kennedy-owned buildings. You can only look at the compound from a distance.

"Jack and Jackie had their house there next to that great big one that belonged to Jack's mom and dad," Shirley mused. "That was nice of her, but then she always sucked up to Jack's father because he had all the money."

"Nobody cares about the Kennedys anymore," Brooke said.

"You're probably right but I'd like to see Chappaquiddick next."

"What's that?" Brooke said. "More Kennedy heritage?"

"Sort of. Except it's more Teddy Kennedy heritage."

They didn't make it to Chappaquiddick Island, but they did see the Dike Bridge, the very place where Teddy Kennedy drove his Lincoln into the water and accidentally caused the death of his passenger. Seeing the Kennedy Legacy places where JFK went sailing, where Jackie wore her pert little sundresses and where Teddy got into deep water touched Shirley. She felt as if she'd completed a pilgrimage to the holiest of shrines to the Kennedys, who lived at the top of her Mount Olympus of celebrity gods and goddesses. She even picked up a stone from under the Dike Bridge to take home with her as a relic picked from hallowed ground.

That night Shirley wanted to splurge on dinner at the Black Dog Tavern, the very place where Monica Lewinsky purchased a T-shirt for Bill Clinton, a fact she did not mention to Brooke. The tavern was upscale but dark with dark wood paneling and a big fireplace. They make you wait over two hours to eat.

"What do you want to do tomorrow?" Shirley asked as their waiter finally delivered their dinners. Brooke was a lacto-less, gluten-less vegan something or another, making it hard for her to eat. Her mother did not recognize the dinner she ordered—some strange purple and yellow dish with a foreign name.

"Oh, I don't know," Brooke replied. "Anything that doesn't involve celebrities."

Shirley wanted to suggest getting a movie and popcorn for a pajama party but something held her back—the same something that made her buy a paperback novel rather than a National Enquirer at the drug store, the same something that made her refrain from asking for a doggie bag for the leftover purple food, and the same something that told her to use a quiet voice and to act less excited, the way Brooke did. It was enough that Brooke agreed to go to the Bambi Day Spa with her the next morning. That would have to be enough, anyway, because Brooke was not giving anything else.

The Bambi Day Pamper Spa reminded Shirley of the one she'd seen on "Frasier," when Frasier and Niles went for the Platinum Package. Brooke and Shirley actually had the Platinum Package at the Bambi Spa which was the highest you could get. You had to take off all your clothes and put on this soft pink robe, and then they pulled your hair back with a pink velvet turban, and then they gave you memory foam slippers for your bare feet. *You Guess the Price* certainly did not scrimp at the Bambi, Shirley thought.

The attendants wrapped Shirley and Brooke up like mummies in muslin strips soaked in wet grass from some obscure place in Africa, and they had to lie down on special cots, listen to meditative music and drink vegetable smoothies. They got hair-cuts and mani-pedi's, and then ate a spa lunch of some little white spring rolls and a small but exquisite fruit salad shaped like a bouquet of flowers. In the afternoon two very hefty men came to perform total body massages while meditative music was still playing. Everything smelled like lavender musk. In some ways, Shirley wished Vera was there because the massage would have made her over-the-top happy, whereas you never can tell with Brooke.

"I feel like wet linguine," Shirley said as they walked back to their hotel. "I don't even feel like eating, I'm so relaxed. This has never happened to me before in my life. No wonder rich women are so skinny. You lose your appetite in those places. Why don't we rent a movie?"

"Oh Mom, you don't need to rent them—you can just get them off the hotel's movie channel," Brooke said.

"Do you feel like Cold Duck? I feel like drinking Cold Duck or something loaded."

"Please let's not get Cold Duck," Brooke sighed. "Please let's just order from the hotel."

Shirley started to say it would be cheaper to buy liquor in town and smuggle into their hotel suite, but she bit her tongue. When they got to their rooms, Brooke ordered something in French, and within ten minutes the bus boy was wheeling a gold cart covered with a white tablecloth through their door. On the cart was a tiny vase with one perfect yellow camellia, and a gold ice bucket with two bottles of champagne and two crystal champagne flutes.

They lay propped up on their beds and downed one flute after another. When they were getting to the end of the second bottle, Brooke ordered two more bottles of champagne. She was getting more relaxed and talkative, so Shirley opened up a subject of interest to her.

"Tell me about the new boyfriend Siddharth," Shirley said. "When can I meet him?"

"That would not be a good idea," Brooke replied.

"I've never had an Indian lover. Are they any good?"

"Oh yeah."

Brooke giggled in spite of herself.

Shirley giggled back. "How good? How good is good?"

"He moved out once and I thought I'd kill myself."

"Why did he move out?" her mother asked.

"I was being a bitch."

"I can believe that," Shirley said.

They both were giggling badly. Shirley's sides were hurting from it. They were seriously drunk and on the verge of becoming Silly Billies together.

"Touché," Brooke said, moving to clink her glass against her mother's. "You asked me something, so I'm going to ask you something. Why in heaven do you have to talk so much?"

"I just do. You know what?" Shirley said, slurring her words. "You never once said it was nice I won the trip."

"It's nice."

"Thank you for once."

"They probably put you on the show because they liked you," Brooke said.

"I think it was the T-shirt," Shirley replied. "The portrait Vera drew looked just like Yip the Lip only she made him look handsome. He's actually butt-ugly in person."

"Everybody likes you," Brooke said. "Even when I was little, my friends liked you better than me."

"It's because I'm talkative," Shirley explained. "I can carry any conversation."

"No, it's not just that," her daughter said, "it's also that you win people over to your side. Like that woman with the dog at the spa. She was crazy about you."

"The one with the Burmese Mountain dog?"

"Whatever. You had her worshipping the ground you walk on."

"I just know how to fix Burmese Mountain dogs' potty problems. All your Burmeses get potty problems and they're not that hard to deal with. I just gave her a few tips, that's all."

"But it's not just her," Brooke said, "Everyone likes you. Everywhere you go. Everyone likes you."

"But you're elegant," Shirley said. "And you have a beautiful vocabulary. I wish I had vocabulary."

"Whatever," Brooke said, pouring herself another drink. "But I hate your celebrity thing. It's tacky."

"I'm trying to control it."

"And you know what else I hate? I hate that you drove me to that grammar school. The school outside our neighborhood. That was one lousy idea."

"That school was better than ours," Shirley said. "Besides, that was a long time ago. You shouldn't bring up a long time ago. If you're going to fight, you have to keep it to nowadays."

"But I didn't have anything in common with those rich kids," Brooke said. "It was a rich school, the one outside our neighborhood."

"But you do now," Shirley said. "You have everything in common with them now."

Her words hung on the air. Silence. Silence.

"I guess," Brooke said finally. She was slurring her words. "But I did have one thing they don't have. Something they'll never have. And it's something you gave me. And I'm grateful for it."

"I don't believe it. I don't believe I did something right," Shirley said. "What did I give you that those rich bitches don't have?"

"You gave me a bullshit detector."

They both giggled uncontrollably.

"They could sure use one at the Bambi Pamper Day Spa," Shirley said.

"Yes. They could. No rich kid has a bullshit detector, and bullshit detectors are very useful."

"It wasn't all BS at the Bambi. The massage boys were cute. And they were built—oh man, they were built," Shirley said.

"They were absolutely adorable," Brooke agreed.

They were finishing the third bottle of champagne when Shirley brought up the hair dryer. The hair dryer was a very important topic for Shirley. When Brooke went away to college, Shirley had not been able to afford good clothes or anything extra for her. Brooke had a scholarship that paid for her room, board and tuition, but no matter how much overtime Shirley put in, she did not have the money to buy her daughter all the extra things the other girls had. With one exception: the hair dryer. The hair dryer was the exception. The hair dryer was the best and most expensive one made, and Vera had gotten it for her at a discount because she worked at a beauty salon. Shirley often pictured the other girls in the dorm wanting to borrow Brooke's fancy hair dryer.

"I bet everyone wanted to use that dryer," Shirley said with pride. "Five minutes and you're out the door. You must have been really popular because you had that machine."

For once Brooke did not have the heart to tell her the truth, which was that the other girls in the dorm had their own fancy hair dryers, and most of them did not even do their own hair.

Instead she said, "Yes, Mom—the hair dryer was a big hit."

Brooke's eyes filled with tears for she knew how much her mother had sacrificed for her, and that was the thing that was always between them.

"I'd do it all the same again," Shirley said as if reading her daughter's thoughts. "It was all my choice to do it."

"I love you," Brooke said. "I love you, Ma."

"I'd do it all the same," Shirley repeated.

After that night, the one Shirley called the Night of the Dash Pajama Party, the rest of their vacation went by quickly. When it was time to drive to the airport, Shirley looked at her daughter and said, "Call me, huh?"

"When I get home." Brooke smiled and put her arm around her mother. "I'll call you. I had a nice time. I really did. I'll call you."

"I had a nice time too."

"I'll phone the minute I get home," Brooke promised. "I'll phone." Brooke was reluctant to leave—Shirley could hear it in her voice.

Shirley had a window seat on the six-hour flight back to Los Angeles. It was only her second time on an airplane, and yet this time she was less nervous. She could even enjoy the view of Microsoft clouds and turquoise skies. She felt grateful to *You Guess the Price*. She felt grateful to Vera, and to the Franklin Stone Manor and the Bambi Pamper Day Spa, and to Martha's

Vineyard. She stared out the window. The truth was she felt the most grateful to her Blessed Mother, the Blessed Mother Kardashian.

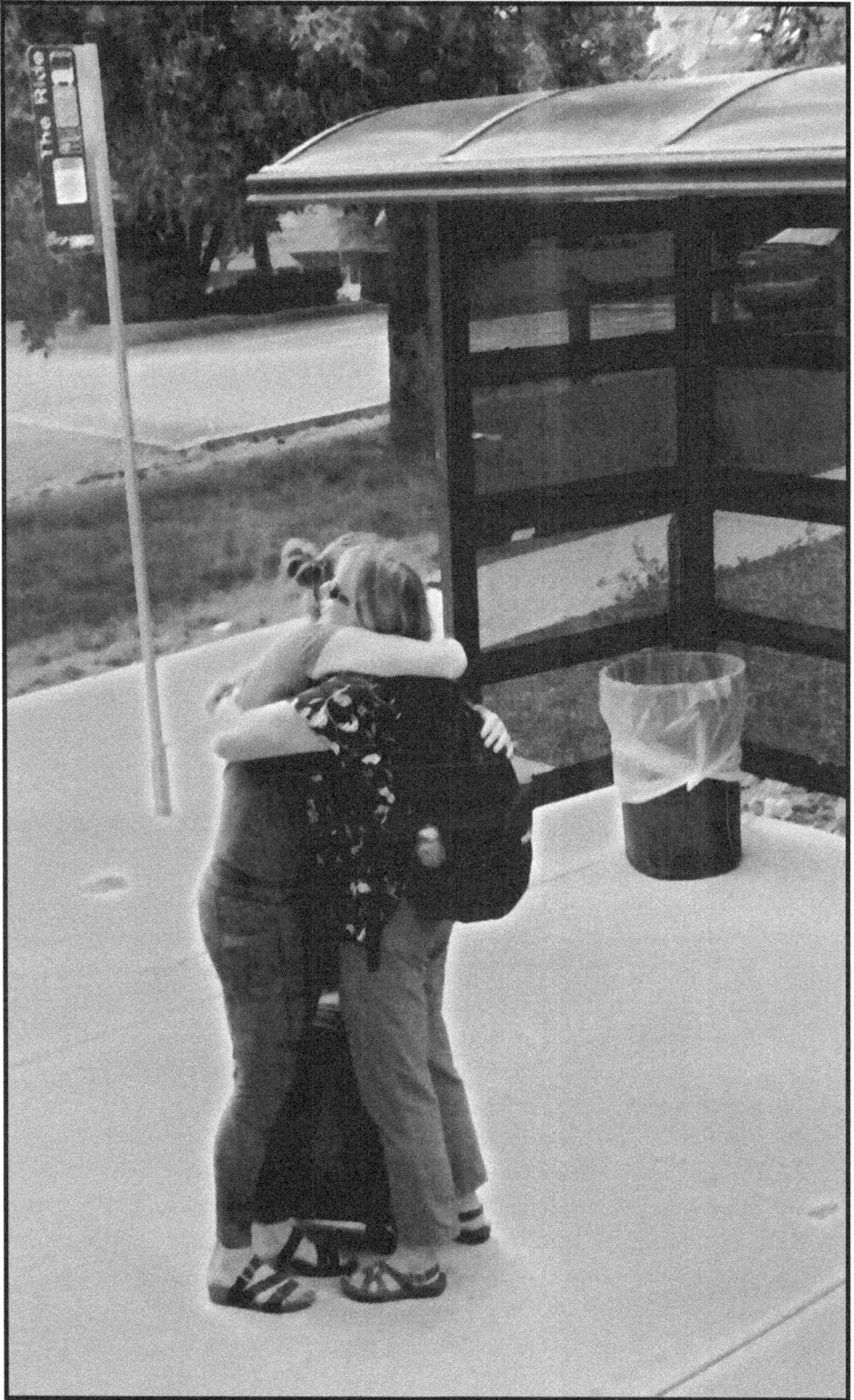

DANISA BELL

PRINCESS

I once heard Ree Ree Walker call Mandi and her mother poor white trash. It was right out in front of our building at George Washington Carver Homes, Goshen's only housing project. I didn't understand it then, back in 1996, for we were only six and seven, Mandi and I, but Mandi was more than just poor. She was *dirt* poor. And incredibly so. Some nights for dinner she ate jelly sandwiches with Vienna sausages. And once when I spent the night with Mandi, the next morning for breakfast we had butter and sugar on hotdog buns with dill pickles and cold black coffee. Whenever I would go after that, I would sneak food into my overnight bag. One time we had Twinkies and ham slices; another time, a jar of peanut butter and a box of Ritz. And we would fill our bellies late at night under the sheets with a flashlight while her mother slept.

Mandi didn't have a lot of toys like the other kids in Carver Homes. No bike, no Barbie dolls, no nothing really. Just this little fat half baby doll named Ruthie that she almost always carried with her. And Ruthie was always naked. She had chopped-off brown hair and no legs, only arms and hands with shiny purple nail polish where the fingernails would be. And when you laid Ruthie down, one of her eyes would close in that peculiar way that made you think she was winking at you when she wasn't, while the other stayed fixed on the ceiling or the sky, depending upon where you were at the time.

Once though, Candace Taylor, who was ten and liked to boss around us younger kids, and always with her hand on her bony brown hip, told Mandi that she was lucky, rich or poor, toys or no toys, because she was white. "One day you gonna marry a doctor or a lawyer, Mandi, and go to London and Paris. All white people go to London and Paris!"

But Mandi didn't care about being white, or about doctors or the European enticements of London and Paris. "No way, Candace!" she shot back. "Me and Ruthie are staying here! For the rest of our life! We like it here!"

"Yeah, Candace," I chimed in. "She's not going to get married! She just moved here in kinnygarden! And we're blood sisters, see?" I held up the tip of my pinkie finger for her to see the barely visible prick I had made with a safety pin.

"Yeah, see?" added Mandi, holding her pinkie finger in the air next to mine.

"You shut up, Tatiana Williams!" said Candace. "You just think you're better than everybody else!"

"No I don't!"

"Do so! You wanna be white like Mandi. Why don't you just go in the house and read one of those fancy books your momma buys you so you can get skipped another grade again since you know so much!" The other kids exploded into a thunder of laughter and began to nod in agreement with Candace. All but Mandi.

Suddenly I could feel the pain of every dark emotion pulsing through my veins and rushing to the tips of my throbbing fingers. I wanted to lash out at Candace. Tell her she was stupid and didn't know anything, but Candace was bigger and stronger. I looked at Mandi. We were the same. Same height. Same size. We both had ponytails and both liked to pull the cheese off our pizza and eat it last. And now we were sisters, no matter what happened. Now we had the same blood. I took her by the hand, and we went back to our own building to play with Ruthie.

)(   )(   )(

Instead of toys, Corsica Pate allowed Mandi to write and draw on the walls in their apartment with crayons and colored chalk. "A way for her to express herself," Corsica Pate would always say. "Mandi is so creative." But the other parents just shook their heads and said that was one crazy woman. First for living in the projects when she was white, and second for letting that little child scribble up their apartment.

And although she wrote and drew on the walls, what Mandi wanted more than anything else was to be a fairy princess. "Just like Snow White," she would say. "Like at the movies." Mandi didn't have a long flowing gown, or seven dwarves to follow her around, but every day when we came home from school, Mandi would change into her provisional princess outfit her mother had pieced together for her from the Goodwill.

It was a pair of purple cowboy boots that were too big for her. They had fake rhinestones and made a loud echo on the stairs of our apartment building when she would run in and out. Along with her purple cowboy boots, Mandi wore a turquoise chiffon skirt with multiple layers that jutted below the waist like a ballerina's tutu, and a long-sleeved pink fitted T-shirt with a picture on the front of, who else, Snow White! But the thing Mandi adored most about her princess attire was the little plastic tiara we all had gotten from Kenya Murphy's birthday party when she turned seven.

"Look! I'm a princess, Tati!" she would say to me. It was the finishing touch to an already astonishing assemblage of garments. Over time, a small part of the headband had broken off, and several of the fake diamonds had fallen out. But Mandi would sail through the apartments on my bike in her ensemble. Free. Happy. Her blond hair licking the air behind her like a hot white flame.

And on the days when the wind was anxious, Mandi and I would find the flowers. Sometimes in front of the buildings or between the parked cars; sometimes right inside the hallway when the door to our building had been propped open by the Walker twins, who would let the loud music from the stereo in their apartment radiate into the hallway and streets. There were red flowers. Yellow ones and white ones. Plastic funerary bouquets that would tumble across the street from Eastwood Gardens Cemetery, also nicknamed Rainbow Hill because of the enormous spectrum of color that exploded before your very eyes upon cresting the gentle incline of Sprayberry Avenue. Our housing project sat on the right, and the cemetery across the street on the left. Mandi would collect all of the bouquets she could find. "We can build a giant palace made of flowers, Tati!"

"That would be awesome! A palace would be exceptional!" She would pull me by the hand, and we would run off in search of more bouquets.

Corsica Pate had been delighted by the pretty flowers when she found us playing with them for the first time in the bedroom she and Mandi shared. "Wow! Beautiful! Where'd you girls get all of these?" she asked. We had gathered twelve or thirteen bouquets from around the complex that day. And just the same as if she had seen a ghost, Corsica Pate gasped. She covered her mouth with both hands and left from the doorway of the bedroom. She returned dragging on a freshly lit cigarette. Long deliberate puffs like cousin Brax took on the tiny "homemade" cigarettes I'd seen him make for himself and the Walker twins through his cracked bedroom door. "Dammit, Mandi, honey," she said, after exhaling high into the air from the side of her mouth, "please don't bring these things in here. They're bad luck."

She squatted and began gathering up the bouquets. Her cigarette dangled from the corner of her mouth like a kickstand holding up a bicycle. Corsica Pate reached across the floor for some chalk and tossed a piece to each of us.

Mandi screamed and threw the chalk back at her mother. "No! We're gonna build a palace!"

"No, hon. No palace. Not with these." Corsica Pate left the apartment immediately with them, not knowing that Mandi and I had already stored twice as many under her bed in the days before. And when she returned to the apartment, the flowers she had carried out were gone, along with her cigarette. She walked over to the stove in the kitchen and bent down and lit another one.

Ⅹ   Ⅹ   Ⅹ

The March wind had become wild. Traffic lights bobbed up and down on cable wires above the intersections. Roof shingles disappeared from housetops, and the bright funerary bouquets danced down the avenue from the feet of headstones at Rainbow Hill. We played house in the grass in front of our building, Mandi and I. She was the mom and I was the pretend dad. Ruthie was our daughter. Just before we headed off to put Ruthie to bed under a bush, Mandi was suddenly captivated by a stunning bouquet that floated down the street like a Texas tumbleweed. It landed for just a second across the street from our building before resuming its course down the avenue. We jumped to our feet to watch. "Tati, look! It's purple!" Mandi pointed to the vibrant spray at the edge of the cemetery across the street, quickly escaping our view.

"Ooooooh, Mandi! That one is exceptional!" I stood and watched the bouquet with anticipation. If only it could find its way across our street. This could be the finest of all that we had; the rare pearl in our hidden treasure. Yes! This one we must have!

"It's purple!" she said again. "And I can see glitter on it!" Mandi was entranced. Any trace of reason that a six-year-old could possibly possess, any prior reprimands from Corsica Pate to abandon all hope of a palace made of funeral bouquets had blown away with the greedy wind. Mandi dropped our mutilated half baby doll daughter in the grass and tore into the street like a lightning bolt to seize the dazzling cluster of flowers.

I did not call her name.

I did not remind her of our mothers' admonitions about crossing the street. *Yes! This one we must have!* And when she had taken just a few quick steps, it happened.

Her small body was sent sailing through the air like a missile from the abrupt impact of a white Ford Mustang. Just like that. Just like that.

She did not scream. I did not move.

She did not turn to reach for my hand. I did not call her name.

All of my words sank one by one like a million little stones into the pit of my stomach and weighed me down. Agony rose up from my belly into my throat. Cars stopped. Men ran into the street. Women screamed and picked up their babies and turned away their tiny faces. Teenagers pointed and watched in horror. Then I, I picked up Ruthie from the grass and held her tight. I squeezed my eyes shut and quickly buried my face into the prickly chopped hair of her scalp. Mandi did not get up.

I turned and went inside.

❌   ❌   ❌

The news about Mandi spread quickly. Mother flipped through the channels at news time. Mandi's first-grade photograph had been run on every channel in the state. One after the other, like a broken record, they called her Amanda Lynn Pate, the hazel-eyed, golden-haired girl from the projects, the unlikely princess who collected graveyard flowers to play with because her mother couldn't afford toys.

She had become an overnight sensation, and people came from all over the tri-city area to lay purple flowers at the site of the accident. Real ones, too, beautiful with thick stems heavy with grief that didn't blow away with the March wind. And even though Mother told me that I would not see Mandi again, I waited for her to come home.

On the third day I went upstairs and knocked on the door of Mandi's apartment carrying Ruthie in my arms. There was shuffling on the inside like things were falling over, and eventually the door opened slowly. I almost didn't recognize the woman who answered. Her normally skinny brown hair that hung well past her shoulders looked as if she had been wrestling with monsters. Her face was red and puffy. She wore a pair of large black sunglasses that made her look like a giant fly.

"When's Mandi coming home, Corsica Pate?" I held the doll baby up for her to see. "I put a pretty dress on Ruthie and made her a bow for her head." And although the dress had come off of one of my larger dolls and hung well below Ruthie's amputated legs, and the bow did not cover the freckled follicles of her mutilated scalp, she was beautiful. Corsica Pate never said a word.

At the sight of Ruthie and her new dress, she collapsed to her knees in the doorway of her apartment and began to bawl and pound her legs in wild hysteria.

)X(   )X(   )X(

Corsica Pate did not have the money to give Mandi a proper burial. I was eavesdropping under the guise of reading my favorite book, sprawled out in front of the television on the living room floor. The women that came over some Saturday mornings to sit and talk and have coffee and bacon were all sure to come on this particular Saturday following Mandi's death. Their voices suddenly became low, as they often did when they spoke of things like sex or men or money, and they didn't want me to hear.

And so it was, Haisten-Hathaway Funeral Home, owners of Eastwood Gardens Cemetery with all its stunning flowers and glossy headstones, would cover the entire cost of Mandi's funeral. My heart plummeted at the mention of her name. When Ree Ree Walker sat down her cup of coffee and said in her heavy voice that none of *us* should ever expect that Haisten-Hathaway Funeral Home would ever do the same for one of *our* children as they were doing for Amanda Pate, Mother quickly chimed in and said it wasn't so, and didn't she remember the good thing that they did for Lester Jones back in '92, long before any white woman and her little girl ever came to Carver Homes.

"You keep thinking that, Gloria," Ree Ree Walker said. I peeked above the spine of my open book to find her looking at me and shaking her head. "You think if it had been the other way around, and that it was Tatiana sprawled out in the middle of that street like that, that Haisten-Hathaway Funeral Home would shell out that kind of money for *her*? Think again." The three other women nodded in agreement.

"Ree Ree!" my mother said, placing another plate of bacon on the table. "Hush! She'll hear you."

"Better she find out now while she's young."

Ӿ   Ӿ   Ӿ

I wondered about Ree Ree Walker that night as I lay in bed. Why she always seemed so angry when the neighbors would talk about Mandi and her mother. I wondered about *poor white trash*, and what it really meant. And if Mandi was trash, did that mean I was now trash too? Did God let trash in heaven? I wondered about *us*, and *them*, and what it was that made us different; made so many angry. About Candace Taylor, and doctors and lawyers, and London and Paris. Why did she seem to know it all? I wondered about Carver Homes and the world beyond it; about the man named Lester Jones and what secret thing the owners of Haisten-Hathaway Funeral Home did for him back in '92? I wondered as I lay there, drifting off to sleep, what did I need to find out while I was young? And about Mother and why she told Ree Ree Walker, "Hush! She'll hear you."

Ӿ   Ӿ   Ӿ

Seven days after Mandi's death, it happened.

The most elaborate event, some say, ever seen in our town. The residents of Goshen turned out in numbers, and even more people traveled from nearby cities. Mother and I stayed close to Corsica Pate, riding with her in the limousine. The only family she had to speak of was a twin brother named Corey, who sat next to her all morning, patting her hand and occasionally putting his arm around her when she cried out in agony. Corey was nearly tall enough to be a circus sideshow attraction, and when his outstretched arm was not around his sister, he gave me peppermints from his deep pocket that were sticky as glue and almost impossible to free from the wrapper.

The windows on the limousine were dark and shiny. Once the door had been shut, all the noise disappeared except the sound of Corsica Pate blowing her nose into the same wrinkled handkerchief she'd had all morning. I wanted to bring Ruthie along to say good-bye to Mandi, but Mother said it would be more than her mother could handle and that Ruthie should stay behind. "Not today, Tati. Leave her behind. Especially today." Mother took Ruthie from me and tossed her onto the sofa before locking the door behind us.

She had become my new best friend, Ruthie. I took her with me everywhere for weeks after Mandi's death, especially to bed at night, when the realization of my best friend's absence weighed me down like a massive boulder, pressing out my tears onto my pillow.

I peeked curiously through the dark windows of the limousine. News cameras were propped outside the church and lined up like trees at the bottom of the steps in anticipation of a grand spectacle, and Goshen residents who did not attend the funeral dragged their lawn chairs to the edge of the street and posted them along the curb to watch the procession as it passed by.

Our car glided slowly along the street. It was led by a motorcade of police cycles with flashing blue lights. More than I could count. Excited children anxiously pointed at the symphony of flickering lights. The day was sunny. The March wind had died.

The officers escorted a horse-drawn carriage with a tiny pearl-white casket not much larger than a toy chest. Two satiny black horses, with their regal gait, meticulously chaperoned Mandi's casket to Rainbow Hill as it rested peacefully in a bed of rich purple carnations. And the most fantastical sight of all, more purple carnations, tiny ones, and white and lavender rosebuds had been intricately fashioned to form a miniature palace that was suspended in the air around the casket and supported on four silver posts that extended from each corner of the carriage.

I wished at that moment that Mandi could have been there to see it: the elegant purple palace abounding with flowers and glory, fit for the finest princess. It was the most beautiful sight in the world.

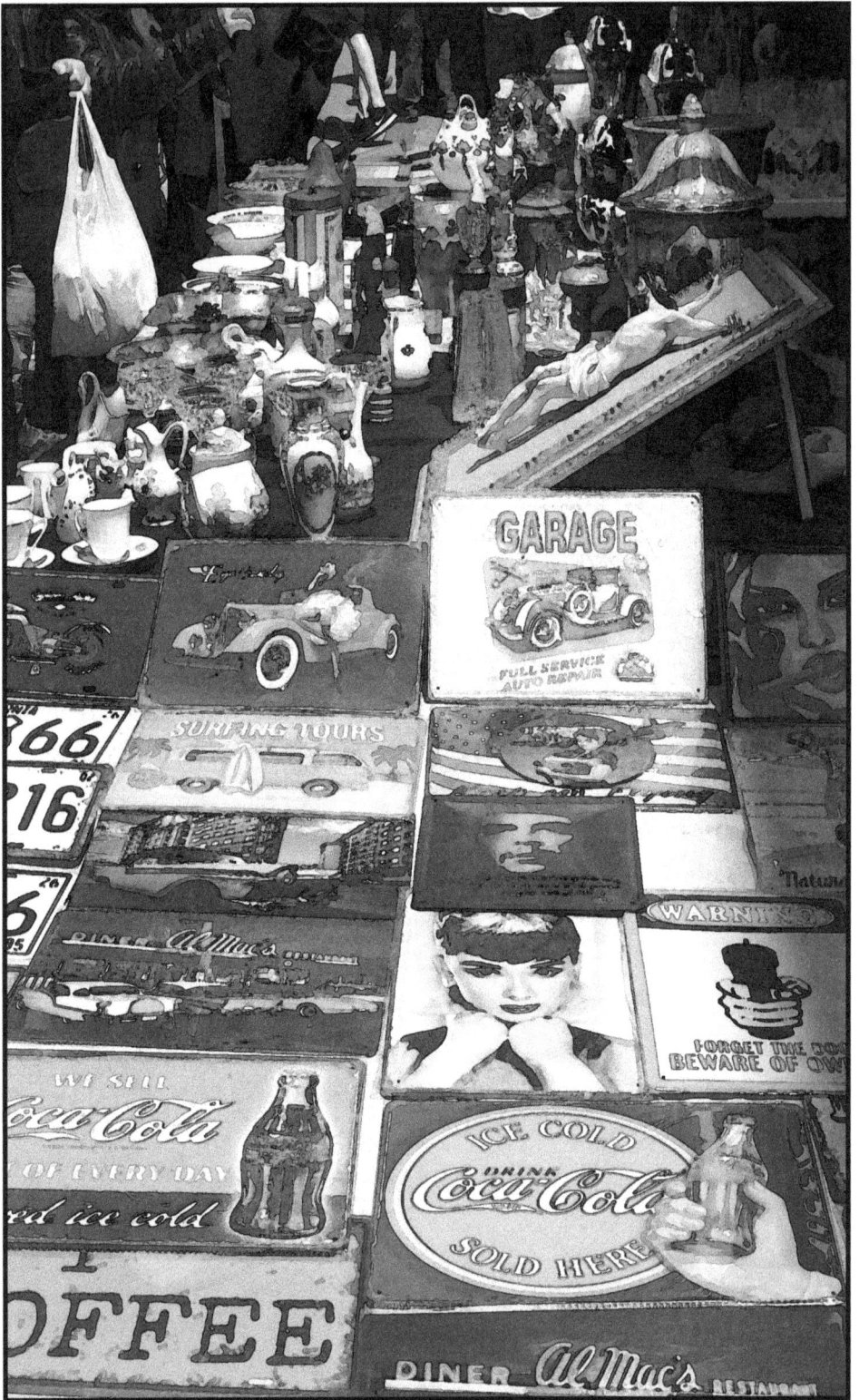

J. ANDREW BRISEÑO

HENDERSON STREET BAZAAR

There were eight large crates of baby bottle nipples near the hearse, well over three hundred nylon backpacks, an antique icebox painted purple, and my dead father. They had put the coffin more or less where the old man would have stood and haggled, stood a picture on a stand next to the box with a small cardboard sign that read "Big Dan's Last Deal. 1949-2012." The two gentlemen from the funeral home were unsure of where to stand or to whom to offer their condolences. Theirs were the only neckties for a mile in any direction. It was not yet nine in the morning and already eighty-five degrees on the asphalt, baking the smell of brake fluid out of the tar.

I was jealous of the undertakers though, because they had a good reason to be uncomfortable. I remembered being a little kid, calling out my father's wares while the disinterested crowd shoved and poured past. This used to be my home, even if I hadn't been back to *la pulga* in five years, not since I'd started school back east. In a Spanish Conversation and Grammar course, I'd learned that *pulga* meant flea, that an open air market was *un rastro*. I had told him that over the phone, and he'd said "So you're the Mexican now?" That seemed like a long time ago, before the coma, all the nights sleeping in the hospital, and then going back to Dad's house, wondering if my car was safe parked on the street. Thankfully, the arrangements had all been made in advance, everything was taken care of. All I had to do was be here.

If you could believe him, Dad hadn't missed a weekend at the Henderson Street Bazaar since I was born. Death, it seemed, was nothing next to thieves and tornadoes. The very regulars stopped to pay their respects. One man, at least fifty, all beard and grizzle, reached into the casket and shook Dad's hand.

Being near him wasn't really the problem. After two weeks on a breathing machine, now he looked at ease, appropriately comfortable in the T-shirt and jeans he'd insisted on being dressed in. The problem was everyone else. From all directions, strangers kept putting things in my hand and asking how much

I wanted. What is the value of a used handsaw? I remembered vinyl records costing fifty cents each, but when I told that to the twenty year old with the mustache, he bought the whole box without even looking through it. Had the market on Perry Como appreciated significantly? I didn't know.

For years, this had been a running gag with Dad. We'd be on the phone or sitting on the porch after dinner when I could get back, and he'd start talking about how they wouldn't be able to keep him from turning a profit even after he was dead. "Shit, I'll be long gone, looking down or up at y'all, and they'll still be buying what I got for sale. And you know what I'll be doing then? Laughing. Cause then you'll have my job."

Somehow when I'd thought about it, there was more funeral to the thing. I thought having my dead father in a polished pine box would slow business down. But people walked up just to see if it was real, then, seeing it was, faked interest in something so as not to seem garish, ended up rummaging through several nearby bins. This was part of what he'd meant—one last sales pitch you just couldn't turn down; he had planned it this way. I knew it.

$$\times \quad \times \quad \times$$

Dad grew up in Old Northside Fort Worth, the fifth of six, back when Mexicans weren't supposed to cross Main Street. He'd lost two uncles in World War II, three cousins in Korea, a brother, two neighbors and a little league coach in Vietnam. Mexicans made better targets, they said, especially in the snow. Even those who dodged war because they were lucky in age or the draft lottery or polio still stood a strong chance of dying young. There was Uncle Paulie stabbed down at the dance hall, Ernesto electrocuted by the cable box. According to Dad's calculations, five men out of seven in our family wouldn't make it to forty. Those who did, and who also avoided the bottle, the track, other men's wives—practically all of them worked for the plant or the railroad or the steel mill, never left the neighborhood, raised kids who would never leave the neighborhood. He never let me forget it, would count out the uncles and the cousins on his fingers, work the long division on a gasoline receipt. Two souls in fifty found a way out of Northside.

For him, the phrase "out of" was relative. There were no curbs on our street, even though we lived in the very heart of the city. We parked Dad's rusty pickup inside the fence every night, just to be sure. But we owned the place and the neighbors never said anything about the stacks of folding chairs in the front lawn. Dad would tell me that he didn't get up feeling tied down, and when he said it I think he was telling us both.

He would bring odd bits of his work home to me. I would close my eyes and stick my hand out, and he would give me a fragile book with the pleasant scent of rot, or crackling maps describing countries that no longer were, intricate vases and sculptures, a gathering of hood ornaments from Chevies model years 56-62, caseless blender innards, the taxidermied head of a ground squirrel mounted with the antlers of a twelve-point buck, forty pounds of slinky. The side of his work trailer read "THERES NOTHING BIG DAN DONT GOT." I knew the grammar was wrong long before I realized the sign wasn't true.

Whenever he brought me something to look at, he would put in a box just so he could watch closely while I opened it and poked and prodded, pushing buttons and levers, trying to figure it out, what the trick was. He always waited till I gave up before telling me where it had come from, and there was always a lesson. That's honest cheetah, Daniel he told me, holding out a spotted throw rug he'd gotten at a lot auction. I was watching on TV where they don't have an ounce of fat on them. Not one ounce.

Dad called all his junk treasure, and in addition to the two treasure sheds and the treasure bus, he also had treasure laid out across what survived of the lawn, the porch, and the corners of our small house. Good thing your mother's not around, he would tell me, rest her soul she would never tolerate this mess. But no matter how much there was, everything was neatly organized, neat enough for him to be able to find anything he needed without having to dig. You have to know what you got, he said, that's always the first thing.

Every Saturday, he would get out of bed at 3:30 and start loading the trailer. The sound of the scraping and grunting would wake me up, and I'd join him, help him with the bigger items of the day. By six o'clock I was making breakfast, and by seven we were pulling in to spot P-38 at *la pulga*, the flea market just north of downtown.

The Henderson Street Bazaar was right next to the river, land too low for anything permanent. Someone had arranged for a forty acre pour of cheap aggregate concrete, and someone else had built large metal shades over half of it. The spots under the shade cost three times as much as the ones like ours, half a mile from anything except the back fence and the stink of the silt-choked river. Dad was convinced that merchants willing to pay a hundred and fifty dollars so as to not have to hang their own tarps weren't worth dealing with. Even though we did as much shopping as we did selling, we never went under those shades. We weren't avoiding them, so much as there was nothing there we needed.

Shade encompassed just part of Dad's overarching theory on commerce and enterprise. He was certain price tags were ruining America, that only a fool could think of just one price. I remember once I watched him tell three buyers in a row that a glass skull was two hundred dollars, only to sell it to a mousy woman with no chin for a twenty dollar bill. "Now she, she knows what the fuck that's for," he said as she walked away clutching the skull close to her chest. "Six to one she still has it twenty-thirty years from now."

Money was something we never really talked about it. I knew we had some—Dad always had a pile of folded cash in his back left pocket for work reasons—but I also knew that we never shopped at stores for anything but cold food. Everything else: clothes, canned goods, furniture, flatware, all of it was second hand, overstocked, misprinted, fell-off-a-truck, and bought on the cheap.

But despite the extra cost, Dad sent me to the parish school at Immaculate Heart, probably because it was close enough to walk. It was a somber school in a brown brick building run by a cloister of nuns who all seemed to have at least one man's name. Sister Mary Stephen. Sister John Mark. My eighth grade year, they pulled all the boys out of religion class and filed us into the auditorium. A white man with silver hair and a tan suit was on stage, standing next to a sandwich board with a fancy logo and the words "St. Stanislav Academy: A Private Preparatory School for Boys."

We sat in the stiff creaking wooden chairs and listened to the recruiter tell us that the school was in the foothills of the Smoky Mountains, that there was a fishing pond, a swimming pool, and a bowling alley. Students could live in semi-private rooms where they had their own phone lines. They played lacrosse. It sounded like life in a deodorant commercial. At lunch that day, we took turns making fun of the guy, who had this over-refined way of talking, like he made a point of saying confectionery instead of the baker's.

That afternoon on the way to an auction out in Jacksboro I told Dad about the slide show we'd seen, with the old buildings that look like castles, and the rolling terraced hills. To me, it was funny, and I even started trying to do the recruiter's accent. I kept waiting for him to laugh. Instead he asked me if I wanted to go.

I didn't, but instead of saying no, I said, "Three to one a place like that costs way more than its worth in the long run anyways."

"That's mine to worry about son, not yours."

I still didn't think Dad was serious, didn't think it was possible. The nuns had taught me that the capital of Tennessee was Nashville, but I had never been there, never been much further than the monthly swap meet a few hundred miles east of town. The whole idea of Tennessee, of school away from home, of not living just east of the interstate—it was a dream I'd never thought about having, too strange to be wonderful. But I looked over, and Dad had the same face that he used to get when he brought me stuff to look at, which he had hadn't done in years.

)X(   )X(   )X(

A tiny woman with designer eye wear, no chin to speak of, hair left to gray in wide chunks, walked up to me. She's probably older than Dad ever was. Business has been so brisk that at first I don't understand why she's talking to me because she doesn't have something she wants in her hand. "You must be his son," she said. "I'm so sorry for your loss."

I shook her hand when she stuck it out, and because I wasn't sure what else to do, I held on to it. She didn't try to jerk away, let her hand sweat into mine. She took it to mean to keep going. "Your dad was a great man."

I looked her in the eye. The thing was she was right, Dad was a good man. But how was she or anyone here supposed to know that? I wanted to say something dark and shitty to her. And I could have too. This was a one day affair. Dad would be cremated that evening. In a week I'd be back in Indiana. If there weren't any hitches selling the house, I might never come back at all, not just the flea market, the city, maybe the state. I could say or do anything I wanted; the feeling was crippling.

Still I couldn't just say thank you either, so I didn't say anything, just walked off into the crowd, the woman and then the funeral director calling after me. The aisle was moist with traffic, and I let the flow of the crowd push me away from all of it. When I got to the end of the row I turned right, toward the covered part of the market, where I'd never been and never seen Dad go.

Out in the sunshine, people sold whatever they had on hand, but here most of the stands seemed dedicated to one specific purpose or another: jewelry repair, fabric by the bolt, glass bongs, a double site selling not a thing but white socks by the trash bag full. There was a tingle of sleigh bells in the distance, and I saw an old man selling coconut ice cream bars to a pack of hopping children. It didn't smell the same without the heat, and the crowd walked faster, like they had someplace to get to.

Sandwiched between a tire salesman and an on-site auto decal installer, there was a small table with a bright red cloth over it. It was covered in tiny fountains fashioned to look like dripping faucets and beer cans pouring themselves forever, held up by nothing. The idea behind them was simple, they had a clear feeder tube that ran from the base to the can or the spigot, hid by the water itself. But for a minute there, maybe because there were so many in one place, it seemed impossible and in spite of myself I waved my hand over the table to check for wires I knew weren't there. I picked up the nearest one, which looked like a can of Pepsi; it was terribly light for its size, and had a tiny orange $25 price tag. I decided I would buy it, knew then I would keep it forever, a little memorial to what I didn't even know. I pulled out the wad of money in my back pocket and flipped out a greasy twenty I'd been paid with and one of the brand new fives I'd gotten from the bank last night to make change. I held the money high, and looked around, and even whistled. But no one came to take my money so after a few minutes I had to walk away.

With no one around to tend it the site had been abandoned, left just as it was. Some unspoken code of the flea market had dictated that now I could be alone. The coffin jutted out into the aisle, and everything around it looked not smaller but larger by comparison, more conspicuous. I went and I looked.

I would say that he looked peacefully asleep, but I have no memory of seeing him sleeping. He didn't look tired though, and I thought that was something. Also, he was the only one out there who seemed comfortable in the heat, which he probably would have gotten a kick out of. I tried to think of something to say to him. Or whatever it was that I wanted him to say to me. There was this feeling like a swelling, like a pressure pushing my skin against the humid air, that had been building up for years. I waited for this to bubble over, to tumble down. But it wouldn't.

I saw the undertakers behind me. They were checking their watches. When I let them take the coffin, they would wheel it back into the hearse and drive across town, where they would roll the corpse out of this rented casket and into a cardboard box. They would burn him at a thousand degrees, until his soft tissues had turned to gas. Because he was a large man, this would take more than three hours, and then finally there would be nothing more for the fire to do. The splinters of bone would be ground in a machine made only for this purpose and then returned to me. What I was supposed to do then, Dad hadn't specified. I closed my eyes, and took a deep breath, and I smelled sour beer and the denseness of human sweat, and a lot of effort. And that was right, how it ought to be. I nodded, and the two gentleman in suits removed and tucked away the fabric that hid the wheels, and pushed my father back into the hearse.

It was after six o'clock, and the other sites around me were emptying. The foot traffic in the aisles was replaced by vans and trucks, each waiting for their turn to load up whatever was left unsold. When Dad did this, there was almost never anything to pack back up—he was a master at bringing and doing just enough.

I looked at what was left, the bottle nipples, and the winter coats, the chests of drawers and the mirrors, the dish tubs full of loose sockets, the display case with the dead moths, the other things that turned out to not be worth it this time around. I thought about the other two sheds and the bus that I couldn't even get to open. I looked to the spot where the casket had been but that too was gone. And so I looked at the spot where Dad was supposed to be.

Why had he brought me back here? Was this his last mystery—the last chance he had to show me something, and if so what was I to glean? I turned it around in my mind like a cheetah skin throw rug, like a bucket of hood ornaments, like a box of treasure not yet even opened—still capable of so much.

But I couldn't make sense of it—I didn't know then what I had.

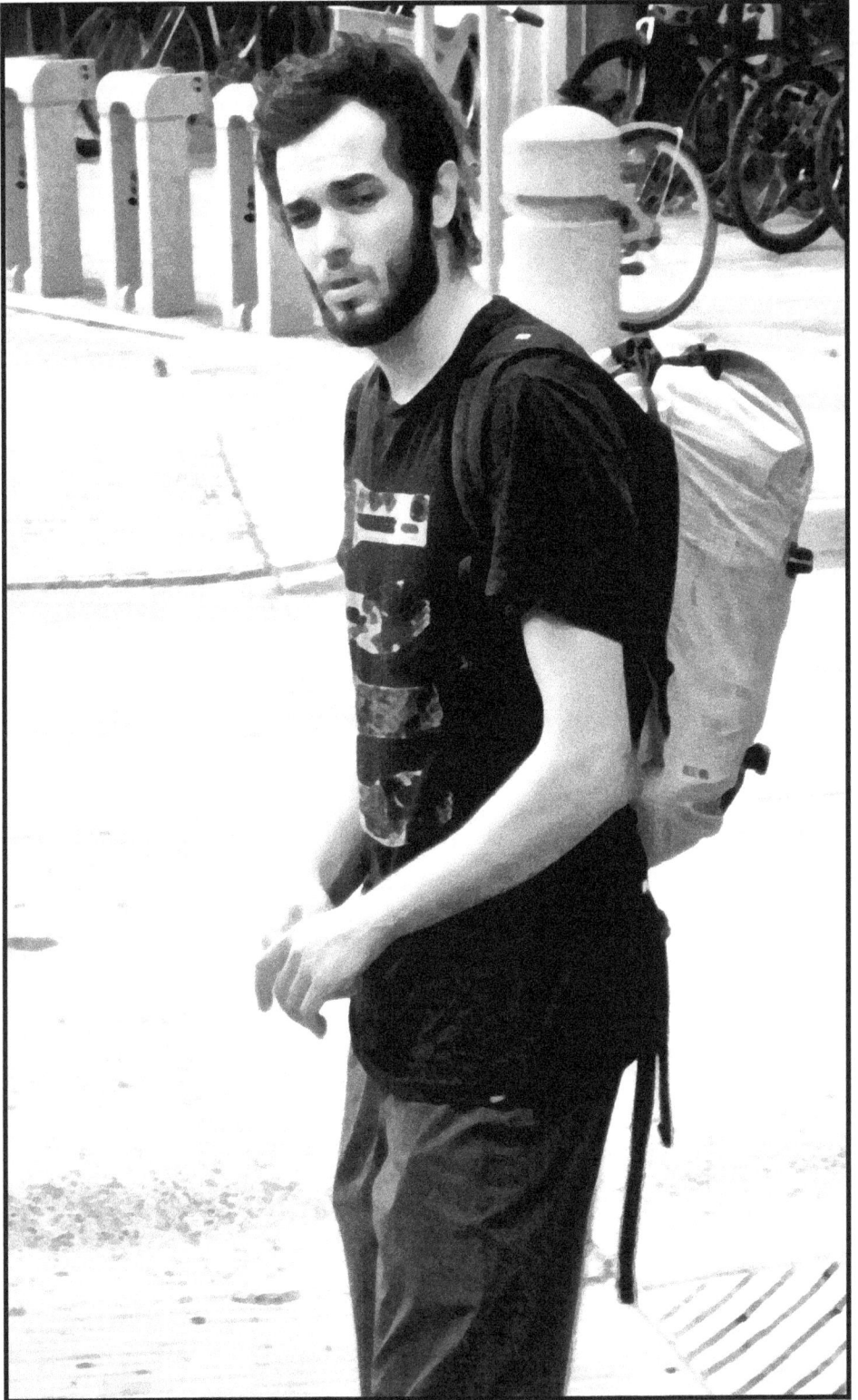

ROBERT STINSON

BRINGING RASPUTIN HOME FOR CHRISTMAS

I had come home for Thanksgiving that first year of college but remember almost nothing about it, except that I drove with an upper-class girl whose number I plucked off the dining hall ride board and who talked on and on about problems she was having with her boyfriend. Halfway home, sensing that my minimal responses betrayed a freshman's innocence, she began discoursing on the shafts, orifices, and fragrant fluids in Samuel Taylor Coleridge's poem, *Kubla Khan*, glancing at me over the tops of her glasses to suggest there were naughty things a freshman had yet to learn.

This was more interesting than the quiz I was facing after Thanksgiving on another poem, Stephen Vincent Benét's *John Brown's Body*. I had dutifully put that book in my suitcase. But any poem longer than a sonnet seemed more trouble than it was worth. *John Brown's Body* was "an epic poem of the Civil War," our professor had said, "Pulitzer Prize material!" He meant these as selling points, but to me they signaled pages and days of tedium. I remember a sleepy half hour on my bed at home, leafing back and forth, looking for a point of entry and a message for my time—this was the fall of 1960, right after Kennedy's election—and finding neither. Indeed, I thought one place near the end especially sappy. It was where Benét has Abraham Lincoln and Mary Todd Lincoln, before they go off to the Ford Theater, talking amiably about what they would do once he left office: "They would go back to Springfield, find a house / Live peaceably and simply, see old friends . . . ." Benét deftly steps around the assassination, letting you imagine it or not as you please. I decided not to and Tuesday of the next week, back on my college campus, deftly failed the quiz. Whatever else I did over Thanksgiving was less memorable than even those few pages.

Coming home for Christmas a month later was different. I remember everything about that, especially, this time, the train. My school was on the Erie Railroad, in Pennsylvania, maybe four hundred miles west of our New

Jersey suburb. I boarded the train on a very cold evening—December 21ˢᵗ or so—declined a game of cards with three or four other students also heading east and, in the over-compensating heat of our car, soon nodded off. I was startled awake a little after midnight, when the train stopped somewhere in the darkness of New York State and a gang of St. Benedict boys got on and came tumbling in riotous shouts and elbows down the aisle. St. Benny's was a Catholic school whose dour priests—I imagined them dour, all black below the neck, white, pudgy faces above—evidently insisted they wear coat and tie, even for travel. The surprise of their arrival arose not just from the noise but from the sheer incongruity of young men in brass-button blazers with the St. Benny's pocket emblem together with the boys' slurred, drunken "Fuck you!" "Jesus fucking Christ," and, "Fucking that's my seat!" My college, a Methodist foundation, was more sedate. You could smell alcohol in the air, and a boy in front of me had a flat pint of whiskey visible in the left side pocket of his blazer. After fifteen minutes, when a stern conductor came down the aisle to take their tickets and warn them, "There's to be no drinking on this train," they quieted down and, the whiskey in their brains going from giddy to sleepy, most of them slumped back or sprawled sideways, dead to the world.

About 3:30 in the morning the conductor came through the car again announcing a stop, making a kindly pause at my seat to say, "This'll be Binghamton. You change here." Everyone else in our car was evidently bound for New York, but I would change trains for one that plied the Jersey suburbs before ending at Hoboken.

Coming home for the second time and, indeed, feeling the triumph of having blown off a quiz for the first time, I felt older on this trip, above the swearing, not actually needing that reminder that I must change trains, ready to negotiate my passage in the world. The conductor handed my suitcase down to me on the platform, and I tipped him a dollar.

"Thank you," I said. "Thanks very much."

"Yes, sir. All right, sir," he said. "Aboard!"

His train moved slowly on its way, and I stood on a brick platform lighted by a row of dim canopied lamps strung along the station roof's overhang. The waiting room and stationmaster's office looked dark and closed, but next to them was a yellowish square of light in a door which led, even without there being a sign for it, to a little café.

There were no customers, so the man behind the counter was already looking in my direction when I entered. As I put my suitcase down he put his chin up and raised his eyebrows in a wordless question. What would you like?

"Oh, coffee and" —I looked at pastries under a round plastic dome— "One of those doughnuts. Well, say two." They were all, I was glad to see, unadorned with chocolate, powdered sugar or candy sprinkles.

He drew a mug of black, black coffee from a big urn, a "railroad urn," I said to myself, and then put my doughnuts in a little bag.

"Sixty cents."

I paid him, stood briefly in his space and then, self-conscious, headed toward the door.

"Leave this here?" I said, turning back with my suitcase still in hand.

"Up to you, mister, but I don't watch 'em." His tone was not unfriendly. "Bring the mug back, okay?"

"Fair enough," I said, put my suitcase down and pulled open the door. I would take the responsibility.

I liked the cold passivity of the platform lights and the immediate heat from the way my hands fit around the coffee mug. I had learned to drink coffee in the kitchen of a high school friend, whose mother, one afternoon the year before, decided that we graduating seniors should know about coffee. She put a heavy splash of cream in our cups and three teaspoons of sugar. That's the way I had taken my coffee ever since, but the railroad brew was black, and I discovered, cold, happy and alone outside the café, the singular pleasure of separating light from darkness, sweetness from gall, bitter, scalding coffee from doughy chunks of doughnut. The mouth of the cup and my breath steamed in the air, clean and animate.

Before long another train pulled in, albeit 45 minutes before the scheduled departure of mine. In the dim light, its three drab cars were of uncertain color and, unlike the shiny, smooth-riding ones from which I had lately alighted, long since rushing toward New York City, these rocked and groaned on their carriages as the train came to a stop. *Was* this my train? I sipped my coffee, which was losing heat now but in its taste still bracing. The proprietor of my life, I nonetheless wanted to be home for Christmas, so I must be careful not to board a train to nowhere. The man in the café would know, and I did have to go back for my suitcase, but I had made too good a start with him to ask. There was no one else on the platform, which was not a good sign, or at least it would not be in, say, twenty minutes. Then I saw someone in uniform step off the car up behind the engine, so I walked in his direction.

"Is this the train for New Jersey?" I said, well short of where he was standing.

He waited for me to get closer. "Where you going, son?"

"Ridgewood?"

"This is it." He smiled. "Ain't much, but she's all yours."

I smiled, too, ruefully: my bid to join the conspiracy. It worked.

"Thirty-five minutes, mister," he said.

The train pulled out, on time to the minute, I in a middle seat of the middle car, which was, indeed, all mine. The conductor came down the aisle right away, said, "Tickets," punched mine, and moved on to the last car without a further word, as though he had never seen me before. I had regained my privacy, my anonymity.

But not for long, because I heard the door between my car and the last open, and watched another passenger, in an uncertain gait as the train gained speed, make his way down the aisle. He slid into a seat across and two up from mine, then looked back at me and said, "Where you going?"

I wished I were a St. Benedict student, without the drinking, of course, but with the coat, tie and emblem, outward signs of inward grace. Wrapped in my oversized loden coat, which said just that I was cold, I could only resort to minimalism.

"Oh, just traveling."

"Going home for Christmas?"

"That, too," I said.

"I'm going."

He was older than I, by ten or even twenty years. I did not want a conversation, for I was pretty easily able, looking at him, to assemble those years in my mind. There seemed to be no heat in the car, but the man had on only a light jacket, unzipped over a plaid shirt with a wide spreading collar, conspicuously less stylish than the button-down, body-hugging shirts men were wearing now—like the one I had on under the loden. His thinning hair was combed back and wet from a very recent wash-up. He was clean shaven, but the cheeks were too pink, scrubbed with harsh soap, Lava, perhaps, meant more for end-of-the-day dirty hands. The eyes were red-rimmed, either from the soap or from drinking. He blinked a lot.

"You in college?" he said.

Before I answered he got up and sat on the arm rest of the seat across from me, letting gravity pull his chest down and shoulders inward. He was no threat, except for the tedium of my having now to talk to him.

"I am, yes."

"I didn't go. What's your major, if I may ask?"

"I don't have one, but maybe, well, I don't know. Maybe history."

"Would it be? Because I read a lot of history."

"Yeah?"

"I read biographies. Two, one on Abraham Lincoln and one on Rasputin."

"The Mad Monk," I said.

"Except he wasn't crazy."

In senior year of high school, I had learned about Gregori Rasputin, the lecherous Russian mystic who wormed his way into the court of Nicholas and Alexandra and, on the eve of the Bolshevik Revolution in 1917, became the Empress's confidant. Our social studies teacher, Mr. Mercer, was mostly intent on showing the class that the Russian Revolution was a chapter of accidents and stupidity, not, in some large sense, pushed by History. Mr. Mercer was always saying, "It could have been avoided. It wasn't 'in the cards.'" Remember, this was in the height of the Cold War. The stupidity lay in Czar Nicholas' letting his wife and beady-eyed, hairy Rasputin, the Mad Monk, divine state policy from signs and wonders.

"No?" I said. Not crazy?

"He was a healer, like Jesus, another great man. Lincoln wasn't crazy, either. He was a healer, 'to bind up the nation's wounds,' if you remember your history. Nicholas and Alexandra's little boy was a hemophiliac, a bleeder. Rasputin could cure him. Prayer. Hypnotism. When you read them together, Rasputin and Lincoln, you see they were both great men. I read in the public library. I also take books home."

I could see him there, the first patron at the door when the librarian appears in the inside vestibule, turns her key in the lock, and opens for the day. He has his own seat, his accustomed seat, anyway, at one of the long tables nearest the stacks, near the 820's, biography. It's a small library, so probably there isn't much distance between the L's and R's, not many people worth a biography whose names start with M, N, O, P and Q. Or perhaps there was nothing on the spine for Napoleon nor even the book jacket for Maureen O'Hara that sufficiently inspired him. His habitual unemployment means he has time but also space in his mind—walking to and from his furnished room in a house sided with tattered asphalt "poor man's brick" —for other people's adventures and for whatever models he makes of them. He has space on his dresser for the books he checks out, next to his comb, toothbrush and nail clipper.

I said, "Not great the same way, though?"

"They were both assassinated. I like to read about those."

Yes, in books next to his gleaming straight razor. I really did not want this conversation. I said, "Yeah?"

Just then the conductor entered the car and came up the aisle. The library man leaned back to let him pass, and the conductor said, "The heat will be up in a few minutes, men."

"Thanks," I said, and, hoping to detain him, "I guess these cars are pretty old, and anyway they just made up this train, huh? Takes a little time."

"Yep," he said, but continued up the aisle and into the next car.

"Lincoln was just shot, though, so there's a difference," the man continued. "Rasputin they poisoned and shot and clubbed in the head and he still wouldn't die, so then they drowned him. First a bunch of Russian nobles lured him down to a secret chamber, saying they would introduce him to a woman he hadn't been with yet. They put cyanide in these little cakes. He devoured them. *Devoured* them. And, you know, when's Rasputin going to die? He drank their wine, and they had cyanide in that, too. Nothing. Do you know what they called him?" He waited for an answer.

"No," I said.

"The Holy Devil. Then they shot him with their revolvers, so he had to be dead, right? But when they came down to see if he was still dead, he got up and grabbed at one of them, so they all clubbed him over the head several times and next wrapped the body in a piece of carpet and drowned him in the river. About this time of the year. Somebody who wasn't in on it noticed blood under the bridge, and when the police came, the conspirators said it was from a dog that was killed during a wild party. You know how it is, they said. The police didn't believe this and had to break the ice to fish out the body, and there was water in the lungs, so you know what that means. Just before Christmas, 1916."

He formed an "O" with his mouth and puffed out so we both saw his breath cloud in the air.

I nodded and made an appreciative tightening of my lips.

"You think you'll study that if you study history?"

"I suppose."

"They cut off his penis and now it's in a museum. He had a lot of Russian women interested in him, not just Empress Alexandra. Thirteen."

"That many?"

"Inches."

Mr. Mercer had not gone into that. He spent a little time on how hard it was to kill Rasputin, but the palace plot against the Mad Monk and its being too-little-too-late to put some sense into the palace itself was his main lesson.

The library man put his hands out and moved them away from each other, measuring, a little more than a foot. He smiled with amazement. Thirteen. Then suddenly he extended his right hand toward me. "My name is Brody," he said.

I touched his fingers but drew my own back before we could properly shake. I didn't say my name.

"That didn't mean he was crazy," said Brody. "He didn't wash, though. Long hair, beard and everything, with food stuck in it. The book had a picture, an actual photograph, showing little flecks of stuff in the beard. He was dirty but not necessarily crazy."

"No?"

"Lincoln was equally great, and he wasn't exactly crazy, but he did get very depressed. Will you be studying that?"

"I sure will."

Brody nodded and looked away, as though at least that much had got settled.

"Actually," I said, "I have some studying to do right now."

"Yeah, you better," he said. I was glad he did not ask what. I did have a sheaf of papers in the pocket of my loden, the course listings for second semester I was supposed to go over with my faculty advisor after Christmas vacation. I took them out, and Brody pushed himself up off the arm rest, walked purposefully up the aisle and settled into a seat near the door.

Relieved, I did look over next term's classes but soon dozed off and did not wake until I heard the conductor's voice in that lilting command-and-question cadence they all seem to use: "Middletown! Middletown?"

Dawn had only just been breaking during my conversation with Brody, the blue darkness reinforcing, in me at least, a sense of unwanted intimacy. But now, as the train slowed for Middletown, the light in my window was bright, and no wonder, for Middletown was in the midst of a joyous snow storm. Our car came to a stop across a downtown street, blocking what must be the main thoroughfare. Crossing gates had swung down and the streaming clang-clang of the bell sounded less like a warning than a herald of the train's arrival. My window frame was a Christmas card scene: intrepid early morning travelers sipping coffee on the platform; not far up the block, the townspeople, their ruddy, untroubled faces tucked between colorful hats and scarves, going in and out of a news stand and, next door, a bakery, where, every time the door opened, a warm bread-smell must be puffing onto the sidewalk; everybody stepping carefully along sidewalks inches deep in drifts. My own town would look like the season, too, in another hour or so, and my father and maybe little sister, in their long wait for me, would be among the people clapping mittened hands against the cold.

I looked up the aisle to see if Brody was taking any of this in. Given my vantage point and the high seatbacks, I couldn't see where he was, so I stood up, stepped forward a bit and discovered he was gone. Back at my seat, though, I saw him outside.

He was still wearing only that thin jacket, colorless in a more brightly dotted scene, and, on that account, unmistakable. More to the point, Brody was just turning away from a last look at the train—more than likely from staring into my window.

Okay, I thought. I want you home for Christmas. Go into that bakery, will you? Pick up some bread for the folks and some Santa Claus cookies. A jolly man in a clean white beard. I kept my eye on him, for the moment standing alone on the platform, no suitcase nearby, but then the train started to pull forward again, Brody receded, and I could not see who met him, who handed him a cup of coffee, saying, "We knew you'd need this. They never have the heat on in that train! Aunt Ginny came in on it yesterday and she was half frozen. She's over at the bakery right now, so let's get her and get home. Mom has your old room ready." I needed this monologue spoken on a snowy street of red brick houses with chimneys smoking crisply in the cold.

And I thought, my family will be putting *me* on the train in a couple of weeks, so I will be coming back through Middletown, Binghamton and further west for more schooling. God knows I need it. But, Mr. Brody, don't board the train. Stay right here. Live peaceably and simply, see old friends.

MICHELE MARKARIAN

WHO ON EARTH BROUGHT HIM?

Kim walked into the ballroom of Lovejoy Hall feeling nostalgic for something that wasn't even over. It was her college graduation. Four years of a music scholarship at a prestigious upstate New York women's university and just as she was starting to feel like she fit in, it was time to leave.

College had been hard for Kim. She was the first person in her family to even attend university, never mind graduate. Her parents couldn't afford the school's tuition, but between college loans, financial aid, and her waitressing job, Kim, despite being an anomaly, managed to squeeze by. Most of the girls came from money. Very few of them had jobs, other than to get good grades and date appropriate men. Kim kept herself hidden from them. None of her classmates had been to her childhood home, met her family. She worked hard and got good grades. She liked to think that in the four years she had attended the school, she had passed for one of them.

"Kim!" It was her older brother, Wayne. He had driven here, along with their parents and younger sister, from the small town in Massachusetts where they had grown up. She saw her sunburned parents tottering behind him before collapsing into chairs—they had been at an all day picnic, and had a little too much to drink, but grinned happily at their girl, their college graduate. "What are you drinking? Beer, yo? It's on me." Wayne flashed a twenty dollar bill.

"Gin and tonic," said Kim, wishing she had dressed up. She was wearing a sundress from the picnic, and had forgotten that these people changed for cocktail parties. "Stupid," she murmured, knowing that it was this kind of detail that set her apart. Her glance fell on Sherry, her favorite suitemate. Sherry was wearing a tea length dress with pearls. You'd never recognize her from earlier in the day, when she'd been wearing shorts and a polo shirt, playing softball.

Kim was just about to join them when she heard Debbie Ford ask,

"Who on earth brought *him?*" Kim followed Debbie's gaze and saw that it was directed towards Wayne, who was ordering from the bar. The back of his black motorcycle jacket had a menacing look to it. Kim knew that motorcycle jackets were not part of the couture, and not just because it was June.

"What's white and male and wears a motorcycle jacket?" Kim heard Sherry say.

"What?" replied Terry Cooper.

"Who cares?" said Sherry smoothly, and everyone laughed. Kim looked at Wayne, looked back at Sherry, and decided to bolt. Screw them all. She was tired of living between worlds.

"Kim?" asked Sherry, grabbing her hand as she brushed past. "Kim, there you are! What is it, sweetie? You don't look like yourself." Sherry was concerned. She rubbed Kim's arm.

Don't touch me, thought Kim, looking at Sherry with a gratitude she hated herself for feeling. "Uh—I'm gonna miss you guys," Kim stammered as a tear made its way to the corner of her sunburned face. It was true. They had shown her a different world, a different way to be. But it wasn't real. In two days, Kim would be going back to live in her cramped childhood home, in her drab Massachusetts town, to look for a job.

"Oh, I'm going to miss you too," said Sherry, hugging Kim with her free arm. "You know what you need? You need a drink. Doesn't she girls? Gin and tonic?"

From out of the corner of her eye, Kim saw Wayne, clutching a Budweiser and her gin and tonic, searching the ballroom quizzically. She nestled her face into Sherry's shoulder and lowered her eyes.

GILLIAN ESQUIVIA COHEN

OUR KIND

Ava dreamt of the house three times before she knew she was pregnant. In the first, she and a man she understood was her husband—an ivory knit sweater above polished loafers, aspiration embodied—were prospective homeowners at an open house. While the man sat on his heels inspecting the plumbing in the kitchen, Ava wandered about, opening doors. Behind one she found a bathroom, dated to the point of quaintness. Unlike the rest of the house, the bath had not been sterilized of its people: bottles huddled in a corner of the counter, a damp towel lay limp and defeated where it had fallen from its hook. The closet conserved shelves of neatly folded terry cloth and beneath them, a small door. "Honey, there's a laundry chute!" she shouted into the empty hall. She lifted the hatch and looked down the metal throat into the basement. Below, an empty hamper gaped expectantly at her. She took a hand towel from the shelf and tossed it down. The hamper gave a start; then, regaining its equilibrium, bobbed gently, sending small, rippling waves off in every direction. The lily pads around it rose and fell, like the respiration of a sleeping child, and the stand of reeds just beyond swayed gently in the breeze. On the dark mirror of the water's glass, she watched the reflection of a crane take flight.

The second was a refracted memory of when she scuttled through the crawlspace that led from the end of her friend's bedroom closet back behind the wall of the master bedroom. In real life, she had made the expedition with Sara one rainy day when they couldn't play outside. In her dream, she crawled alone. Beyond thin planks of wood that seemed so impenetrable from the other side, she sat and listened to the sigh of sheets pulled taut on a bed, the groan of floorboards beneath stocking feet. Some vestige of a child's fear at hearing what she should not pricked at her—of tumbling down the rabbit hole, an Alice who cannot make her way back out—yet this time she knew she could sit there all day and never miss dinner, never be caught.

In the third dream, the sky was the greenish violet of a new bruise and the house inside was dark. She walked through the abandoned rooms, opening drawers and rifling through artifacts. The art magazine with the scandalous photo of gloved hands censoring naked breasts on the parlor hassock. The heavy chemistry textbook with its honeycombs of chemical compounds, the yellow legal pad adorned with the filigree of her friend's father's script beside it. The peach-pink compact and its neat ring of pills in the mother's bedside table. She wandered the house, squinting in the dim hurricane light, snooping in the taxidermied corpse of the lives of Mr. and Mrs. Arlington, two people who were not her parents. Just before she awoke, she stood at the kitchen window and looked out at the woods, watching the trees sway in the heavy wind, waiting for something to emerge from their darkness.

"I haven't seen these people in over a decade," she told Elisa. They sat across from one another at a tiny table in an overpriced cafe, sipping bitter coffee and trying not to wince. "I haven't thought about them or Sara since high school."

"Maybe it's not so much about the people but the house itself. Freud would say—"

"Oh yes, please. What would the good doctor say?"

"Freud would say that the house represents your body."

"So I'm snooping around my own body."

"Or maybe it's your unconscious telling you you need to settle down and nest. How many apartments have you lived in since we met? That has to be wearing on you."

"But why Sara's house then? Why not have dreams about my parents' house, if all my unconscious wants to tell me is nest?"

Elisa waved the question away with her hand. "I don't know, I don't know shit about dreams. You know what you could do? Talk to a psychic."

"Or a therapist."

"Or you could buy tchotchkes."

⟨ ⟨ ⟨

Ava trolled thrift stores for ceramics and colored glass and asked her artist friends for studies to hang in her fifth-floor walk-up. Michael frowned at the explosion of red and yellow signifying her friend Emma's orgasm. "You should frame the first chapter of my thesis instead," he said. She had been sitting on the bed reading and pretended to continue even as he called for her through the brusque opening and shutting of cabinets in the kitchen. There was a hollow thump followed by an explosion of cursing and she knew he had hit his head again. The apartment was too small for him, or he was too big for it. He had the feel of a high rise under construction with just the ground floor complete and an artist's rendering of what it will look like in five years shouting in faded enthusiasm at passersby. She wondered if the problem was not the things in the apartment but the people.

)(   )(   )(

"The lease is in my name though and it isn't up till September," she told Elisa.

"So kick him out!"

"Right, because that would be so simple."

"You could stay with me. Give him a week to get himself organized and get out. You'd have to move your stuff over to my place first though. Books and DVDs, your nice towels. Your kitchen stuff!" Elisa gasped. "Don't let that fucker walk off with your wok!"

"He wouldn't do that."

"Excuse me? Are we not talking about the same guy who went crying poor-mouth to you—what, a month after you met? All poor, misunderstood philosopher who could change the way people thought about ethics and 'the nature of mercy' if only he had a quiet place to finish his thesis? And is he done with said thesis, by the way? How many years later?"

She thought about it and discovered it was indeed easy to imagine finally returning home only to find things her hands had adopted mysteriously spirited away from the kitchen, the living room, the bedroom. Her calls would go unanswered, only to be returned when he knew she would be at work or in class. She would take her phone off of silence and find messages about how he was sorry he had missed her call but he was just so busy writing the final chapter. He would definitely walk off with her copy of *The Genealogy of Morality* and if she called him on it, he would say that she never really understood it anyway so he had a right to take it. If she called his attention to the irony of his stealing a book on the subject of morality, he would say, "You see? You didn't understand it at all."

)(   )(   )(

Once she had her answer, she sat down on the dingy bathmat and though a corner of her mind pointed out that she had never before let anything but her feet touch the grey terrycloth, she promptly told it to fuck off. She checked the Accuracy Window again, compared its two pink lines against the diagram in the instructional insert and another voice floated by, one that told her that the test could be wrong, yet she knew it wasn't. She leaned her head back to rest on the edge of the tub and looked up into the skylight. The plastic bubble was scummy with mildew and pollen and dead leaves crowded the casing. She squinted at the shard of scuffed blue and decided that what she needed right at that moment was more sky.

✕   ✕   ✕

When they asked, Ava told her parents she wanted a break from the city. She slept in her childhood bed, read the best sellers her mother picked up at the market and when her father invited her out, ordered dessert from the restaurant's rotating display case, its glass bleary with nose and finger prints.

On her fourth morning she started walking. At first she kept to country roads, winding along the paved cowpaths where cars rarely passed, looking at houses and imagining different lives. She idled before clean lines and ample lawns, picturing herself lying on porch swings or reading in the embrace of bay windows, and hurried past the split-levels and single story ranches with their contents vomited onto the yard, the trailers with their flags of laundry waving unabashedly at passersby, the barefoot children, faces smeared with Red #40, heirs to the long legacy of the shuttered mill.

Ava had grown up in the shadow of the mill, as they all had. It stood dead-eyed and mute just beyond the square, pressing itself onto the consciousness of the town, refusing to be forgotten. As a child Ava had been convinced it was haunted; as a teenager she had trespassed with a boyfriend, slipping under a lolling tongue of plywood to explore its caverns littered with condoms and needles, the blackened hardwood floors still slick with a hundred years of oil. In school they first learned about economic decline in third grade, when they were taught that the town had once rivaled Boston. They learned then that they were the heirs to collapse, children born of rubble. The teachers tried to dress them up in feathers, calling them phoenix, but for most their efforts were washed away in the first rain. Without wings, many classmates had wrapped themselves in polyester blankets with singed edges and snuggled close to space heaters. Others had umbrellas and galoshes and parents who would drive them to homes where fires were lit for ambiance. Ava's slicker was too small, exposing her plumage to the wind and rain, but she ducked from doorway to doorway and learned to dash through the open spaces between houses with her wings folded up inside her sleeves. She left a few crimson feathers in puddles along the way but still managed to gain acceptance to a respected liberal arts college and move out.

Turning onto Main Street, she spotted the crown of red brick peeking above the trees. She walked down the hill past the oldest colonials, known to her by name, the market where she worked in high school, her elementary school, the meeting house, each building as familiar as family. When she came to the mill, the dissonance disoriented her. The iron gate, glistening with new paint, stood open; a little boy in a sun helmet ran across a manicured lawn; a woman carrying burlap bags branded with the name of the organic grocery store in the city walked up to the entrance and waited for a uniformed man to open the door. When Ava raised a hand to shield her eyes from the glare coming off the windows, she noticed the vinyl banner announcing that just three units remained unsold. The little boy ran up to the doorman. He held a long stick as if it were a rifle and showed the man how he could aim and shoot at imaginary tigers. Ava summoned her memories of the interior of the mill and tried to picture luxury condominiums. The little boy darted behind a tree, aiming his rifle. "Bang! Bang!" Ava watched the boy run to another tree, closer, then train his gaze on her. Watching her, he walked up to the fence, the rifle held by his side. "A native!" he whispered. He pushed the over-sized sun helmet back to fully expose cold blue eyes. Ava wrapped her fingers around the bars of the fence and smiled at him. The boy bared two rows of sharp little teeth then barked at her like a dog.

)X(   )X(   )X(

In the grey light of early morning, she remembered the cemetery. Something that hadn't existed for her since she had graduated from primary school, it came knocking at her memory as she lay in bed, slowly waking into her body.

The stream didn't run like she remembered it, the distances recorded in the muscles of her legs when she was short clashing with her adult height, but finally she came to that sudden clearing in the woods that had seemed so surreal when she and Sara first found it all those years ago. In the middle of the woods, after battling brush and dodging branches for an hour, she arrived at the vacuum: a mile of old carriage road that seemed to appear suddenly in deep woods and disappear just as abruptly, as if dropped there from on high. Sense memory led her to the cemetery, so overgrown it was nearly impossible to spot from the road. It was a family plot, probably begun by some of the first settlers in the colony, with few more than a dozen visible headstones. Most of them were unmarked and many of them were small. They stuck up out of the weeds at angles, the land flashing its crooked smile. A lot of children lost to smallpox, to winter. The tiniest ones, the size of drugstore paperbacks, marked the graves of stillborns.

As children, she and Sara had mourned the youngest lives lost. They pulled the weeds from around the headstones and lay tiny bouquets of wildflowers at their base. They imagined the lives of the unnamed buried there, drawing on what they learned about colonial life in school. Only two of the headstones in the very back looked finished the way the ones in the old church cemetery did. Esther Hopkins, mother, and Ezekiel Hopkins, son. 1786–1819, 1805–1814. Theirs were carved granite, the mother's adorned with a cross over a bible, the son's with just his name. He had been only nine. Nine years old herself, she had imagined different ways Ezekiel could have died but falling through the ice, skating on a winter afternoon, was the one that had stuck with her. She remembered being disappointed that Esther had died five years after he had. It would have been so much more poetic had she died that same year or the following one, of a broken heart. As children, it seemed so plausible that someone would die of a broken heart. It seemed to happen all the time.

She had stopped thinking about the tiny graves around the same time her classmate became an aunt. When she arrived home from school that day, she had related the news to her mother and instead of sharing her enthusiasm, her mother's face clouded. "How old is this girl's sister?"

"Fourteen."

"What did you say the girl's name was? The one in your class?"

"Theresa."

"Do you play with her often?"

"No, not really. Sometimes at recess."

"It's better that you don't play with her too often."

"Why?"

Her mother was quiet for a moment. "Theresa and her family aren't our kind."

)K(   )K(   )K(

She lay down on the grass and gazed up at the blur of green and blue. She had never been afraid of cemeteries; they had always been peaceful places for her. Growing up, she had sometimes taken naps there in the summer, the shade so cool, the ground so soft, as if hands were holding her aloft, cradling her to sleep. She tried to now, but sleep didn't come. She sat up and brushed the weeds away from the tiny graves. Were you to dig there now, it's likely you wouldn't find anything at all. Just dirt. You could dig for hours, for days and find only dirt and rocks. She wondered how long it took for bones to decompose. A baby's bones weren't as well formed, as permanent. They probably decomposed faster. The ones who didn't make it to nine months disappeared, reabsorbed back into the soil, into the earth's womb, she was sure. No trace would be left, unless the mother decided to find a small, flat rock to stand as a reminder of its absence.

)K(   )K(   )K(

At first, the woman's face, shut tight like a box, was a second door raised against her. Then Ava gave her name and Mrs. Arlington opened, hugs and smiles and exclamations of happy surprise. She swept her inside the house on a wave of linen and pearls that left her in the room where she had tried out so many adulthoods. It looked different but felt the same. Pipe smoke and cut flowers and something else she couldn't place translated into warmth, safety, and ideas of how things ought to be that were absent from her own home of cigarettes and TV dinners. The feel of that room curled inside her body and tugged at the deepest, oldest parts of her. She was six years old, playing Chutes and Ladders, breaking windows and saving kittens stuck in trees. Sara moved her token up, up, up, climbing one ladder then the next, while Ava got stuck in a cycle of sin and redemption, ascending one ladder only to fall back down the next chute. Gluttony, sloth; tummy aches and dunce caps. Lust, a hand in a cookie jar, was the longest chute. It tossed her back to the bottom of the game board, while Sara counted her squares and won the blue ribbon.

Draped across the love seat, Mrs. Arlington asked her about her life: school, work, relationships; then she itemized Sara's many blue ribbons and related her plans as if they were things in a store that just needed to be picked up. She asked what Ava's plans were and Ava spoke in the subjunctive, sitting stiffly on the edge of the sofa, smiling between sips of iced tea and wondering why she had come. She finished her tea and asked to use the bathroom.

After washing her hands she stood in front of the mirror, pressing cold fingers to her cheeks, the corners of her eyes, her lips. She remembered the time Sara had gone into her mother's make-up to paint her like a Russian nesting doll. From the far corner of the glass peeked the closet, its door ajar in invitation. She slipped her finger into the crack and eased it open. Beneath the rows of neatly folded hand towels was the tiny door. She lifted the hatch of the laundry chute and looked inside. Directly below her sat a little girl, murmuring to the stuffed rabbit cradled in her arms.

"Hi," Ava said.

The girl looked up at her. "Hi."

They observed each other in silence as the house breathed.

"My mom used to braid my hair and tie it off with ribbons just like that," Ava said.

The girl fingered one of her braids then said: "Sometimes it hurts when she does it. She has to pull really hard to make it stay. Says my hair's too slippery."

"Mine too. That's why I cut it short. See?"

The girl touched her hair, considering Ava's bob. "What's your name?" she asked.

"Ava. What's yours?"

"Violet."

"What are you doing down there, Violet?"

"I'm waiting for my mom."

"Where is she?"

"Upstairs, visiting Mrs. Arlington."

"Don't you want to come upstairs and be with her?"

"Not yet. It's not time yet."

"Oh no? When will it be time?"

"Soon."

"And what will happen when it's time?"

Violet looked at her with a violent seriousness. When she spoke, she spoke slowly, molding each word with her mouth. "When it's time I'll get real loud. I'll scream so everyone can hear me, even with the door closed. I'll scream so loud the door will break and everyone will see me. They'll see me and they'll see my mom."

Ava straightened, putting some distance between herself and the chute, but knew not to break eye contact with the little girl. "But you won't do that now. You won't get loud yet, will you?"

Violet looked down at her stuffed rabbit. She drew her fingers gently down its head and back and Ava thought she saw it move. "No, not yet. But soon."

)X( )X( )X(

The sun was dangling from an evergreen bough when she left the house. A breeze swept the day's heat up out of the ground and untangled it from rose bushes, making room for the evening cool to settle in its place. Threads of oldies music, the pop songs of a youth long grown old, unraveled from distant radios and names were called to dinner through the evening calm. Children's laughter, light and bird-like, pulled her along the road, up to the playground. A dozen children ran between metal bars and along wooden beams, trailing wild hair behind them. Swings creaked as legs pumped them higher and higher till they launched into the air.

Off to one side, bordering the woods, towered the slide. A string of children ran up its ladder and shot down the metal chute then rushed to overtake each other on the dash back around to the steps and up again. They followed their frenetic circuit up the ladder, down the slide, up the ladder, down the slide, up, down, up, down, as if it were a game.

Then there was a commotion, confusion, and the circuit halted. The children on the ground and waiting on the ladder looked up at the boy at the top of the slide. Gripping the handles, the boy slowly stood up. At first his face was a tight screw of concentration and nerves; as his eyes panned the wide expanse of terrain laid out below him, wonder, then joy radiated from him like a lesser sun. Impatience sawed at the voices of the other children behind him as they whined at him to hurry up but the boy ignored them. They tried to knock him down with insults and when that didn't work, the two children highest up on the ladder began hitting at his legs and back and tried to pry his fingers from the handles. The others descended the ladder and joined a growing crowd of children watching the boy make his beatific stand at the top. He stood there, smiling at everything, at nothing, even as his spry body shook from the blows.

Ava watched him in awe, silently rooting him on, even as she wondered who would arrive first: the boy's mother or an ambulance.

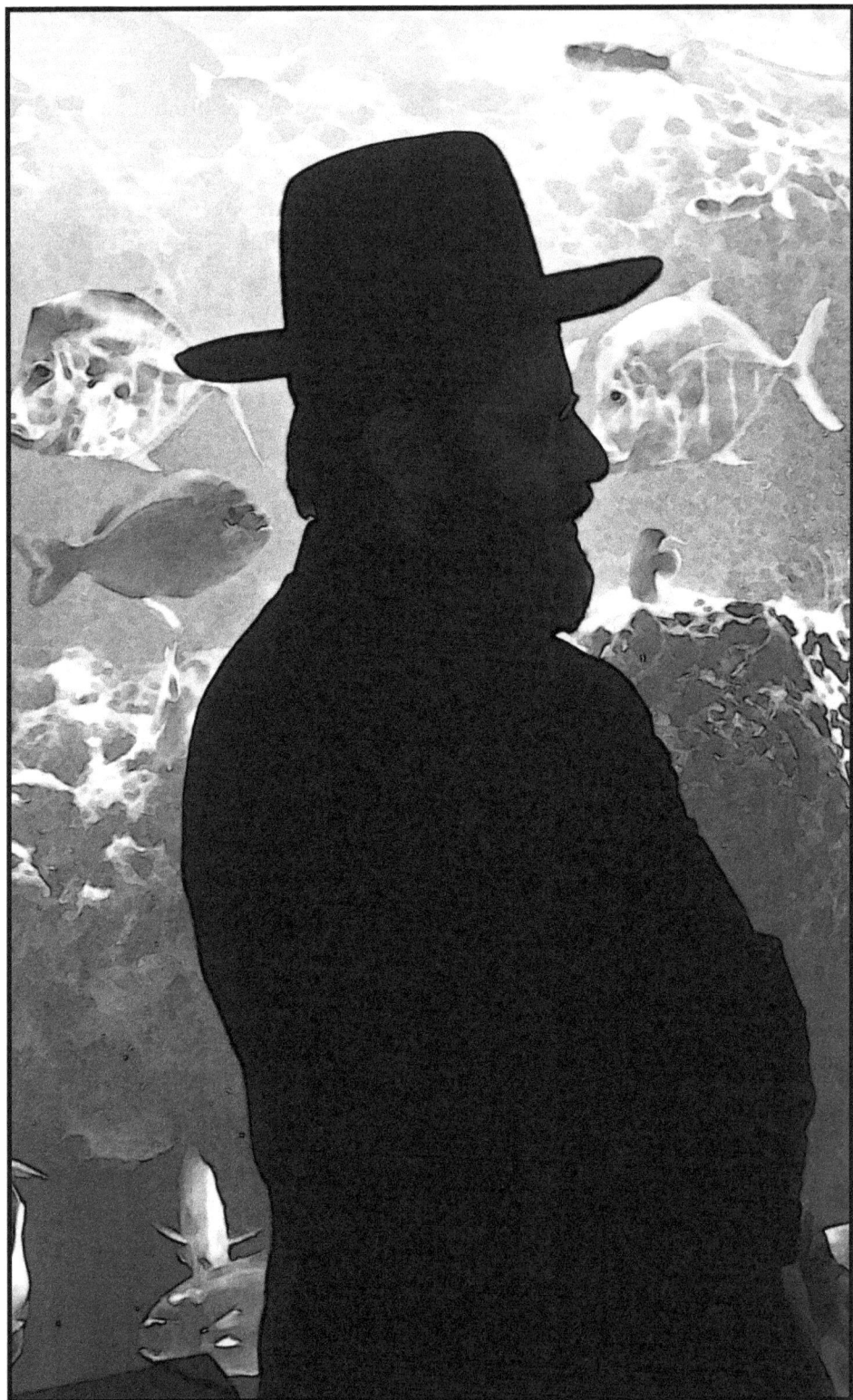

DANIEL M. JAFFE

HIDE AND SEEK

"So that's it then?" Rabbi Katz's intonation is flat, resignation coating defiant question.

"Yes, I—" Mae clears her throat, tries to match his tone "—I guess that's it." Her words are clearer to her than her intentions.

"You've decided," he says. "Just like that."

On the surface, his is a simple declaration of fact. But underneath, she knows, his words nearly burst with challenge. Does she know how to speak the same way? "I've decided," she says, "yes."

"Without discussing it with me first." Greater authority in his voice.

Mae looks down at her fingers lacing and unlacing. This is her house, her life. He is here at her request, in her own Collingswood, NJ, home for the first time. The home that she owns. Should be his white fingers fidgeting, yet he sits calmly opposite, sits on her forest-green sofa as if belonging here. Is this the power of spirit? To feel the Lord's comfort everywhere?

"Mae, shouldn't we have discussed this?" A switch: now he is imploring.

She takes charge of her fingers, stills them in her lap, looks directly into his brown eyes while maintaining the blankness of her own. "We're discussing it now."

"After you've decided."

She can do this. Her life, her daughter's life. Her decision is best for them both; he cannot change her mind. She relaxes her face to soften it—her cheeks ease, her teeth unclench, her lips part to breathe. Women appear to men more reasonable when soft.

His lips move too, as if to speak, then become still, move again. "Your hair looks pretty without the yellow kerchief. Fluffy."

"Thank you." Had she been wearing the kerchief when—? Of course, she always wore it when working. Dust. She notices the raised beauty mark halfway between his lower lip and chin; her daughter has such a raised beauty mark. "Your mustache looks very trim."

"Thank you." He tugs at it. "A little more gray, I'm sure."

She watches his brown eyes wander over her living room, the white walls, the glass-fronted china cabinet she found at one garage sale, the white dishes with blue trim she bought at another. Can he tell they're second-hand? Does he care? Does she? Last year's calendar that she keeps on the wall for its photograph of Dr. Martin Luther King, Jr. in pressed suit and tie (the Rabbi blinks—does he know who Dr. King was?). The pale green area rug frayed in spots. Is the Rabbi seeing or just marking time while plotting to reverse Mae's decision? Why would he even want to? Doesn't matter: her mind is made up, and she invited the Rabbi here just to tell him. For no other reason.

"Mae," he asks, his voice thick salve, "why didn't you call *before* making your decision?"

Mae had, nearly three years ago, telephoned him at work, had called more than once to share the news and shape a plan. He spoke with her at length, explaining in great detail the Jewish view that life begins not at conception, but at birth; Mae responded that Baptists view beginnings rather differently. Rabbi Katz then requested that Mae kindly refrain from telephoning him at work, his secretary apparently having questioned why "a woman with black urban twang" kept telephoning.

He had to know that Mae would not call him at home, for what if a headache kept the Mrs. from running her usual afternoon errands and she were to answer the phone? Having employed Mae for seven years, the Mrs. would surely recognize Mae's voice, twang or not. Especially so soon after Mae quit—"A sick aunt in Ohio needs me." Mae had lied to that good lonely woman always fixing Mae lunch and eating with her at the olive kitchen table, always asking after Mae's health and her boyfriend's, telling Mae the Jews had once been slaves too, "so our histories are not so different, yours and mine." The Mrs. said this while reaching across the olive kitchen table to pat Mae's hand. White on black.

"Always pay attention," Mae's late mother had taught her, "to which folks treat you like help and which like family."

Mae reaches up to finger the strand of white pearls she put on this morning for the first time ever, a goodbye gift from—

"Why didn't you call *before* making your decision?" the Rabbi says, repeating his question.

Mae drops her hand, just sneers. "What difference does my decision make to you? I thought you'd be glad, not having to send any more checks. It's not like you ever visited us—her."

"But every time I send a check, I feel connected." His voice drops to a whisper. "Just knowing that maybe one day I might see her . . ."

"One day," Mae whispers. "Which day?" Mae scratches her rust-colored corduroy arm chair. "Not her first birthday. Not her second." Mae's voice doesn't rise to the screech she hears in her head because she is uncertain whether his apparent caring is a good thing. Has she been wrong in deciding, finally, to sever all connection? "Where are my manners?" she asks, standing. "Some coffee?"

He stands from the forest-green sofa, his rumpled, open-collared white shirt and black pants sagging, his black jacket hanging in creases. He says, "Mae," and reaches out over her unpolished brown coffee table.

She retracts her hands. "I make mistakes, Rabbi, but only once."

"That's not what I meant."

"I'll bring coffee."

"I don't want coffee."

"*I* want coffee. Kindly sit down."

In her kitchen, Mae leans for a moment against the white refrigerator yellowing here in patches and there, takes several deep breaths. She invited him only to do the decent thing and tell him to his face that this would be their final communication. To tell him how well she has turned her life around. And maybe—just a little maybe—to see if she felt anything now. Not that she'd felt much back then other than spur-of-the moment passion, the comfort of a compassionate man in a moment of need. Still, before marrying Morris, she must be sure. And there is something she's been needing to ask, a question lodged so deeply in her throat these last years, she's been able neither to swallow it down nor cough it up.

She sets the kettle on the gas range, spoons freeze-dried granules into blue mugs. She doesn't bother taking out milk or sugar, remembering that the Rabbi takes his coffee black. Not that she ever saw him drink coffee, but while Mae dusted the study bookcases or mopped the kitchen floor, the Mrs. always gossiped about him, his habits, his routines. "Such silly things to be telling you," said the Mrs. more than once. "But a *rebbetzin*—that means a rabbi's wife—can never talk about him to anyone in the congregation. You understand?" He drinks coffee black "to remind himself that good things are tinged with bitterness." He gargles with unflavored mouthwash because he says "you can only trust medicine if it tastes bad." He maintains piles of papers on his desk because "clutter breeds creativity." The Mrs. always balled his socks—"otherwise he's as likely to wear one brown and one blue since his mind is not on things of this world." Mae remembers how that idea intrigued her, a man whose mind was not on things of this world. Different from most men she'd known, men whose minds were forever on their construction work aches and pains or their taxicab upkeep or basketball, football, baseball. Men and their balls.

During the first six years of Mae's employment, she never glimpsed the Rabbi even once since he worked at the synagogue on Thursdays, Mae's day at the house. But then he hired an assistant—"the congregation's just exploded," explained the Mrs.—and the Rabbi took to working afternoons at home.

Mae listens to the blip blip blip of water pouring into the blue mugs as the steam warms her eyes. She swallows, remembering that first Thursday afternoon he worked at home while the Mrs. was out doing errands. He shook Mae's hand and nodded in greeting. None of her other bosses' husbands had done that. A few words of conversation one week and then the next. The Mrs. usually running errands in the afternoons.

Mae stirs the two mugs with a spoon, stands them on a white dinner plate, carries them into the living room, sets the plate on the unpolished brown coffee table, takes one mug, sits down on her rust-colored arm chair. A small noise from upstairs, perhaps Betsy Wetsy falling to the floor, or a buckled shoe.

"She's here?" asks Rabbi Katz, turning pale.

Mae nods, marveling at his skin's capacity to become even lighter. How thin his face.

"I want to see her," he says.

So, now he wants to see her. "Not a good idea." Sip. Hot.

"I've never seen her. I have the right to see her."

"You've never seen her. You don't have the right to see her."

"You invited me here while she's upstairs. You wanted me to see her."

Mae sips again, feels the bitter burn on her tongue. Always a smart man, even able to read her grunts from another room: "You shouldn't be lifting that sofa by yourself, Mae, let me help you"; or "they sell pads now to protect your knees while scrubbing corners—I'll buy one for you next week"; or "I'll tell my wife we need a separate vacuum cleaner for upstairs so you don't have to lug this one up the steps." And that day after Mae's boyfriend walked out for good, the way Rabbi Katz sensed from her sullen frowns a deep need for comfort, the way he spoke to her while she mopped the kitchen floor. Words of comfort, then a hand on shoulder. The electricity of his hand on her shoulder leading to her head on his shoulder. His arms around her. Back pats and embraces leading to—

They couldn't look at one another afterwards, Mae muttering scolds at herself, he sitting on the bed, head in hands, weeping softly, leaving her to dress and then empty the mop bucket in the basement just as the Mrs. returned carrying grocery bundles. Mae wondered while pouring out that bucket in the basement's white utility sink, while splashing herself with the Rabbi's kitchen floor filth, wondered whether he were weeping for the Mrs. or for himself. Surely not for Mae . . . in any case, she'd never think to ask because tears are private.

"I wanted you here for me to say goodbye," Mae explains now. "Face to face, the decent thing. That's all." And to ask a question if she can manage to hawk it up. Sip and swallow melting heat down her throat.

"You knew Dottie would be upstairs, but you never intended for me to see her? That's why you asked me here. To hurt me."

Mae knows this to be true, at least in part, and feels the blood of shame rush to her face. She doesn't bother turning away because she knows he won't be able to detect her flush.

"Please, Mae, let me see her. Just once. A quick hello."

"And how would that be good for Dottie?" Mae's voice sounds sarcastic, but her meaning is sincere. If he can come up with a convincing reason, will she change her mind?

"Just tell her I'm a friend come to give you a wedding present." He reaches into an inner jacket pocket, pulls out a checkbook.

This, Mae thinks, is not convincing. "A white friend? A white *man* friend?"

"A former boss, then."

No, he is not convincing at all. "And would you tell Dottie hello or goodbye?"

"She's my child. My only child!" he pounds fist on knee, the first outburst of violence from him she's ever seen. "Do I need a reason to see my daughter?"

"You've never come here before. Did you need a reason to see your daughter?"

"You never invited me!"

"Did you need an invitation to see your daughter?"

"What is this? You tell me you don't want me in her life, but you're angry I didn't force my way into her life?"

Mae knows he's right, sips more and feels the coffee burn tracks down her throat. She considers posing her question as if it were a fairy-tale challenge— answer correctly for the right to kiss the fair princess. But she doubts that the Rabbi knows the correct answer, and she does not want to feel the sting of the wrong one.

The Rabbi shakes his head, slumps back on the forest-green sofa, the waist of his white shirt bunching and blousing over his belt. He asks softly, "What do you want from me?"

"Nothing, Rabbi. I never wanted anything from you." Not for herself, true, but she did want something for Dottie. But only if he'd give from wanting to, not from being forced. "You think I expected you to take Dottie into your white home and raise her there with the Mrs.? With me as the Mammy? Or are you telling me that if I'd asked, you'd have left the Mrs. and your congregation and your world and moved in here with us?"

"Mae—"

"I didn't think so. It's not like you loved me."

With shaky voice, "And that's my shame, Mae. For love I could have justified my sin."

"Your sin." That's what she and Dottie are to him. His sin. "You shouldn't feel guilty, Rabbi. After all, I didn't resist your holy touch. That's my shame." Mae sits up straighter in the rust-colored arm chair. "Put away your checkbook. You've paid every month like Dottie was your mortgage. I thank you for that." She nods the way she's seen queens do at flunkies in the movies. "I work hard, and my boyfriend's an accountant, Morris is. He'll provide for us just fine one day. A good man. Loves Dottie."

The Rabbi's eyes dart from side to side. "Have you told him?"

Of course the Rabbi worries about this; Mae's proven her silence, but heaven knows what Morris might choose to reveal, right? "Don't waste your worry on Morris. He's never even asked, just assumes Dottie was from my former boyfriend, a man of light complexion, convenient for you."

Mae sees relief pass over the Rabbi's face. She wants to spit.

"You're a good woman, Mae, you deserve good things. Please let me see

Dottie just this once."

"I think you should leave now."

He sighs, pinches the bridge of his nose. In pain? Good.

"Fine," he says. "I understand. If I'd been a better father—"

"If you'd been any kind of father and not just some Jewish banker!"

His face goes blank. She clamps a hand over her mouth, then brings it down. "I apologize, Rabbi. I didn't mean it." Didn't she? Was she incapable of such meaning? Both hands twitch, hot coffee splashes from mug to lap. She jumps up, sets the mug on the white plate on the unpolished brown coffee table, swipes at her lap.

"Mae!" The Rabbi springs up.

"Just a few drops. I'm fine."

He rushes quickly around the coffee table.

"I'm fine," she repeats.

He kneels. A rabbi kneels right at her feet and takes her hand and sandwiches it between the two of his. "I'm sorry, Mae," he says, his pale white face tilted up to hers, his eyes. "I say to you face to face, humbled on my knees, how terribly sorry I am."

Nice. But now? "Get up, Rabbi."

He stands, embraces her. Her arms remain limp at her sides. What has she done, bringing this man into her home? She tries to wriggle free, can't. "Rabbi, let me go!"

He presses his lips against her forehead and mumbles something she does not understand. It is this kiss, this presumed blessing, that burns through her skin and head and descends to dislodge the question nearly gagging her for so long, dislodges it like a clot into the bloodstream heading for the heart. She whispers, "If I were white would things have been different?"

He releases his hold on her, stares in silence.

"If I were white," she continues, "would you have dared touch me in the first place?"

His face wrinkles in great pain.

"And if your daughter were white," she continues, her voice so very much louder now, "would you have stayed away this long? Would you have stayed away at all? I'm waiting for an answer, Rabbi. I expect the truth from you."

"Some truths aren't pretty."

"Truth is always pretty."

"Some truths are ugly."

"The truth shall make you free, says the Bible. So tell me the truth now and I will never bother you again."

"The truth," he says, his hanging head that of a guilty child. "Okay then. The truth. Here's the truth: skin color's not relevant to me, it never was, I'm not a bigot. That's the truth." Then he shrugs and looks away and Mae knows something more is coming. "But," he continues, "if you had been Jewish, and Dottie . . . then . . ." He looks up, his eyes unreadable. He shrugs again.

Although Mae never imagined this among possible answers, she recognizes this as truth from the way it sears. So obvious now that it's out. Like all truth.

Rabbi Katz extends his hand toward her, palm upward. He holds the position. Mae's throat feels tight, no longer from her questions, but from his answers, prickly and choking. She can barely swallow, glares harder than she ever has.

The Rabbi nods to himself, lowers his hand, nods again with unfocused eyes, eyes escaping somewhere. He turns, shuffles a few steps toward the front door, lingers as though waiting for her to summon him back and say everything's okay now that the air's been cleared. Mae sizes him up, looks at the black and gray hair wisps over his jacket collar, the hunch of his shoulders, the sag of black pants. His unpolished shoes. No, she thinks, he has not won the right to kiss the fair princess. What a mistake she made. What a mistake.

Mae strides past him, grabs the brass knob and opens her front door. A soft whoosh of cool air. She looks away from him, up at her front hall ceiling light, a simple white bowl fixture over a simple white bulb. Mae hears him step onto her wooden front porch, listens to the creak of steps as he descends, to the click of heels on sidewalk, the opening squeak and slam of car door, the engine rev. Departure.

She waits until his car no longer sounds, then looks out her door, beyond her gray wooden porch at her young sugar maple tree, its remaining leaves blazing so proudly red in the November sun. She looks down her block of attached houses, some fronted with brown brick, others with chipped white paint or colored aluminum siding. Mowed lawns sprinkled with fallen brown and orange leaves, bordered by chain-link fences or more-or-less trimmed hedges, rose bushes pruned for the impending winter. Her street, her neighborhood. Her world.

MURALI KAMMA

IN THE NEW WORLD

"I'm here only because of my daughter," he said, not looking up as he closed the menu.

Kumar had already said that a few times—using the same words, in fact—but he was obviously reminding me, as if he knew why I had invited him to lunch. It seemed like he wanted to deflect any criticism of him. Or perhaps he was seeking reassurance.

"Of course," I said, "it doesn't surprise me. I'm sure your daughter appreciates it. You gave up a good career, a good life—"

"Don't get me wrong." He raised his head, his eyes widening under his bushy eyebrows. "I'm not saying I made a big sacrifice. I came because we wanted to move here. But, you know, it's not easy being a new immigrant at my age . . . not easy to be jobless, face uncertainty."

He was being dramatic. Kumar had been offered a retail position, but according to his wife, he rejected it because of the low pay and status. An earlier job had lasted only a few days—or rather, nights—because, as he put it, staying awake when everybody else was sleeping was not for him. I wondered if he'd been fired. He'd reportedly worked at another place, but that job too had been short-lived, apparently. And then he did something bizarre, alarming his wife.

Calling me one day on my cellphone, as I was returning to the office after lunch, she told me about it. A resident in their building had seen Kumar at a traffic light near the highway, holding a sign that read: "Experienced project manager seeks work commensurate with qualifications."

Furious and concerned, she demanded an explanation when her husband got home. He jokingly said that one had to use creative methods to find a proper job. When she threatened to leave him, Kumar quickly backed off and said that he'd done this only a couple of times, briefly. He wouldn't do it again. In any case, motorists seemed to think it was a prank.

Flabbergasted, I didn't know what to say. Was he losing it? This was her second phone call to me, and I wondered how Kumar would react if he found out that she was calling me. While she was practical and resourceful, he came across as a dreamer with unrealistic expectations. She had no qualms about working long hours at a supermarket, which offered health insurance for the family and provided job security. But it wasn't easy, and her husband's vacillation frustrated her.

"Please talk to him," she implored, her voice breaking. "You're one of the few people here he knows and trusts. He'll come to his senses if he listens to you."

I was doubtful, though I didn't say so. I'd already shared his resume with prospective employers, made calls on his behalf, and given him tips and leads. I even provided a reference. He got some responses, but nothing solid had panned out yet. Telling him to be patient, I'd asked him to accept— like his wife—a lower-paying retail job until something better came along. If retail wasn't his cup of tea, there were other possibilities. Kumar wasn't enthusiastic, so I decided to let him find his way. He was a grown man, after all, and there was only so much I could do.

Of course, that's not what she wanted to hear. Without interrupting her, I entered my building and, holding the phone, climbed the stairs to my office. I'd stopped using the elevator, seeing the stairs as a good opportunity for getting exercise on weekdays.

Just last night, she continued, her husband had said he was ready to go back, ready to give up on his American dream. He missed his old life, but didn't expect her or their daughter to accompany him. Kumar would return alone. Once he was established—which shouldn't take long, according to him—he'd send money. His needs were few. With her help, they'd be able to put their daughter through college.

Mournfully, she added, "It's crazy. I don't know what's happened to him."

I was stumped. Then, finding my voice, I mumbled some soothing words and said I'd be happy to talk to him soon over lunch at a restaurant.

)X(   )X(   )X(

"The prices here are high," Kumar said, looking around nervously at the other diners. "We should've gone to the buffet place I was telling you about."

"Come on, Kumar, I already said this was my treat. Easier to talk here.

The buffet place gets crowded—and frankly, the food here is much better."
I was glad we'd managed to snag a corner booth that gave us some privacy.

He nodded glumly and, without looking at the menu again, said he'd
have whatever I was ordering. I didn't know what to make of him. I wasn't
trying to downplay the struggles of new immigrants, but Kumar had been
such a go-getter that it was astonishing to see the transformation. Two decades
ago, few students in his class had been more promising and ambitious than
him. Being younger, I joined the same college after him, but my cousin had
been his classmate and it was he who'd asked Kumar to get in touch with me.

Kumar's shoulders stooped as he sat. But despite his hangdog appearance
and thinning grey hair, one could tell that he wasn't a dour—or old—man.
His face was still unlined, and he'd shed some pounds in recent weeks, giving
him a leaner look. Kumar only had to smile, which I hoped he'd do more
often, to reveal a sunnier and livelier side.

Before meeting him, I learned through my cousin that, prior to his
move to the U.S., Kumar had risen swiftly through the ranks in the corporate
world, attaining a respectable position. But something had changed. Sure,
moving to a new country can be challenging. And yet, on our first meeting,
soon after his arrival, he'd been upbeat and full of energy. The possibilities for
his family seemed rich, and he was very hopeful about his prospects.

So what happened—why had things gone downhill that quickly? He
was dejected, even depressed. Years ago, my cousin said, people had spoken
well of him, seeing him as an up-and coming young man with a bright
future. And indeed, in his old life, Kumar had to a large extent fulfilled those
expectations. In his new life, though, he seemed lost, reminding me of a man
who slumbers for so long that when he wakes, unexpectedly, he's bewildered
by all the changes around him. It's a new era, with the unfamiliar rules and
customs making him a stranger. Moving to a new country could be like that,
I suppose. Kumar hadn't found his bearings—yet.

Paying the bill, I realized we weren't talking about what Kumar was going
to do, how he was going to make progress. Our conversation was desultory.
As we drifted from topic to topic, I avoided bringing up the topic that was
uppermost in my mind. His demeanor and subdued manner discouraged me
from asking intrusive questions. I didn't want to come across as a busybody.
Bringing him to this restaurant had been a mistake, only reminding him of
his diminished status. It was too fancy. I thought it'd be a nice change, but I
had miscalculated.

Now, as we walked out, I couldn't think of anything to say. Pep talks and platitudes seemed pointless when, as his wife put it, he was so "proud" that he wouldn't settle for a modest job. Looking for a suitable position in his field demanded his full attention, he'd told her, leaving him little time for other work. But Kumar had nothing to show for it, and she was getting tired of his shenanigans. How long could they continue like this?

"Kumar, I haven't been to your apartment," I said, as I opened my car door. "Let me drop you there."

"What's there to see? It's a shabby apartment in a shabby building." He laughed mirthlessly. "Sometimes, before I open my front door, I'm greeted by a bag of dog poo."

"Did you complain?" I said, shocked.

Smiling, he shook his head, and by the look on his face I could tell he thought I was clueless. I had a good, well-paying job and my family led a comfortable life in an attractive, secure neighborhood where we owned a house. What did I know about his trials—such as the bigotry and uncertainty he had to face in this bewildering country, which he was finding so hard to decipher and get ahead in?

For me, though, Kumar was hard to decipher. He seemed both proud and needy, presenting a curious mix of arrogance and vulnerability. His struggle to live with diminished expectations and status was painfully obvious. Had he suffered other indignities that he was unwilling to share? I was sympathetic, but I knew an attitude adjustment would help him enormously. I just didn't know how to convey that without offending him.

"Well, I'll see you," he said. "Thanks for the lunch. I'll let you get back to work. I can walk from here . . . it's not far. Let's meet again."

"No worries, Kumar. I know you don't want me to drop you, but I'll tell you something before we part. Your wife called me a couple of times."

Kumar stared at me. When I saw his face turn red—in embarrassment, certainly, but perhaps also in anger—I was filled with regret for being so impulsive. Was he going to berate her for calling me?

"She's worried," I continued. "We feel you're drifting—and need help. She turned to me out of desperation."

"Oh, did she?" Kumar's voice dropped. He seemed deflated. Perhaps what I said didn't surprise him, and he probably knew that his wife had instigated the meeting.

"I think we should talk more, Kumar, maybe over tea. I don't have anything pressing at the office. Your wife can join us if she's interested."

"She's at the store now, but come to the apartment," Kumar said unexpectedly. "You can have tea there. My daughter and wife will be home by four."

We didn't talk as I drove, and since the traffic was fairly light at this time of day, it didn't take long to reach Kumar's neighborhood. I found a parking spot on the littered street, which had a few potholes and was lined with grimy, graffiti-scarred buildings. Not many people were about. Although Kumar's apartment building looked gloomy, it was in a better shape than the other buildings. Opening the creaky door, we entered a narrow passage.

"The lift . . . elevator . . . broke down again," Kumar said. "Let's take the stairs."

It was a little dank and dingy inside, with stained walls, and the building was eerily quiet. We heard the loud, monotonous siren of a firetruck as it went down the street. When we reached the third floor, Kumar took out his key and unlocked the door.

"No dog poo today," he said, entering. "So that's good news."

"Why don't you move out? I know it's an expensive city, but if you keep looking, there are possibilities—"

"Yes, we've thought about it. We didn't know any better, but the school is decent. Our lease won't expire until next year."

The modest apartment, furnished with mismatched items that seemed to have been bought at thrift stores, was neatly kept and not uninviting. If I had to guess, it was Kumar's wife who'd turned this place into a home, a welcome refuge for the family in this crumbling neighborhood.

"Have a seat," Kumar said, gesturing at the most comfortable chair, which was near a worn sofa that had lumpy yellow cushions. "I'll make some tea."

There was, directly across from the well-padded armchair I was sitting in, what looked like a wooden TV stand. But instead of a TV set, what I saw was a tabla set, with the two drums resting on a bottle green tablecloth. It triggered a memory.

Kumar was a musician. As a young man, I suddenly recalled, he used to play at a professional level in my hometown. It's strange how the mind works. Even when I was chatting with him or my cousin, I hadn't remembered Kumar's musical past—but now it all came back to me in a rush. Although I'd never seen him perform, and the music group lasted only a couple of years, I knew they'd been well regarded by aficionados. As a teenager, I'd seen a flier promoting their concert, which my cousin and a few other people I knew had attended—and liked.

While the group didn't last, Kumar had apparently kept up with his music. When he returned with the tea, I pointed at the tabla and said that his commitment to music was commendable, given his current situation. And here, I added, he was deprived of an audience, not just the monetary compensation. Passion was the fuel that seemed to keep him going.

Chortling, he handed me a cup before sitting on the sofa.

"Keeps me sane, but it makes the guy downstairs insane," he said. "That's why we get presents like dog poo. But I'm very careful. I play it only for a limited time in the afternoon when there aren't many people in the building."

I was tempted to ask him to play for me now. First, however, I had to tell him something important. "Kumar, here's an opportunity for you. My son takes lessons at a music school that's looking for more instructors. They're doing well. I'm sure they don't have a tabla player. They'd love to have somebody like you . . . somebody of your caliber."

"Really?" His eyes lit up. "Sounds interesting. Is the school close to your house?"

"Not far," I said, resting the cup on my lap. "It's accessible for you because there's a station nearby. It won't take you more than thirty minutes by train. I'll be glad to talk to them."

Kumar put his cup on the floor. Then, in a gesture that surprised and touched me, he folded his hands and simply said, "Thank you."

HEATHER TOSTESON

TARGET FIXATION

If there's one thing I've taught my son that will serve him really well in life, it's keep your eye on where you want to end up, not on what's in your way. I've seen too many guys crash when they don't. I taught him this for dirt biking and stock car racing, but I think it applies to life as well. We aim for what we're looking at. It's called target fixation. It's a physical response. You're racing around a track and the car next to you spins out and crashes and if you look at it, before you can think your own car is slamming into the metal, the wall, bursting into flames. *Keep your eye where you want to be.* If I've told my son once, I've told him a thousand times.

People were surprised when I had my son on his own dirt bike by the time he was five. He'd been riding a two-wheeler since he was three; he was ready. I explained this to my wife's family, but they still thought I was crazy. Life's dangerous, that's just a fact. It's how you take it on that makes the difference. You're never too young to learn that.

I should know. I came here from Tamaulipas by myself across the desert when I was twelve years old. My mom had six more kids to raise and my dad was dead. I was the oldest, so it was up to me to help her. My goal was really clear. I had my eye on more food for all of us. I worked in the fields, then construction. I still remember looking at the food on my shelf in that first apartment in Rio Grande, my amazement at what I'd been able to do: Feed myself until I was full. But I knew I had to do more. I joined the military when I was eighteen. Served in Vietnam. Got my green card. Got my GED. Became a citizen. Sponsored every one of my brothers and two of my sisters and paid their way. Now I work for the Border Patrol, fixing their motorcycles and jeeps so they can go out and catch people like me. Go figure.

You ask what I've kept my eye on through my life? I mean, after I was sure I could keep a refrigerator full and once I'd brought my family up here? The answer is my kids, especially my son. I've tried to teach him everything I know. Fast as I could because you never know how life is going to turn out. I taught him how to hunt, fish, rebuild an engine, detail a car, race a dirt bike and a stock car, box as hard with his left as with his right, how to flip a guy in a fight.

How much of that he's going to be able to use at MIT is not so clear to me. But it's what I have to give—and I have to say this for Jordan (his mother's choice of a name not mine), he's learned all of it. I have no fears for him in that way. He can take care of himself. He can also (and I think this isn't so usual with engineers) hear beneath the words, with his heart and his gut. He's not going to get took.

I've taught my son all I know so he can do better than me. I remember when he was thirteen and he passed me on his dirt bike during an off-road race, just sailing out over a rock, riding on one wheel then settling back in, not giving me a glance, keeping his eye where *he* wanted to be—at the head of the whole goddamn pack. Near blinded me, the feeling I had. It wasn't pride. I taught him what I know, but he was the one who knew how to use it. I think what I felt at that moment was full—like life at that moment held more than I had ever imagined, all I could possibly want.

I wonder if my dad, if he'd lived, would feel that way looking at me. I remember so little about him. He was dead by the time I was ten and at least half that time he was off working somewhere else—first in Mexico, then in the States. All I can remember about him is he had this really sweet voice, deep but sweet, so when he said, "*Mi hijo,*" it slipped right into you, dark and rich and warm as chocolate. And he was tired, he had the most tired eyes I've seen in someone ever. Tireder even than my mom's her last year when she was dying of cancer. Tireder than my wife's, who feels more weighed down than she'll ever admit by the life she's chosen to live for me and the kids. The one that feels so rich to me, given where and what I come from.

☒   ☒   ☒

My wife is college educated. She's an epidemiologist with the county board of health. If there's an outbreak of hanta or Nile virus or food poisoning, she's meant to investigate. She does that using numbers. *Chance, bias, confounding*—those are the three things to look out for she warns our son—like the words don't just apply to diseases, they apply to love, friendship, schooling, road races. These words are red flags to her. They are things that can distort. They can invalidate your findings.

I'm not so book smart, but the words never stop meaning, least as far as I can see, what they always did. Chance is what brought us together. If I hadn't stopped into that college bar that evening in April thirty-five years ago, if Candace hadn't just been dumped by her boyfriend of three years because she "wasn't the one he needed to ensure his advantage in the corporate world" —well, Jordan and Juana (my choice) wouldn't be here, that's for sure. You can say higher—or lower—forces were at work. You can say there was a divine plan. Or that two total strangers, after shipwreck, clung to each other on the off chance either of them could swim.

Does it explain why we're together now? Does it need to?

"What's the glue?" Juana asked me right after she got engaged last year. I almost said fear of drowning, but instead I said what I always do to Jordan: *target fixation.* "We never took our eyes off where we wanted to be, honey. We never took our eyes off family."

In other words, we looked out over each other's shoulders, at our own private and wide stretch of desert sky, our bodies doing what a man and a woman's body do best. And then we both kept our eyes on the very best there was in our shared, chance destiny, these two great kids who just fell from heaven into our laps and looked up at us as if we were, each of us, something unbelievably special. They were biased, maybe. Maybe completely biased in our favor, like we were in theirs. Who wouldn't want to aim there?

These days I think about why Candace and I are still together after thirty-five years because both my kids are marrying young too. Jordan's marrying up, like I did. Juana's marrying down, like her mother. I feel like Candace failed her daughter, but I don't like saying *I* failed my wife. It's like Candace knows the reality of target fixation from the other side, the helpless crash and burn side. She feels it's pointless to try to reason with Juana.

"Juana's heart's made up, Julio," Candace has told me several times. "You want to try to change it, try. Just leave me out of it. She knows I'm going to stick by her whatever her choices."

Candace's not saying I won't. She's talking about her own family up in Phoenix, how they act like the distance between Phoenix and Las Cruces is greater than between New York City and LA, Mexico City and Seattle. They have the kids up to see them there, Candace too, but not a one of them will set foot in our house. It's like they're afraid they'll catch something. Spanish flu maybe, although neither of my kids speaks Spanish like it's natural to them. When their attitude isn't pissing me off, I think it's kind of funny because the one place Candace has been a real hard ass is our house. She wants it to look just as good as the one she grew up in. Better, actually, since I'm handy with repair and remodeling. If her parents and her three sisters were to come, they'd think they were in their own homes. Except for the number—and color—of the people living in it.

It's not like we're isolated here. Two of my brothers and one of my sisters live in the area and we're in and out of each other's houses constantly. Holidays, the rest of the family drive down from Chicago, over from LA. It's crazy and good. At those times, Candace stands out here just as much as I would in Phoenix. Our kids have her height. In the right context, like school, they can pass for white. Juana especially when she dyes her hair, which she used to do before she met Vicente. It's not just their looks, it's also their accents and the way they carry themselves and their mother's book learning that help. But they fit right in with their cousins too. That's never going to be true for Candace, anymore than it would be for me with her people. I never thought she minded though I've never asked her straight out. It seemed that maybe the difference felt good to her somehow, that without having to work at it, she was a standout. I have always liked looking at her from across a room, so tall and white skinned with her straight blonde hair brushing against her shoulders, her blue eyes always so serious, her mouth lifting a little at the edges as she surveys the room to make sure no one is feeling left out or drowned out. What I see is not happiness exactly, but tranquility, some pressure on her heart easing momentarily.

For there are pressures on Candace's heart, real pressures. It's not just her way of getting to me, letting me know what she feels about the drinking, the other women, me being me. I'm shamed to say it wasn't me but Jordan who took her seriously and made her see a doctor. She's got something wrong with one of her valves, the mitral, and that means half the time her blood's washing back instead of forward, a turbulence that robs her muscles of oxygen and leaves her breathless, tired. They can fix it. Give her a mechanical valve or take one from a pig. Being a mechanic, I know which one I'd pick. Troubles me to think of my wife's heart fixed with used parts from a pig. For one thing, there's no warranty.

But here Candace isn't taking anyone's advice except the doctors, and sometimes not even theirs. They want her to do this soon as possible. But she says, "I've survived with this for fifty-four years, I can survive a year more." It's the weddings. She's focused on the weddings. She's not going to take her eye off them for a moment. Which is why the kids decided, without consulting either of us, to have a joint wedding earlier than either of them planned. They have told their mother to schedule her surgery for a week to the day after the ceremony, so they'll both be back from their honeymoons.

"What's the hurry?" I asked Jordan and Juana. "Your mother's health comes first, doesn't it?"

Juana and Jordan looked at each other uncomfortably.

"It's what *she* wants," Jordan said finally.

"Why?"

"She doesn't want to stand in the way of our happiness."

"That's what you told her? Postponing the weddings would make you unhappy?"

Jordan stood up. He's thinner than me but five inches taller. Tough.

"Of course not, Dad. But if it's going to make her happy, we'll do it."

Juana shook her head, her face reddening a little. "It's not that, Dad. It's Vicente. She's worried about his status. She thinks the faster we marry the more likely it is he'll get a green card."

Jordan smiled. "And she's afraid Marisol, if she's given a few more months to think, will decide she can do better." Marisol graduated summa cum laude to Jordan's magna and is going to Harvard Law in the fall, married or not. Jordan is an add-on to her life plans, not the focus.

We're good parents, both of us, but it is breaking our hearts to see our children following in our footsteps, and, at the same time, we're doing our best to encourage it—including double weddings. I'm having a hard time getting my mind around that and I can't, hard as I try, look beyond it either.

I'm thinking about it today because of the bachelor party tonight, which I see as my last time to prepare either of these young men for what's facing them. Then comes the wedding, where I've got to say something to everyone, but to Juana in particular, about setting your sights high, staying focused. I just wish for her I could have said it earlier. But what am I going to say, "I don't want to see you making your mother's mistake?" She wouldn't listen to me anyway. Candace and I divided the children between us real early. Juana loves me but she looks up to her mother. Jordan, it's the other way around. Where one sees strength, the other sees weakness. So, it's only her mom has a chance of changing Juana's thinking, but Candace doesn't seem to have the interest.

I don't think the boys are making mistakes in who they're choosing, so tonight feels easier. It's a full moon and we're dirt biking off-road in the desert: Jordan and his two best friends and three cousins, Vicente and his two brothers, me and my brother Rafael. I've borrowed bikes from my buddies, checked them all out and filled their tanks, tested their headlights. They're all loaded on my truck and Rafael's.

Candace and Juana and Marisol are having a spa day, then going to an evening praise service, then a night out at a very fancy restaurant, compliments of Marisol's wealthy divorced mother, flying in for the occasion from her second home in Miami (her first is in Caracas). Marisol's father, equally wealthy, now located in New York, flies in tomorrow with his third wife, who is five years older than Marisol—and also a graduate of Harvard Law. They are going to be joined by Vicente's mother, who is illiterate and comes from the highlands of Guatemala, three nieces from my side and Juana's best friend Alison who, like her, teaches ESL to immigrants, illegal or legal makes no difference.

"I wouldn't trade places with you," I tell Candace.

"Ah, but you haven't seen the masseuses, Julio," she says. She laughs genuinely. Something has happened with Candace since the diagnosis. You can see it in her eyes, hear it in her laugh. It's like some weight has been lifted from her spirit that we thought was just part of her basic nature, a sadness, a heaviness, a fatality. It's like she has no worries now.

I can't help feeling this is a bad sign, which is strange because for years I've told her not to worry so much, it just makes you grow old, doesn't change what's going to happen one way or the other. Candace calls that my "culturally foreshortened risk horizon." I call it keep your eye where you want to be.

But I don't like this shift in my wife. It's like nothing bad can happen to her, she's free of something, she's feeling so light if she didn't have the kids she'd float up above the mountains like one of those hot air balloons, just a bright red dot slowly disappearing into the clean, cloudless blue.

As we're driving in the truck, I try to explain this to Jordan. Vicente and his brothers are riding with Jordan's friends Sam and Ernesto, and Rafael's sons are riding with him.

"You think Mom has a mood disorder?" Jordan asks. "You think she can't just be feeling happy that finally what is bothering her has been diagnosed and something can be done about it? That her kids are getting settled at the same time? That they're going to experience the same joys that have made her own life so worthwhile?"

I look over at him. He smiles—and it gets to me, everything he's saying and not saying.

)((   )((   )((

When we get to the pull-off, Rafael and I open up the backs of the trucks and set up ramps and the boys wheel all the bikes down. I'm working on a Bud and so is Rafael. I offer them around. Rafael's sons take them, so do Jordan's friends Sam and Ernesto. Jordan looks like he's going to say something, but doesn't, just bends down and double checks the height on his bike. Vicente and his brothers refuse. They're church goers like Candace and Juana (that's where Vicente met Juana, through the church's ESL tutoring program where Juana was volunteering), so they're going to act like they have no vices—at least in places where it might get back to the powers that be. I respect this. Vicente is keeping his eye on where he wants to be—and he's bringing his brothers along.

I offer a beer to Jordan again, and he shakes his head and smiles. Marisol probably said something—or Candace. He's not going to pass it on, but he's going to respect their wishes, be the guy they wish I would be. My son is a good-looking guy. I look around and think, damn, we are a fine sight, every one of us.

I hand around reflective vests. I borrowed them from work, so they have the Homeland Security logo. "Everybody keep them on at all times," I say, looking directly at Vicente and his brothers so there's no confusion. "Jordan's going to take the lead," I go on. "I'm bringing up the rear. We're heading away from the mountains, so if they're in front of you, stop and turn around. Everyone keep your lights on. Don't look down at the ground right in front of you, if you see it then, it's too late. Look out a good twenty, thirty feet, where the light first hits, so you have a better chance of responding. If you've not done this before, take it slow, get a feel for your bike, your own center of balance before you accelerate, pay attention to the changing levels of traction with sand, grass, gravel, rock. Aim between the prickly pears and the agaves—not at them. It should take us a half hour to get where we want to be. There'll be a truck there with supplies. A bonfire ready to light."

Rafael and I've been working days to get this all to flow smooth. I look at all these handsome young men. In the glare of the headlights their faces are shadowed and over-exposed at the same, and for a second it feels like the first day in boot camp and it gets to me, it really does, how young we were, and how at some level it is no different now, we're just as ignorant of what we're getting ourselves into, Rafael and me, in this new stage in life when our kids have grown and left us, just as unaware as we were back then. I don't think that is something you can teach anyone, what real relation the past has to the future. It's changing, it's always changing and we're always its turning point.

The group naturally sorts out, with Jordan and his friends, who've ridden with him for years, in the lead, then Rafael and his sons, then Vicente and his brothers, then me. 3-4-3. 3-4-3. I keep scanning as the groups fan out wider and wider, each rider finding his own path through the creosote, yucca and ocotillo, wanting some feeling of freedom, the illusion that it's just between them and a moon so bright it's thinking it's really the sun and the stars stabbing through the sky like light from a tin lantern.

I can see something has come up minutes before I get there—all the lights converging, lighting up the metallic sides of the trailer of a large semi. Somehow it's gotten itself straddling a wide arroyo, the rear wheels of the cab on the rim of one bank, the rear wheels of the trailer on the rim of the other. The arroyo is about four feet deep. It looks unnatural, how exactly it is balanced, like it was picked up and carefully set down just so. What the fuck, I think. I immediately start trying to imagine how to move it, that's just the way my mind works, I'm a fixer.

Jordan and Rafael are over at the cab talking to the driver. It isn't until I came up to them that I realize the driver is a woman. She's laughing and crying at the same time.

"She was following her GPS," Jordan tells me, his voice kindly, expressionless. The highway is miles back, she's been driving all this time and never registered she was off the road? How can you be so clueless? I wonder. We all wonder. But nobody is saying because it's a woman and she's crying more than she's laughing. A guy, he'd be cussing himself out so loud he'd have no room for advice.

"A miracle of balance," I tell her, putting my hand up to shake hers. "You want to come and see for yourself? I'm Julio. I'm sure my son and my brother have introduced themselves."

The guys are staggered along the length of the trailer, marveling. I can see Vicente, like me, is playing various scenarios through in his mind. You go forward, the trailer might flip. You go back, you'll up end the cab.

The woman we help down is blonde as Candace, tall as her too. She looks, by moonlight, to be in her early twenties. She's thin. Big boobs. "We could hire her," I hear Sam whisper to Ernesto.

"Mind yourself," I tell them. I'm busy thinking what we need to do. The boys need their night out. She obviously needs a tow, and it isn't coming from eleven dirt bikes.

"You're going to need it craned up," I say.

"I don't know what I was thinking." She puts her hand to her forehead. "I mean, I saw this stretch was different, but I didn't register it as deeper. I just kept telling myself that the GPS had a better sense of direction than me. I thought I was on a dirt road, that I just couldn't quite make it out in the dark. I was just scanning everywhere for asphalt, and that voice kept saying turn left, go straight ahead for one mile. "

"Your daddy never teach you not to believe everything you hear?" I ask.

"From men, sure. But this was a woman. She sounds like my mother on her good days. Once I felt myself going down I gunned as hard as I could but it was too late. I made it all worse. Worst. They don't teach you about this in driving school." The young woman shook her head, the tears gleaming on her cheekbones. She had a thin straight nose, thin lips that made her look tough until they trembled. "Don't mind me, I'm losing it. I tried my dispatcher. I tried 911. There's no reception out here. Just cactus and coyotes." *And eleven strange men on dirt bikes out for a good time.*

"But the air is clear," I pat her arm the way I might Marisol's. "Take a deep breath. We'll get you out of this."

"Shit, Valerie, you're a real idiot. Your first big job—and your last." She made to hit her forehead, but wiped her cheeks instead.

"Where are you coming from?"

"Ohio."

"Know what's in here?"

"Household appliances. Refrigerators, dryers, dishwashers, and washing machines."

"Ouch." They'd have to empty the trailer before they lifted it, but who wanted to be the one doing the heavy lifting if it came unbalanced. Death by Bosch or Kenmore. There are better ways.

"At least it isn't flat screens," I say.

She smiles, drawing her breath in with a trembling sound, like a little girl getting over a tantrum.

"Dad—" Jordan begins.

"Anyone have reception?" I call out although I know the answer. We chose this location so we'd have a real night out, no one able to reach us.

"I'm off schedule. I was supposed to deliver this evening. They're going to dock me," Valerie says.

Oh honey, I think, that's just the beginning.

"Nothing's missing. So far as you know, nothing's broke. They're not going to bring heavy equipment out in the middle of the night. Why don't we have someone drive you back to town, find you a motel. You can organize things from there."

"I can't leave." She's standing in the arroyo now, her hand over her mouth, tears streaming. "I can't believe I did this to myself."

"You're going to sue GPS, Google maps," Sam tells her. He's just been accepted into law school. He is looking Valerie up and down with appreciation. "If I was farther along in my studies, I'd help you. Pro bono."

"I'm sure you would," Ernesto hoots. "Pro boner."

I tip my head at Jordan and walk aside. "Someone's got to drive out and call for her since she won't leave the truck—you know, for fear of illegals. Someone has to stay with her, of course, because she can't get back in that cab. You and Vicente, it's your last night of freedom. Take everyone on to the campsite, enjoy yourselves."

"You planning to stay with her, Dad?" Jordan asks, his voice too relaxed, even.

"Rafael just came to please me. He's complaining about his back. He'd be happy to spend the night in his own bed."

"We could leave the guys here and drive out and get the other truck and drive it back. They could party in the meanwhile."

"It's not a good idea," I say. "So many men and one woman. Anything happens, we'll have a lot of problems."

"Same goes for one on one," Jordan says. "And this isn't the time to raise such questions."

"What do you suggest?" I ask. Something happens at that moment, as different as can be from the feeling I had when Jordan passed me at thirteen never looking back. This feeling hollows me out. *My own son does not trust me.*

"Whatever your mother thinks, the women in those bars were just that. Women in bars. No one to take home. It never went too far. I let her think so because I was tired of the suspicion, the accusations."

"Those hang ups at the house? The women asking for Julio? You *planted* them, Dad?"

I straighten up then, furious. "I don't have to answer to you."

"But I'm going to have to answer to Mom, Juana and Marisol tomorrow," Jordan says.

"And what are you going to say? We left a woman all by herself in the desert?"

"We offered help but she refused it. She's an adult, capable of deciding for herself."

"She's not refusing help. She's refusing to leave the mess she made."

The moon lights up the silver sides of the trailer. It has a picture of Rosie the Riveter on it. *We do more for less. Put us to the test.* Like *sin papeles,* I think. Talk about selling yourself short.

Valerie is heading back to the cab. "I wouldn't do that, sweetheart," I call out. "Too unstable."

She looks back at me, suddenly insecure. Her cab is home. She's even bought floral seat covers. She ignores me and goes back to the cab and opens the door.

"I have to write down the GPS readings."

"Right," Jordan mutters. "They're what got you here."

"She needs to feel in control," I say.

"Be careful. Move slow. Get everything you need," I coach. "Have a blanket, water, food? A flashlight? Hand them out here."

"And a book," she says, handing things down to Rafael.

After some discussion among the boys, the upshot is they all ride back together on their bikes to the trucks we left at the pull out. The bonfire goes unlit. The booze in the other truck will be added to the bar at the wedding reception.

Rafael and I sit out under the moon and the stars talking quietly, while Valerie, wrapped in her red flannel blanket reads and weeps, weeps and reads. She is reading *The 7 Habits of Highly Effective People,* which she picked up used at one of the truck stops. Obviously she hasn't gotten very far into it and given how hard she's crying, I don't think she's going to take in what she does read.

"You don't have a romance or nothing?" I ask. "My wife's a scientist but she likes Nora Roberts."

"I think I need all the reality checks I can get," she answers. "This is surreal."

So Rafael and I lie on our backs and stare up at the sky that is a deep blue under the April moon. Whatever wisdom I had to share with my brother, I shared years ago. My son and Vicente, they will have to learn for themselves. For the first time, I let myself think about Candace's operation, how dangerous it is, how unready I am for the consequences in either direction.

"You think she regrets it?" I ask my brother.

"Not looking at what's right before her eyes?" Rafael answers, misunderstanding me. "Believe me, it's not a mistake you make twice."

The next morning when I walk into the house, dusty and tired and sore, the first tow truck has already radioed out for a tall crane, just like I thought. Candace was the one got them out there at dawn. After Jordon stopped at the house and filled his mother in on the situation and gave her all Valerie's information, Candace immediately started making calls—while Jordan and his friends and Vicente and his brothers went to a bar and drank beer and sang rancheros until dawn. Now Juana's accusing her brother of corrupting Vicente, who has a terrible hangover. She's afraid Vicente is going to stumble over his vows—maybe forget his English completely. His Spanish too.

Candace, when she hears the whole story from Rafael and me, gets herself patched through and invites Valerie to the weddings.

"Two for one," she tells Valerie. "Think of it as a favor to me. From what I hear, it sounds like you could pass for a member of my family. Since they're not coming, I'd welcome a stand-in. You can pretend you're my long lost cousin."

"Sounds like she'll clean up nice," Candace says when she gets off the radio.

The sun pouring in the window is not kind to either of us, but it is fair.

"You'll clean up well too," Candace says to me. Then she pauses, straightening the papers on which she'd been writing notes about the operation, the wedding, the calls she'd been making for Valerie. "It was kind of you and Rafael to stay there with her."

"We're sore as hell. I feel fifty-eight going on eighty. But we would be feeling this way in any case. What the hell were we thinking, Rafael and me?"

She brushes my hair, what's left of it, back from my face and studies me. "Whatever the kids like to think, I knew what I was getting myself into when I chose you, Julio. Whatever happens, I want you to remember that. I have no regrets."

"Enough of that," I say. "I have my eyes fixed on our future and you should too."

That's what I say, but I am also thinking as I kiss her how a marriage can be just like my wife's heart, with that valve whose leaflets don't always close tight, that contraction that is meant to send the blood and oxygen out to the body but instead sends some of it back so we come up short of breath and of the hope that comes with it, how sometimes we can fix that and sometimes we can't, about what it would be like if I told my kids that today: Keep your eye on the goal, but sometimes the goal floods back in on you. I'm thinking maybe they already know. Know they are both true. We need to keep our eyes on where we want to be—and nature can push back, reverse our momentum whenever it damn well pleases. You got to be prepared for both.

When we get to the hotel, we're looking good. I'm in a tux with a red rose on the lapel. Candace is in a red silk dress, looking fresh, like she just woke up from a long nap. But I take Jordan aside and tell him I'm going to escort Candace up the aisle myself.

"You walk too quick for us. It's your age, you can't help it. She walks with me, your mother's going to look like she's the stronger one."

Jordan just nods. He has other things on his mind. Marisol's mom and dad are arguing about where the step-mother is going to sit. While the parents' voices get louder and louder, Jordan puts his arms around Marisol and she clings to him like a little girl. Juana is giving Vicente the silent treatment. I give that marriage a year at the most, but people did the same with us.

As we walk up the aisle, Candace whispers, "Oh, if only my family could see us now." She squeezes my hand whenever her breath gets too short, and I slow down. The give and take, it is as good as it has always been between us in the bedroom. By the time we get to the altar, we've both worked up a sweet sweat.

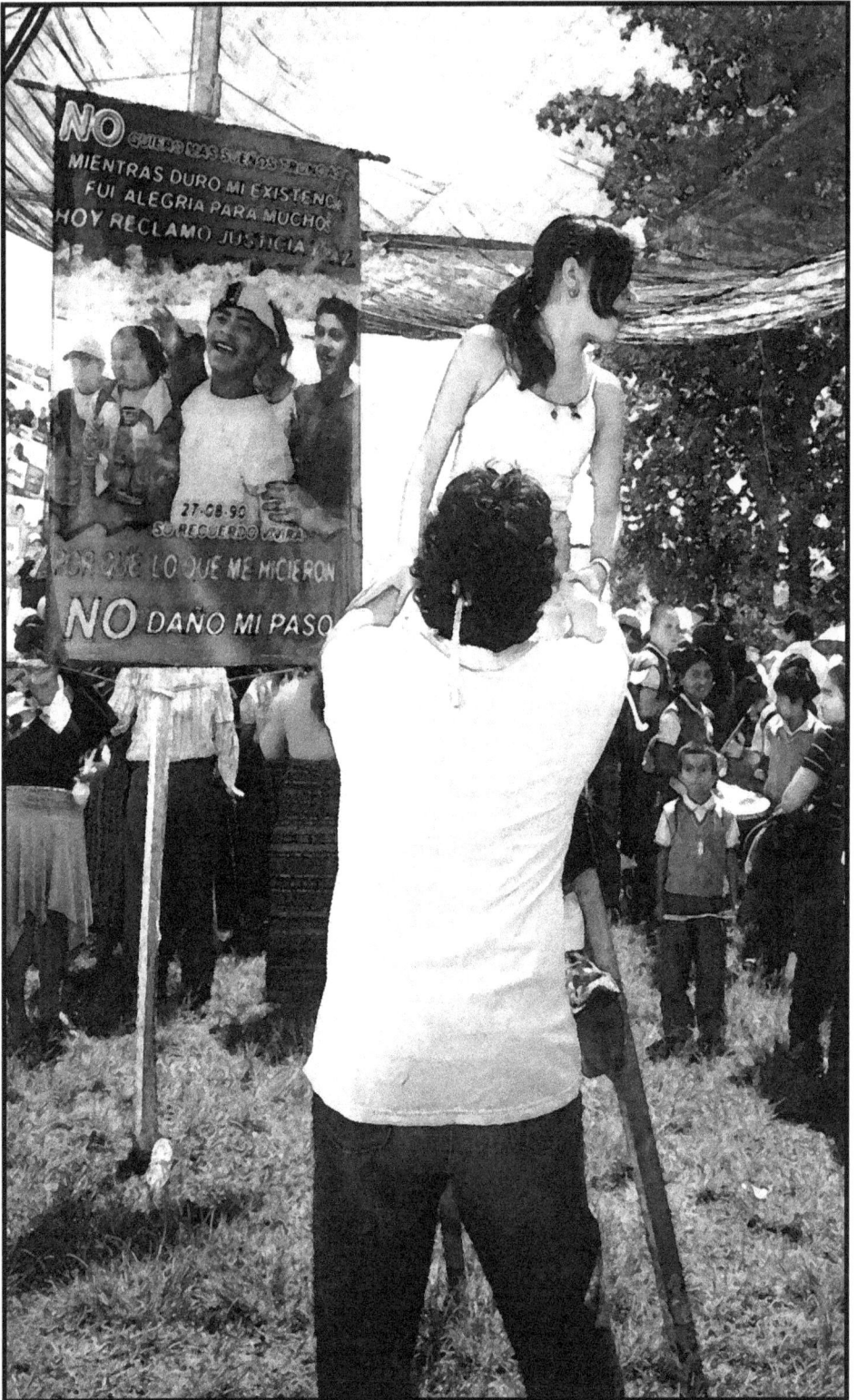

IV. ADVOCACY: WHAT WE FIGHT FOR

SARAH BIGHAM

OUR BETTER ANGELS

Years ago I interned at a mental hospital, primarily on a ward housing long-term male residents with dementia or severe mental illness that, at the time of their diagnoses decades before, required lifetime in-patient care. After so many years in such a facility, I wondered, how would anyone even begin to adjust to life outside these walls? In fact, the few who wandered off during outside walks were reported to return almost immediately, knocking on the windows to be buzzed back inside to the home they had known for so long.

Reality enhancement was a current fad, requiring certain employees to prompt residents to anchor themselves, however briefly, in the current time. As a college intern I was essentially invisible to the psychiatrists and doctors-in-training, so while I was occasionally rounded up by the nurses to sit in on the reality enhancement group sessions, the medical team members leading the sessions never made eye contact with me, let alone directed me to use the prompts. One man in his seventies with rheumy eyes and a preference for suspenders would routinely ask for his wife. "When's she gonna get here?," he would ask plaintively or demandingly, depending on his mood. The reality enhancement psychiatric interns were required to tell him, each time, that his wife was deceased and would therefore not be coming for any more visits. Every time, this man with dementia, whose capacity for short-term memory had evaporated years ago, would burst into tears, sobbing onto his threadbare T-shirt, hanging his grayed head and wrapping his arms around himself until that fresh memory of loss exited his mind. I was haunted by what I regarded as emotionless cruelty and felt as if I was watching torture—waterboarding of a different sort.

The nurses and orderlies always thanked me profusely for my time, but I knew I was the one who benefitted most. My time on the quiet hospital campus of brick buildings taught me more about life and people and differences and respect than all of the courses that made up my psychology major. This was an old-fashioned hospital with wards composed of twenty-plus beds in one large, open space, surrounded by the TV lounge, a seating area, bathrooms, and activity rooms, with a locked and windowed nurse's station in the middle. Based on the setup, it seemed that at any moment, Nurse Ratched could have made an appearance, but the ward staff I encountered were all extremely caring people.

Prior to interning at this hospital, I thought the jokes about tin foil hats were simply made up by comedians. But I learned that foil was indeed serious business in a secure psychiatric facility. Some residents carefully hoarded small squares of the stuff to place strategically and somewhat unobtrusively in their hair, pockets, or pants to protect themselves from the various invasions swarming around us. Radio signals, light waves, secret government organizations, and alien communications were frequent sources of concern.

I also learned a lot about race and gender and socioeconomic status. As a middle-class white woman from a small town, I saw for myself that the doctors and administrators on campus—those with the most power—were nearly exclusively white and male. As for the orderlies and nurses, the food preparers and the cleaning crew, the maintenance workers and the painters— the people who ensured that the residents were clothed, housed, fed, and cared for—-they were black. Most of the patients were also black. One day when the doctors were not on the wards I realized that I was the only white person with a badge in a large building with many staff members. I realized then how blind I had been to how it must feel to be seen as a representative for a larger group, how blind I had been to how the larger world worked, and how blind I had been to the opportunities I had that others never would. Most of the residents of the ward were quite elderly and, as a young college student, I remember being struck by how differences in melanin that might seem so prominent elsewhere, were far less dichotomous here as the older folks of all races turned a crepe-like shade of gray as they aged. Perhaps, in the end, we all finally see beyond the color of our skin.

The lessons about race and privilege have remained with me. Much like the hospice volunteer training I went through years later when I was reminded to check my assumptions at the door and be with the patients and their families as they were, I learned at the state hospital how important it was to try to check my privilege as well. This is no doubt something I will spend a lifetime attempting to get right and I know I have stumbled many times along the way, but I hope I am making progress.

The pervasive thoughts of mind control and tin foil and protecting oneself from invisible invasions are also things that have stayed with me for years. I am fascinated by radios and how we can tune in to stations using a box with some dials—hearing sounds through the air. What else is out there? I am not alone in these thoughts. I have been to the Very Large Array in the New Mexican hinterlands where huge white satellite dishes are aimed at the sky. The scientists working at laboratories such as this *want* to have contact. My ward residents wanted to avoid it. The contrast is both fascinating and disturbing.

Recently, I was outside in the garden, admiring the soon-to-arrive sunset when I realized that our neighbor's TV antenna was glowing. Mesmerized, I made a concerted effort to observe the antenna again, over subsequent evenings. The phenomenon continued. In just the right light, at just the right time, the out-of-date, unused antenna that our high-tech, big-screen TV neighbor has not yet dismantled takes on a shimmering silver color unlike anything I have ever seen and it looks, in part, like a spaceship. "Maybe those men on the ward were on to something," I think, as each time I step back into my house and close the door to temporarily block my view of that antenna.

But most of all, I remember what the ward residents taught me about compassion, resistance, and basic human decency. I refused to participate in the reality enhancement exercises and, when given the opportunity, would spend time talking with the residents about the memories they did have, or wanted to have. For the patients whose words had left them, sometimes sitting together in silent companionship like old friends seemed like the best way to spend time between activity sessions.

I would sit with the widower to chat about the weather. When he inevitably asked about his wife, I did what I hope someone else will do for me someday if my beloved wife dies before I do and my mind has begun its journey to be with her. I would touch his arm gently, smile, look him kindly in the eye, and say that I was sure she would be along soon. He would grin, tilt his head back into the rays of sun coming in through the ward's huge wall of windows, and nap as he patiently waited for her arrival.

MARY KAY RUMMEL

GIFT

I did not know then to give thanks
for a classroom full of children
who felt imprisoned.
What could I call in response
to the boy who grabbed my hand,
to the girl whose hungry heart
was busy embezzling mine?
Needs so naked I closed my eyes,
until their courage dissolved
my teacher-fear of failing.
One boy, silent for months, for years
swam out of desk shadow
into the churning morass
of his mind and voice
riding the waves
of his soul's own making.
School's a prison. Once you get in,
you can't get out, he wrote
and then kept writing.

JOHN LAUE

A TEACHER SPEAKS OUT

*(To the people who think
good government means cutting
the capital gains tax)*

Yes, I've seen them:
the girl whose father
had been having sex with her
since she was ten;
the brother and sister
whose parents were addicts
and gave them $30 a month
for all their expenses;
the sixteen year old
living in an abandoned car;
the boy who told me casually
his father had been drunk
and angry at him
and had crushed his kitten's skull;
the girl pregnant at fifteen
with her second baby;
the tiny one whose father,
tired from working in the fields,
held her hands in boiling water
because she'd overcooked his dinner;
the child whose mother told her every day
she wished she'd gotten an abortion
instead of giving birth to her;
the seventeen year old
who'd been on heroin
for three zonked-out years

and hung out in gay bars
to have sex with lesbians
but thought she could change her preference
by becoming a Christian;
boys (and girls) who cruised the streets
at night with shotguns
hunting for members of a rival gang;
kids who were heads of households
at fifteen; suicidal kids,
incest kids, victims of rape, abuse,
molestations; all those who came to me
with minds and bodies scarred,
delinquents, schizophrenics,
borderlines, addicts, alcoholics.

And the poor, thousands of them
coming through the doors
with pathetic hungry eyes.

Yes, I've seen them, taught them,
loved and counseled them
for twenty years while you walled up
in wealthy enclaves,
balanced budgets on their shoulders.
But you should know: the seeds you plant
are yielding wild explosive fruits,
strange, starving crops that fail to ripen.
The time's approaching now
when even you will feel their fall
unless you wake and share the wealth.
I know! I've seen them all!

DISCOURAGEMENT

They stare at me
with various eyes,
angry, bored,
resigned.

Some haven't a single
pleasure of the mind
except sports news or
strategies for makeup.

Their ignorance, apathy,
and restless inattention
seem impossible to teach.

Year by year I feel like
I've been worn down,
my resolve eroded
by their weathers.

I fear becoming like
the hopeless kids
who sit here blankly,
purposeless, lost.

I hold my tears
till I get home,
then cry for them
and for myself:
the pleasures missed,
the poems unwritten.

LOWELL JAEGER

SOUNDS LIKE BOMBS

Sounds like bombs, one of us says. Our hostess points
across the river, over sagebrush hills on the horizon.
Military Firing Range, she says. *The big guns.*

We stand silent awhile. Feel the cannon percussion
punctuating the drone of tires on the interstate highway.
Hear jet boats on the Columbia blasting
against the current behind the dam. Constant
buzz of hydro-electric power crackling in transmission lines
overhead. Less than a flash upstream

from Hanford Nuclear Reservation,
where progress knocks apart the building blocks
of everything, teasing atomic blaze enough
to vaporize us all. *But let's not
think about it,* laughs our hostess.
She wants us to revel in the sunshine, get comfy
with other guests lounging in the Jacuzzi.

One of us asks, *Why the helmets on the kids
in the pool?* Our hostess throws her hands in the air,
rolls her eyes. Says, *Once in awhile some loser
hooks a golf ball over here while teeing off on hole five.*

Golf carts of well-fed attorneys and brokers
motor by on the course perimeter. Ladies in pink carts
clinking cocktails, trailing after. We smell cigars. Then perfume.
This sequence repeats and repeats and repeats
till we hardly notice it more than the swish
of sprinklers sousing flower beds near the greens.

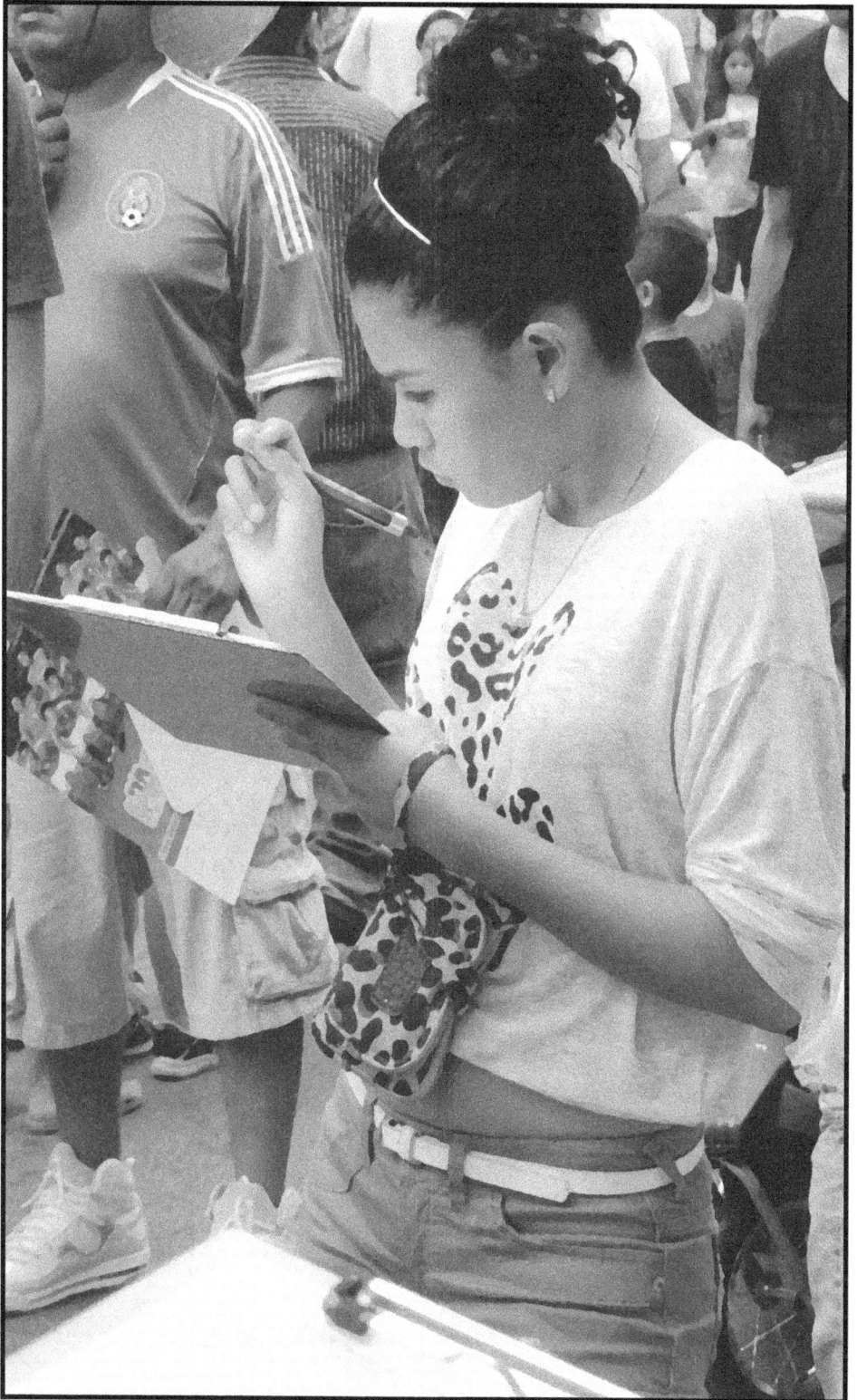

MARIAN MATHEWS CLARK

MY STUDY ON STAY-PUTS

You can do your studies on us migratory types all you want. My sister Rose came home from school last year saying that's what you stay-puts call us. I told her you're probably the same guys yelling White Trash Bastards go home when we drive through Salem. She says, no you wouldn't yell at us. She doesn't think you even talk to us. She says you just check up on how many months we don't go to school and how many kids we have and how many weeks we're hungry in the off-season. I ask her why you don't mind your own business but she tells me you're not hurting anybody, just writing up these studies called "Our 1965 Migrant Population" or "Movements of Migrants in the Sixties," that kind of thing, where you put us in categories.

I tell her you're not the only ones who can sniff out what makes types tick. I'm figuring out stuff, too.

She says, Lily, you're thirteen. Nobody'll listen to you.

But what does she know? I'm doing my own study on one of your kind. This girl came straying into our fields a month ago when strawberries the size of Grandpa's tumor were crouching in their bushes, all juicy and red. Just ripe for plucking, my fourteen-year-old brother Louis said, then laughed to himself.

The last five years at strawberry time on Oregon Sunrise Farms the big bosses have hired Marie, this scrawny woman with hair chopped off to her ear lobes, to drive a painted-over school bus into town to pick up a bunch of jack-off kids.

A month ago, when Marie dumps off her first load for the season, this girl I'm doing my study on catches my eye right off. Me and Rose always watch them close, staggering off the bus at seven, an hour after we get here, and dragging themselves over the rows like they don't know where they are. Maybe their mamas stuffed them into Marie's bus while they were asleep. Me and Rose have the types named, and the first day we usually pick out which stay-puts go with which type. Name The Stay-Put is something I came up with one real bad summer when the sun was beating down hotter than usual and you couldn't roll your pants up because your legs would burn and blister, and dirt and berry juice would creep under the blister and smart like crazy. So you kept your pants rolled down but you felt sweat trickle down your legs all day. Naming stay-puts took your mind off juice and blisters.

This year I have to name them by myself because Rose, who's sixteen, has started hanging around with Butchie, clinging to him too tight to pick much of anything, let alone help me lay out the types. By the end of that first day I have them pretty much lined up, though, except for this one girl I'm doing my study on.

I can tell right off she's not one of the Kick-Asses who Marie will yell at all summer and threaten to can if she catches them throwing berries one more time or smashing bushes when they chase each other over the rows. Last year this Kick-Ass everyone called Red landed in our section with his foot in Louis's flat. Louis told him if he ever saw him close enough to see red, he would beat the crap out of him.

Three days later Marie canned the kid for stuffing the bottom of his flats with dirt, then covering it up with berries. I said that'll show him. Won't show him a thing, Louis said. I reminded him about Ray Halvery in quonset five who got his whole family canned for stealing two flats of raspberries. Ray was crying and the whole family was awful scared.

That's different, Louis said. Kids like Red don't have to worry about coming here year after year, so getting kicked out is nothing to them. I didn't argue with him, but something didn't sit right about the whole thing.

This girl I'm doing my study on doesn't hang with the Gossip-and-Giggle-Girls either. Louis calls them GAGS. They come out here in their little groups and yak all day and cackle over the Kick-Asses stumbling around making fools of themselves. Once I had a row next to a GAG. She yapped with her friends about the extra school outfits she was going to buy with her berry money and how clothes in the stores were running to orange and red and bright colors this year. She said her boyfriend thought she looked best in pale pink, though, so she probably wouldn't buy any new thing unless she wore it at home.

For a minute she sounded like Rose, who moons after some boy every summer. I guess if Butchie said he liked a certain color, Rose might wear it for him, but the only pink thing she has, used to be a white blouse that rubbed up against my red sweatshirt in the wash. Wearing colors for somebody seems silly to me. What good does pink do a boyfriend?

Three days after the strange stay-put comes into the field, I catch Rose by herself. I tell her I've spotted a girl I can't name, that she picks steady, eats alone, and doesn't talk to anybody.

She's strange all right, Rose says, then says she sounds like one of the Bust-Your-Guts, these nineteen and twenty-year-old stay-puts who keep their noses stuck in the bushes from the first berry in the morning to the last flat they haul to the checkout stand at night. Nobody can figure why they act like that, except Marie said once they're probably college kids, stacking up money for school.

I think Rose might be on to something, except the Bust-Your-Guts are older than this stay-put, who's about as old as me, and they're always yelling at each other, how many flats you have? This girl's a by-herself person. I'm just ready to ask Rose if she's ever seen a young Bust-Your-Gut, when Butchie struts up and says, There's my woman, to Rose, who's ready to be anybody's woman this summer, I hate to tell him.

Butchie lets his hand drop to her butt, which makes her forget my study in a second, and she tosses her head at him like she's some kind of princess. I want to tell her she's not so great, with her dishwater straw for hair and the gaps between her front teeth. She does have nice eyes, I'll give her that, but her big boobs that poke out of her blouse are what Butchie's after. In a few years, when they're sagging lower than Butchie's Mama's and Butchie's dropped her, she'll wish she'd stuck with me on this stay-put project instead of chasing after some pimply guy who's always touching at his crotch to see if it's still there, I guess, and who calls her gooshy names like Rabbit Rump or Little Toots. Rose says I don't know a thing about love. I tell her I don't want to if it makes you stupid.

I spend the next week keeping my eye on this stay-put and trying to find something to call her with almost no help from Rose, who's usually the friendly one and could have had a talk going with that girl the first day if she'd wanted to.

Once in a while Butchie has to take care of his dimwit brother, who, Rose says, I'm not supposed to call that because he's something called hyperactive. When Butchie's not around, Rose sticks with me and says I can't do a study without writing facts down and how I'm too young and nobody'll pay any attention. I shrug her off. I don't think even those stay-puts who do studies could pick and write at the same time.

It's going slow without Rose, but she and Butchie have been all over each other for two weeks now. With the way Rose's love life always ends up, I know one of them's got to get sick of the other any minute, so I'm waiting it out. But all of a sudden one afternoon Rose up and tells me they're going to get married. Butchie acts like he's believing it, too. Then Rose tells me she wants a church wedding.

I can't talk for a minute. It feels like she socked me in the gut, but finally I say, You can't do that. I need you for my project real bad, Rose. She's not even listening. She tells me, Lily, you have to help me figure out how I can walk down a real aisle. It's expensive, you know, with the right kind of dress and all, but nobody in the family's ever had a church wedding, and I love Butchie so much I want to be the first. I look over at Mama who just shakes her head and says Rose must have got too much sun to be spouting off like she is.

The next few days, I can't think much about the strange girl because I'm worried about losing Rose, who spends all her time on privy breaks now, rubbing Butchie's shoulders and him rubbing hers, and sometimes they're out of sight, probably rubbing other things. I watch Mama, staring off across the fields, sad-like, thinking about Rose's church wedding, I bet, wishing she could give her that, and I'm wondering how Rose could make Mama worry when we're just pulling out of what we owed the camp store for the days it rained and we couldn't pick.

)(   )(   )(

Grandma used to say, If there's lightning, wait for the thunder, and sure enough she was right. As if Rose's mess isn't enough, Louis gets himself hooked up with these Hang-Around-Guys, HAGS, I call them, which keeps me from getting back to my study for at least ten days. And strawberry season's half over.

These HAGS are stay-puts who think we have free smokes and strong booze and cheap sex, and they hang around long enough every year to see who does and who doesn't, then quit picking after about a week. We've always kept away from HAGS, but this year Louis starts talking to a couple of them, and before you know it they're following him around like he's king of the quonsets.

This one kid, Mike, I know is trouble right off because he's looking me up and down, mostly at my boobs that are starting to show. Our family runs to big ones. My Aunt Sadie, who joined the stay-puts a few years ago when Uncle Dan landed a janitor job up in Seattle, has the biggest ones I've seen on anybody. They cover from her armpits down, and they don't just hang to her waist but push out all over. I always wanted to ask Mary Beth, the cousin my age, what they looked like. But I couldn't think of the right question that wouldn't seem disrespectful to Aunt Sadie. I might have another chance, though, because Mary Beth is lying around the trailer in Seattle, bored, and thinking about coming back out on the road. If she does, she'll meet up with us in August, and maybe I can tell her how my study comes out, in case Rose isn't talking to anybody but Butchie by then.

When Mike starts hanging around, I tell Louis not to trust him, but Louis is restless this summer. He starts spending time with these HAGS down by the sewer ponds a quarter-mile from camp, trading cigarettes and Millers. Mike acts like he's waiting, and Louis is feeling the squeeze to come up with something. But Mike has treed the wrong squirrel. We're broke for any extra stuff. Our money lands in Daddy's hands at the end of the day, and us kids wouldn't think of holding out. At least we never have, though I worry about Rose this summer with all her blab about a church wedding.

A few days after the HAGS show up, Louis starts talking to me on the side about going on a road trip with them. Road trip, I tell him. Who do these guys think they're talking to? Louis shrugs it off like it's not a big thing, but I see him flipping through sleeping bag pages of outdoor magazines in the camp store, and I watch him stare into the berry bushes and sometimes roll up his sleeves, like he doesn't care the sun's scorching his arms. He bumps in and out of those staring spaces, and when he isn't staring he works faster than he's picked since I can remember.

Each night he drops his ticket in Daddy's hand, and Daddy and Mama go to the camp store and buy hamburger and apples and Oreos. Once, Louis says he doesn't think we need cookies and why don't we save a little more money for fall. Daddy says we should treat ourselves along to keep us going, doesn't Mama think so, and she says yes. I shrug, but Rose gives Louis a dirty look and says she wants cookies no matter what.

He says, Okay, Okay, it's just a thought, but I can tell he's nervous. I've seen him looking at those sleeping bags more and more.

The HAGS are sticking with Louis like glue now, and one afternoon Louis asks Mike and his buddies if they can stay for volleyball after the bus leaves. Mike sneers and says, Volleyball? And Louis says, Yeah, well it's what some people around here do for fun even though I don't like it much. I know then he's a goner because he's the camp volleyball king.

I'm in the privy when I hear this, and Louis and Mike are leaning against the water truck twenty feet away. Mike says, You got what you need for the road trip, Louis? Louis says he's working on it, which makes me nearly fall through the hole. Daddy isn't going to shell out for a sleeping bag when we have all the blankets we need for setting up house. Then Louis asks them to stay for supper and Mike, says, Sure, why not, and I feel like Louis has gone crazy.

Mike's the only one who ends up staying, but Daddy still has to buy an extra half-pound of burger to make Louis's friend feel welcome. I go to the camp store with him that night and watch him lay the extra meat and cookies on the counter, kind of like his mind isn't there. I bet he's thinking that with the extra food, we can't put away more than twenty dollars that day for the off-season. He grins at me in a minute, though, and he doesn't look worried anymore. Grandpa always told us, don't let the unexpecteds bother you for more than a minute. Those damned expecteds will get you soon enough. Grandpa's heart wasn't a bit good, and he died of an attack picking cherries up in Washington.

Well, silly Lily, Daddy says. What you thinking?

I say, Nothing, Daddy, then tell him the Oreos look real fresh and that I'm glad he got a package of vanilla wafers because my sweet tooth's hungrier than my meat tooth tonight and he can give Mike one of my burger patties and only buy a quarter-pound extra. He says, Lily, you need to put that meat on your bones, and he looks at my baggy pants where my butt should be and shakes his head. He's used to Mama's butt that sticks out and I think he's nervous that I don't have one. I want to say not to worry and that I'm growing hips and a bigger waist, but I don't talk to him about that stuff. Louis is always parading around, talking about girls' boobs or the size of their butts, but Daddy's quiet about those things.

)(( )(( )((

When Mike walks into quonset ten—our house this summer—I'm sitting on the floor hemming Daddy's overalls that have been dragging the ground for a couple days. If it weren't for Rose being with Butchie all the time, she would be lollygagging on Mama and Daddy's bed right now, batting her eyeballs at Mike like she was looney. But with her gone, Mike's eyes just roll over the empty bed and take in us kids' bedrolls pushed up neat against the wall. He glances at the icebox and the chair where I always sit unless Mama or Daddy needs to prop up in it for their sore backs.

Warm in here, Mike says.

Louis says, It's not usually, but today's muggy. I say, Feels just right to me, and glare at Mike.

Louis and Mike finally duck out the door to help Daddy with supper. Mama's at the showers washing off the berry juice and letting the tired feeling drain off in the water that's hardly warm this time of day.

After I finish the hem, I crawl up on Mama and Daddy's bed, the darkest spot in the quonset. I'm almost drifting off, when I hear voices outside, and Louis and Daddy walk in. I don't think they see me because they're talking private, and Daddy's shifting his weight back and forth like he's making a big decision. Louis is staring at him.

It's just a weekend trip, Louis says, and they said they'd buy gas and even food maybe, since I invited Mike for supper. But they all have sleeping bags, and if I could just get one on sale in the camp store, I could go.

Daddy sighs bigger than I've ever heard him. Wouldn't a bedroll do? he says.

Louis says they all have sleeping bags, and if he could buy one, he promises he'd work harder than ever for the rest of the summer. I'll go out at five instead of six, he says. I can do it, Daddy, I know I can.

Sale things can't be taken back once they're bought, Daddy says.

I know, Louis tells him.

My heart's pounding so hard I think they might hear it, and I close my eyes so I won't have to see Louis disappointed. It's quiet for a minute. Then I hear Daddy say, Okay, Louis. We'll get the bag tomorrow. I'll draw the money out of the fund.

My stomach drops out the bottom, and I want to leap out of bed and say, Forty dollars is three days' food in the off-season, but I can't move. So I lay there quiet and wait till they go out. Then I curse Mike for coming into our fields and Louis for being so damned stupid and Daddy for—well, I can't think of anything to curse him for really, except trying to make Louis happy, and how can you be mad at anybody for that?

The next day Louis is out picking at five, even before Marie leaves to get the stay-puts and has two flats ready to punch in by the time we get there. He picks like crazy all day and only stops once to run to the store for the sleeping bag and put it in our quonset. A few times he stops a minute to check his watch because Mike said they'd pick him up after dinner.

None of the HAGS get off the bus this morning but Louis says they're getting ready for the trip. He doesn't act worried, just picks so hard he gives the checkout boys (the boss' kids) fits because they can't figure where he's stealing berries from. They start snooping along our row until Marie tells them, Do something useful and check on the Kick-Asses, which makes them shoot off across the field like they're detectives.

When we hear the quitting whistle, Louis runs off to camp to eat and Rose hurries to find Butchie. Me and Mama and Daddy stretch, then sit on our jackets for a few minutes in between the rows, looking at the berries, knowing we don't have to pick another one before tomorrow.

There's something about that six o'clock whistle and the few minutes after, sitting with Mama and Daddy, that makes me feel so good after twisting off berries or pulling down beans all day that I don't know if there'll ever be anything else quite so nice. You're stiff and dirty and don't care because you'll be washed up soon, and the rest of the day's the best part, with burgers and Oreos coming and money to pay for them and maybe a game of volleyball after supper. When Rose was free, we would play poker or, after we went to bed, a game of Guess My Most Exciting Thing. Now she's too busy with Butchie for poker and if I want to play Most Exciting Thing, all I have to say is a church wedding and I've guessed hers every time. If she can't guess mine after one try, she says she wants to quit and daydream about Butchie.

Rose has gone way overboard with this Butchie thing. She hardly even notices Louis when Mike doesn't show up that night. Even if I was crazy lovesick, I'd never miss a look like what was on Louis's face. But watching Mike the night before, I knew it was going to happen.

I guess Louis' eyes were too full of that sleeping bag to see these guys are full of shit. That's what I want to tell him at ten o'clock when he finally quits saying they're just late, probably car trouble or something, and after he runs over to the store to see if there's been a call for him. I go with him like I believe there will be, but I know we're wasting our time.

At ten-thirty he says it's better he didn't go because he has things to do on the weekend, and nobody, not even Rose, asks him what things. Then he heads out of the quonset to get a little air, he says, and an hour later I find him sitting by the sewer ponds staring out into nowhere.

I sit beside him, but he doesn't move. Well, you got a new thing to sleep in, I say, but he keeps staring. I start to say I hate stay-puts, especially Mike, but he says, I just want to sit here without hearing anything for a while. So I walk back to the quonset, real slow, thinking about what to do. When I get there, I slip his new bag under Mama and Daddy's bed so he won't have to lay eyes on it. Then I stretch out his bedroll. I don't need to, though, since he doesn't come in all night. I know, because I'm awake all night myself except for a little dozing off.

⟡   ⟡   ⟡

Louis is real quiet these days, and Rose is hanging around more and more with Butchie's family. I don't see how she can think of hooking up with Butchie's mama and daddy and six kids plus the dimwit. Whenever I mention the dimwit, Rose gets crabby and wonders why I can't get it through my head he's a hyperactive. Well, whatever you call him, I say, he hasn't got a bit of sense and flits around worse than a dragonfly.

I haven't given up on my study, but it isn't turning out like I planned. I make one last try to get Rose to help me by telling her I heard Marie call the strange girl Elizabeth. That name, I say to Rose, sounds like she's a queen or something, thinking Rose will come up with a title like Royal Ass. But Rose just sighs and says there's a dress in one of those bride magazines at the store that would make her look like a queen, except it's sixty dollars. She says she guesses the dress doesn't matter anyway because Mama says she can't have a church wedding, and even though Butchie says he'll love her even if they get married on the banks of the sewer ponds, which is nice of him, it isn't the same.

Something does happen I can use for my study, even though Rose says it won't count because it's out the blue, and you have to decide what you're looking for ahead of time. What's the good of studying something if you already know it? I say. The surprises should count even more, if you ask me. Then she says it won't count anyway since I'm not writing things down. I tell her I'm storing things in my head to write down later, which gives them longer to settle in and makes them better than her old stay-put studies. She says, Dry up, and won't talk to me for a while. Lately she gets mad easy.

⟡   ⟡   ⟡

The thing with my study happens on a day Rose stays in the quonset with cramps. I tell Mama I want to pick with Butchie's family to get to know my in-laws, but it's really because they have rows by Elizabeth. I'm picking at the end of the dimwit's row, which puts me right up next to her, and we're picking along neck-and-neck until Marie comes by. For as quiet as that girl acts, she starts talking to Marie about how she's going to come back next summer to save money for college, which I figure is another five years off. I don't see the good in looking so far ahead when you haven't even taken the tests my cousin in Seattle says you have to pass to get in. And Mary Beth should know. She's been going to school steady ever since she moved there.

At eleven-thirty this Elizabeth girl opens her pink flowered lunch box— the same color as her pigtail ribbons—and I see this whopper piece of cake sitting there with a candle on it. I'm thinking, if only Rose was here to talk to her. But seeing as it might be my last chance to store up facts and knowing it's up to me, I take a deep breath like Rose said she did before a speech she gave once, and I clear my throat and say, before I can think about it too much, Whose birthday cake is that? My heart's pounding.

She looks surprised, but then starts talking so much you would think I'm Marie. Mine, she says. I'm thirteen today, and I'm having a birthday party with seven friends coming at five-thirty tonight, and she grins out of this tiny mouth I don't know how any boy will ever be able to fit his lips on. Then she says, And after the party, we're going out for pizza and a movie and after that everyone's staying overnight. She takes a breath and then a bite of cake.

Oh, I tell her.

Did you have a party for your last birthday? she says, then gulps down another bite.

I shake my head, then start picking fast, before she can ask me anything else. But while I'm scooting along the row and yanking the berries out, I can't help thinking about my birthday two months ago where we had cheeseburgers, and Mama and Daddy gave me three dollars to buy anything I wanted, and Louis said he would teach me how to blow smoke rings if I ever started smoking, and Rose said I could use her white low-cut blouse anytime she wasn't using it. I decide I wouldn't want a stay-put party with all those people, probably wearing pink ribbons and talking about boyfriends. Besides, it seems silly to make a fuss over a birthday just because one day you're twelve and the next thirteen and the six o'clock whistle feels the same either way.

)(   )(   )(

The most important thing I find out about this stay-put comes that afternoon when I see she's been working so hard to get into college, she hasn't learned everyday stuff. That comes out when this lopsided bus with the good-behavior guys from the prison goes by on its way to the cherry orchards next to the fields. One guy yells out the window, Picking berries is sissy shit work. Louis, who's come over to help me finish my row, yells back, Dry up, asshole.

Butchie's daddy, whose mouth makes all of ours seem holy, flips off the good-behavior guy, then says, There's a lot of cherries to pick out here if you know where to look. Butchie laughs, and his mama says, If the woodpeckers think they're big enough to get the job done, and the dimwit hee-ha's, crazy like. Elizabeth doesn't laugh a bit but just keeps picking and frowning like Butchie's family's talking Chinese.

Then Butchie's daddy, who's watching Elizabeth, grins at Butchie's mama like he's up to something. But nothing happens for a few minutes because the dimwit darts to my row and kicks dirt in my flat. I know Rose'll be mad if I stir up in-law trouble, so all I do is hold his ankle behind the bushes until he screams like a banshee, and his mama tells him to get his ass over where it belongs.

Butchie's daddy, who might have been on one of those good-behavior crews for all I know, swats the dimwit and then says to Butchie's mama, Better be ready to round up these kids as quick as a flea screws because the convicts are back, and you know what that means.

Everybody's quiet a minute and then Butchie's mama, who's as big a liar as the old man, says, Makes my blood clot to think of it.

Yup, the old man says, that massacre up in Washington is the worst I've heard of since the Alamo. Convicts just went berserk and got loose in a field like this one and the cops said they couldn't tell berry juice from blood when they got done. People lying around with their throats slit and guts hanging out and some pickers they haven't found yet.

I check out the stay-put who's still picking, but real slow now. She's glancing from the cherry orchards to her flowered lunch bucket. Butchie's daddy is still spewing off stuff about eyeballs rolling in the patch where the bad guys were popping them out with church keys.

I'm having a hard time keeping a straight face when Butchie says, I'm glad our family's here together. It would be awful to die alone. He glances at the stay-put who's standing up now, staring across at the good-behavior men.

Her eyes are getting bigger and bigger, and she's twisting on one of her little pink ribbons.

Butchie looks at Louis. Keep a lookout in case we have to run, he says. Louis nods, and I see he's ready to bust. The stay-put's froze to the spot. Then Butchie's daddy stands, like he sees something in the orchard, puts on this frightful face and says, God almighty, they're coming.

Well, with that, Elizabeth's mouth falls open and her eyes go big as potatoes. She unfreezes and takes off in the fastest walk you ever saw that turns into a run halfway across the field. Her arms are waving everywhere.

Come back, Butchie's daddy yells. You forgot your flat. But she doesn't stop until she's out of sight. I guess she gets on the bus because we don't see her the rest of the day. Butchie's daddy slaps his leg and his mama yells, Did you see that filly run? I'm lying in the row, trying to get my breath, and Louis is snorting, he's laughing so hard. It's good to see it.

When six comes around, I can't wait to tell Rose what happened. I have to tell it away from Mama and Daddy because they wouldn't think scaring somebody's funny. After the six o'clock sit-down, I run to the quonset and find her stretched out on Mama and Daddy's bed sighing and moaning. Rose, I say, I have something to cheer you up. It's about the stay-put I'm doing my study on.

She rolls her eyes, but I go ahead and tell her the convict story and about Elizabeth's pink ribbons and how she mowed down the field on her way out. But before she flew out of there, I tell Rose, you should have seen how she looked. All the tan dropped out the bottom of her face, her mouth was hanging open, and her eyes were wild as the dim . . . the hyperactive's.

Rose is watching me close, and I think maybe I'm finally getting through to her. When I finish, I give her a big grin and say, And guess what, Rose. She hasn't got any boobs.

Rose sighs and looks away. She's quiet a minute. Then she looks back at me. Maybe, she says, her eyes clouding up. But at least that girl'll have a church wedding.

My stomach goes all funny, and all of a sudden the quonset air is sticky. I jump up from where I'm leaning on the bed and stumble for the door. Damn you, Rose, I say. And then I run toward the sewer ponds to be by myself, so I can get the look on that stay-put's face set firm in my head before Rose can wreck it.

ANDRENA ZAWINSKI

WOMEN OF THE FIELDS

—for Dolores Huerta

The women of the fields clip red bunches of grapes
in patches of neatly tilled farmland in the San Joaquin,
clip sweet globes they can no longer stand to taste.
Just twenty miles shy of Santa Cruz beach babies in thongs,
Pleasure Beach surfers on longboards, the cool convertibles
speeding Cabrillo Highway, women line as pickers—
back bent over another summer's harvest.

The campesinas labor without shade tents or water buffalos,
shrouded in oversized shirts and baggy work pants, disguised
as what they are not, faces masked in bandanas and cowboy hats
in fils de calzón—

The young one named Ester taken in the onion patch
with the field boss' gardening shears at her throat.
The older one called Felicia isolated in the almond orchard
and pushed down into a doghouse. The pretty one, Linda,
without work papers, asked to bear a son in trade
for a room and a job in the pumpkin patch. Isabel, ravaged
napping under a tree at the end of a dream after a long
morning picking pomegranates, violación de un sueño.
Salome on the apple ranch forced up against the fence
as the boss bellowed ¡Dios Mío! to her every no, no, no.

The promotoras flex muscle in words, steal off into night
face-to-face to talk health care, pesticides, heatstroke, rape,
meet to tally accounts—forced to exchange panties for paychecks
in orchards, on ranches, in fields, in truck beds—to speak out
to risk joblessness or deportation to an old country a foreign soil.

Women of the fields, like those before them, like those
who will trail after—las Chinas, Japonesas, Filipinas—
to slave for frozen food empires in pesticide drift,
residue crawling along the skin, creeping into the nostrils
and pregnancies it ends as they hide from La Migra
in vines soaked in toxins or crawl through sewer tunnels,
across railroad tracks, through fences to pick our sweet berries,
for this, this: la fruta del diablo.

KATHERIN HERVEY

ROARING FORKS

Mick's high as a motherfucker. The meth he scored this morning from his buddy Phoenix courses like electricity through his veins. He stomps and strides to the music banging out of his headphones, greasy hair swaying in rhythm with the bass, his bony hips failing to hold up his sweat-stained jeans. He eyes Angie two trailers down, her hot ass peeking out beneath tiny shorts, her mom sunning her wrinkled body under the blazing Arizona sun.

Inside the trailer, he switches on the TV and plops down on a recliner patched with duct tape, beer in hand. He has lived in this trailer since he can remember, and every inch is etched with memory; like the time his mom threw a knife at him and it landed blade-first in the wall behind him. Or when he jumped on the roof high on PCP and the ceiling caved in, forming a spike he always ducks under. Rage. Desperation. Mick carries these forces deep in his bones. People think he's just a loser methhead, but he can see the hidden strands that attach him to this trailer and divide him from the other side of the tracks.

On the TV he sees a protest is going down a few miles away. People in the streets because an unarmed black man was shot in the head by a white cop. He remembers watching the last protest, and the army of militarized police lashing out with batons, pepper spray, and flash-bangs, beating people—black people—until they buckled and submitted, then lining them up zip-tied on their bellies, bleeding, in the middle of the road.

He cried as he watched, drinking the same beer he is drinking today, alone in the same chair, thinking of the millions of other people watching who have lost their way as if there was a map to life they could find again, buried under empty pizza boxes filled with cigarette butts. Mick has been beaten and arrested by the police more times than he can count, but not for a purpose.

What would happen if he stood up from his chair to join them?

Instead of covering his tears with coughs so the neighbors don't hear? He has already survived beatdowns by police because he is poor white trash. Doesn't anybody get it? That when you are born in a trailer, get it, and live through the beatings, get it, you can only either suck it up or take to the streets where no one hears you. That at a certain point you have nothing left to fear except the fear of not caring if you live or die.

This is his fear. That he no longer cares.

He is crying again, his beer going hot and his high melting in pools of sweat on the chair. What makes these protesters so willing to bare their bodies to the violence on its way? Mick doesn't know, but oh man he can taste their rage in his throat, feel it in his heart like a burning fever.

He just wanted to get high. So he wouldn't see this. To forget. But he can't.

KEN WILLIAMS

BARBARA'S STORY

My day was drawing to a close. My feet were hot and sore, my body tired, and I wanted nothing more than to go home to a cozy house, a glass of wine and warm food. But first I needed to finish my usual Tuesday's work schedule. On this day of the week, come rain, or as it was today blistering hot, I patrolled Santa Barbara's Farmers Market. But only after having stopped at the Salvation Army shelter and, also the main city shelter. I was not looking for produce but wounded humanity.

My job, as it had been for over twenty odd years and would continue for several more, was to be the social worker for the homeless—especially the disabled, which mostly consisted of the mentally ill, substance abusers, veterans and those beaten down by life. I was to secure them a bed at a shelter, disability checks, medical help or simply be a friend who cared about their well-being.

The crowd was thick with a lot of jostling. My mood turned sour. I don't like crowds. Also, at times the younger people who composed the bit players of this festival, with their unlimited credit cards and obsessively in possession of the most carefree and cavalier attitude simply rubbed me the wrong way. My issue not theirs, I reminded myself. Which simply made it worse.

Cutting through the crowd I made my way over to the end of the street. Looking up, I came to an abrupt stop. Sitting on a tourist bench in front of an upscale, hip restaurant/bar sat "Barbara." It was the popular kind of eatery with a fairly long bar with doors that opened to the street. Diner tables spilled out onto the sidewalk cutting into the flow of foot traffic.

Barbara hadn't been on my caseload long. Even though obviously mentally ill, she insisted that she could work and told me she was desperately looking for a job. Today, she wore the same ankle length, dirty white smock that she has worn since she had first come into town. Same dirt-encrusted bare feet. Dirty pillowcases, which held all her worldly possessions, lay scattered about at her feet. Somewhere she had procured a red sweater. Regardless of the heat she had put it on—backwards with the zipper in back. Seeing her in it added more heat to my already overheated body. I pawed at sweat that trickled down my forehead.

I stood quietly off to the side watching the boisterous crowd totally ignore her. It was like she didn't exist. The outside tables were packed. A line waiting to enter had formed at the entrance, feet away from her.

It was as if Sylvia Plath's bell jar had descended around Barbara. She took out a compact, looked into the cracked mirror and began to attempt to brush back her untrimmed and uncombed hair. Next she added too much rouge and too pale lipstick. Except for her clothes, and obvious state of extreme poverty and mental illness, she was like anyone else applying a few added touches of beauty while she waited for friends to join her. Done. Compact and lipstick tucked away into hidden folds of her nun-like dress. She looked longingly over to the joyful crowd with eyes both expectant and sad. She simply wanted to belong.

That day has stayed with me ever since. Barbara, one of many, taught me the painful aloneness that the mentally ill *and* the homeless live with: That they want nothing more than to belong—to enjoy life with good friends, good food perhaps, a night out on the town. Her longing looks scarred my heart that day. The memory of this beautiful woman has become a part of me.

Ж   Ж   Ж

POSTSCRIPT

A few years later the benches like the one that Barbara had been sitting on, which dotted the main street in Santa Barbara, would become a center of controversy when the city wanted to spend tens of thousands of dollars to uproot them and to replace the benches with something that would discourage the homeless from sitting on them. It was another salvo in the powers-that-be's ongoing war against those suffering from extreme poverty in this rich and sun-blessed city. Many in the so-called liberal community, including certain homeless advocates, merely found it objectionable that the city hadn't consulted with them first. When I was quoted in the local paper as opposing the idea it earned me the ongoing animosity of certain city officials and bosses within my agency. These developing battles were the beginning of the trajectory to my decision to finally leave my job. (Along with my protracted fight with the police on the unsolved murders of Ross, Michael and probably Gloria.) A heavy heart, countless dreams and the memories of honorable friends made amongst the homeless was my gold pocket watch after more than thirty years of having the honor of serving the homeless in Santa Barbara.

As for Barbara, I finally was able to get her in front of a Social Security judge after the government had denied her disability claim twice! This old, gruff man did his best to hold back his tears as we watched her fumble through her bags of "stuff," trying to prove that she was capable of work.

Barbara left the chamber. The judge, the stenographer and I were left alone. The judge looked over to me and said, "Where do you find these people? How?"

Barbara was granted disability and soon thereafter left the city. After I quit working for the department, the city decided to revisit the need to make Santa Barbara more homeless unfriendly. . . . The city could use a heart and soul such as this woman possessed.

MARK D. WALKER

MY LIFE IN THE LAND OF THE ETERNAL SPRING: THE COFFEE PLANTATION

Though I had lived and worked in Guatemala for seven years, it was a brief encounter with my young daughter, Michelle, on the San Francisco Miramar coffee plantation, perched on the side of the Volcano Atitlán that would determine my direction in life. It was a few days before Christmas, and I was strolling through the Big House when I came upon her in the living room. She stood, her feet planted on the orange tile floor, hugging her new Airedale puppy, Tiky, and gazing with wonder at the Christmas tree twinkling with colored lights and filled with handmade decorations. Below the tree, a number of brightly wrapped packages sat in contrast to the stark white walls. On the wall were a number of photographs of my wife's family members.

It was a perfect holiday moment until I noticed a dozen small children directly behind her pushed up against the screen door which opened onto the patio beyond. A soft evening afterglow highlighted the children, and I couldn't distinguish their faces behind the screen. They stood, dressed in simple cotton shirts, jeans, and flip-flops, silently peering into the room. These were the workers' children, who lived in little block homes below the Big House. The children were all so cute, so inquisitive, so innocent. None of them dared to open the door and come inside to join Michelle or touch the presents; they were relegated to peering in from the outside.

This scene would be branded into my memory as it represented the vast difference between the options open to these children in comparison to my daughter. Because I had married Ligia, the daughter of the *finca* (plantation) owner, Michelle was part of the family. Seeing the workers' children reminded me what it felt like to be on the outside looking in. I'd never be totally accepted by Ligia's grandfather and key family members, nor would I be invited to do anything but occasionally visit the plantation during holidays over the years, whereas generations of her family had lived on and developed this coffee plantation.

With mixed feelings of sadness, despair, and guilt, I kissed Michelle on the forehead, petted Tiky, and walked through the room and into a long hallway which led to a patio on the other side of the house. As I entered the porch, I found my wife relaxing in a wicker lounge chair gazing at the iconic green volcano, a slow mist covering its peak. I sat with her, asked one of the kitchen girls to bring a glass with ice, and settled in with a few shots of Johnnie Walker, Black Label Scotch Whiskey.

I told Ligia about the children peering into the room at the Christmas tree and Michelle with her puppy and she reminded me, "Well, all the workers' children were up here yesterday afternoon for the traditional Christmas celebration which included piñatas filled with multi-colored hard candies. They all drank water with cinnamon or a soft drink and were given a small bag of plastic toys. Some of the local musicians played the marimba. They had a great time."

Yes, I thought, *but what chances do they have of ever getting beyond the coffee plantation and making a real living on their own?* As a former Peace Corps Volunteer, my focus always started with the condition of the bottom of the rung of society—in this case the finca workers. In the past, at many coffee plantations, the workers would make a pittance and they'd be paid with finca currency which could only be used at the finca's own general store. So, what they could purchase was limited to what the store deemed necessary based on the finca owner's price system. The few plantations with schools only went to the elementary level, and their teachers often didn't show up for work. If they were lucky, some children would make it to sixth grade. Only a few ever made it to a public high school due to a lack of transportation or horrible road conditions. San Francisco Miramar did have a basic health clinic, but many coffee plantations didn't. The workers had access to clean water though some had to go to the river to bathe.

This contrasted with our daughter, Michelle, who attended a relatively expensive private school called La Asunción. She was picked up and let off by a school bus owned by a Spanish order of nuns. Michelle wore a nice, crisp new uniform and always brought home homework.

I realized that I'd always be looking from the outside in, whether on the coffee plantation or working in the highlands of Guatemala. I looked over at Ligia and said, "I'm going to contact my friends at CARE International and my Canadian missionary friend, Alan, and find out who needs help doing some good grassroots development work."

Ligia's response was immediate, "Can you make a living at that? Your pay at the Peace Corps barely paid for food!"

"Yes," I responded. "It will take years to gain the necessary experience and track record in order to work for an international relief and development group, but this is what I want to do."

"Well," Ligia responded, "you've worked in some of the most isolated parts of the country where none of my friends or family have ever visited and have your masters from the University of Texas, so maybe it's time to make a living at what you love the most—helping the kids who need a break."

"For sure. We might as well get some mileage out of those two years we spent in Austin so I could get a degree," I observed. "But I want our children to at least be aware of how lucky they are and to help out kids who aren't as fortunate."

Ligia's response was simple, but direct, "It's up to us to teach them to respect others based on how we treat them, in our home and community."

As the sun ducked below the ocean to the west, the volcano loomed before us, green, lush, and imposing. The mist had lifted and the fire flies began flickering around the many colorful flowers and plants in the finca garden and the worker's children began to walk down to their little homes. One mother called out, "Miguilito, why are you still up there? It's time for the *patrones* (finca owners) to have dinner."

I took Ligia's hand and squeezed it, "We're so lucky that Mariano (her grandfather) and "Coco" (her uncle) have always invited us to relax here at the finca. I've learned so much about life in Guatemala—the good and sad parts."

As I gazed up the side of the volcano, and took in the sweet aroma of the coffee blooms, I realized that the finca would not be the site of my life's work. My calling would be to join those of a like mind, working to assure that children of the most humble families would receive a decent education and aspire to a career of their choice and reach their true potential as God's children.

MARY KAY RUMMEL

CLASS FOR BEGINNERS

René, the van driver teaches us some Spanish, says,
La mitad de la naranja, meaning half an orange,
also meaning my spouse, my other half.
He wants us to stop halfway between
Panajachel and Antigua to shop at Paulina's,
a trap for tourists where we buy serapes
that we will never wear in public but they bring us
the comfort of the sixties and we know
sweet René gets a cut from the sale.
"The blue is good for you," he tells me.
The orange he holds up for Suzanne.

Seeing the beauty, learning to see
the world in which it lives

My mother used to say,
"See how the other half lives,"
meaning those who are not poor.
Now, Mother, I live in the other half
but I am finding it is no half,
only the tiniest tip of the orange
and all the rest are poor.
I like having money.
Can you tell me how to live my life?

I am searching for "la mitad"
the middle ground of guilt

At sixteen I worked part time
at the dime store with Rosita
who worked full time in yard goods,
all day cutting, and measuring cloth.
I went to her house to play cards
in the West Side neighborhood,
poorer than mine on Seventh Street.
Her husband swore in every sentence,
Jesus and *Jesus* and *Jesus.*

René is a teacher but makes more driving
for tourists—one thousand quetzals a month.
He's good at saying, *no es correcto,*
makes us practice conjugations.
When I ask, "What is a *llano?*"
he thinks I say "yawn," and we learn,
yo bastezo, ella bosteza, nosotros bostezamos.

Seeking a way to be closer to the world
and be less a part of it

I wanted to be like Jesus, was already poor,
had nothing to give away so joined the convent,
vowed to own nothing. Even the toothbrush
was "ours." We were given two habits to wear
but we were not hungry. Poverty was the easiest vow.

Searching for "la mitad"
the middle ground of guilt

A gift to be able to visit the home of Zoila,
a weaver in her Mayan village.
She shows us how to make tortillas
over the open fire and eat them hot and fresh.
When we walk up mountain the girls,
Lilian Maribel, Astri Sofilia and Arelisa,

they point out fields of squash, cilantro, beans.
We see farmers working on fields so steep
they are tied so they won't fall. Boys come down
the path with wood stacked high on their backs,
buenas tardes, buenas tardes.
Later, the girls sit at Zoila's new table,
and read to each other in the fading light.

*Seeking a way to be closer to the world
and be less a part of it*

When I was a young woman
I wanted to come to Guatemala
to teach in the mountains
in my black veil and heavy shoes.
When I left the convent I said
I'd never again wear those black shoes
but here I am walking in my time,
"the last half," walking the cobbled streets
of La Antigua wearing nun shoes
on my sore feet, the learner, not the teacher.
I am watching the hands of weavers,
trying to reach them as they move
red and orange threads across their looms.

*Seeing the beauty, learning to see
the world in which it lives*

*One thousand quetzals = approximately $120.00

THE NAME OF DESTINATION

On flying from LA to Minneapolis with two hundred
Hmong people migrating from a refugee camp in Thailand

If the edge has a look, this is it.

The grandmother who can't sit still
opens a plastic bag filled with food,
passes it to the young men and women
who hold babies in embroidered carriers
on their chests and on their backs.

Eyes, dark rings, cheeks, sunken, exhausted.
Nameless, wearing only the name of their destination
printed on white tags, they remind me
of how my great grandparents held their children
in steerage bunks on a heaving ship out of Ireland.

If jumping off happens, it is here.

After landing, a Hmong grandfather fingers
his bundle as he waits at the top of the ramp
for his family, brown eyes flickering.
He's wearing pink flip flops into a cold night
where fatigue, where snow, wind and maybe
a new history waits.

If the edge has a look, this is it.

I don't know what it means to be adrift in the world.
It's possible to forget who we are and what
country, what village we belong to, what bread
we eat and what we are named, as borders unstick
themselves and come together again.

The Hmong hill people buried the placenta
in the place where a child was born hoping
to bring her back at the end.
As if one could return from here to there,
living in one place and being in another.

If edge has a history, this is it.

ELIZABETH BURTON

DAY AND NIGHT

When Amangul's father invited Grace to an event at the local Xinjiang government center, she wasn't sure what to expect. He was president of the Uyghur part of the university, and therefore an important man in Kashgar. To invite her to see the private performance of a troupe of champion folk dancers was an honor not typically bestowed upon anyone outside government circles, so Grace gladly accepted. It was only as the event drew closer that she discovered Amangul wouldn't be among the attendees.

"It's only for significant people," Amangul had tried to explain. "Like my father; like you."

"But I'm just a teacher!" Grace said. "What's so significant about me?"

"You're American." To Amangul, that explained everything.

When the night arrived, Grace donned her best Western dress and took a taxi to the center. Usually, she either walked wherever she needed to go or took a donkey cart, but something told her she needed to arrive in a more glamorous fashion. And indeed, a uniformed doorman was waiting to help her out of the taxi and direct her to the event.

Feeling a bit of a fraud, Grace entered the plush auditorium she hadn't known existed before. Chinese women in evening gowns circled the room, selecting from a lavish buffet of fruits and Chinese food. Looking down at her own clothes, what her mountain grandmother would have called her "Sunday-go-to-meeting" dress, she almost turned around and left. But Amangul's father, a portly man in his fifties, appeared at her side.

"Welcome!" His smile was genuine and she relaxed a bit. "We have a seat reserved just for you." He took her elbow and steered her gently around the buffet table. "You're our honored guest."

"This is all a bit more grand than I was expecting," Grace said, indicating her dress.

"Nonsense! You look lovely; that blue matches your eyes." He touched the tip of her nose the way he would a child's, transforming her worried look into a smile. "I am glad my daughter has such a friend."

"Is this our guest?" A Chinese man Grace guessed to be in his forties suddenly blocked their way. She immediately mistrusted him, his manner so smooth she could have slipped on it. "I am Chang, the Deputy Governor." She could tell he assumed she knew the importance of his title, but she could only guess at the privilege that went with it. "It's lovely to meet such a pretty young American friend."

It was all Grace could do not to raise an eyebrow, but she smiled politely. "I'm pleased to be here." She turned to Amangul's father, who was still holding her elbow, "Thank you for inviting me."

"Ah," Chang said. "He did so at my direction, didn't you Abdulsalam?"

"That I did, sir. That I did." His tone was overly deferential, almost toadying, and Grace disliked Chang even more.

The Chinese man, though, didn't seem to sense her discomfort. His laugh was too loud, as if he were trying to make it carry through the room. "Come," he insisted, "Let's show this beautiful lady to her seat."

The men fussed over her while she settled into the chair, and she fought the urge to chase their hands away. Where there would have been a fancy rug to eat off of in Uyghur homes, here, Grace sat in front of a delicate table with a fine, red silk tablecloth. Instead of the traditional Chinese presentation of food, though, with selections served on a Lazy Susan turntable in the middle, Grace found herself surrounded by half a dozen small plates including all the selections from the buffet. She was grateful she wouldn't have to mingle with the women in the beautiful dresses.

Her relief was short-lived. An attractive young Chinese woman in an ornate Western-styled gown settled into the chair beside her. "And here is Miss Chao," Chang said. "Two lovely ladies dining together!"

"Hello." Grace smiled at the other woman and extended her hand. "I'm Grace."

The woman looked at her with what could only be disdain, but she took her hand. "Chunhua." Her "It's nice to meet you" was said in perfect English but with little enthusiasm. She reached into her purse and pulled out a pack of American cigarettes, offering one to Grace. When Grace shook her head, she lit her own with a tiny red and gold lighter. Grace swallowed a cough.

Chang and Abdulsalam were seated across the table from Chunhua and Grace. "Dinner first," Chang said, "and then, dancing!" *Dancing* was said with a flourish of his hands.

Throughout the dinner, Chang kept urging Grace to eat more of the Chinese food. Grace couldn't identify most of it, but she was proud of herself for at least trying everything. She ate more heartily of the local melons she was used to. Her favorite was a variety of melon which tasted just like the ripest cantaloupe she'd ever eaten, but was crunchy in texture.

Alcohol flowed freely, and Grace and Abdulsalam were the only ones who didn't partake. Despite her background in a teetotaling family, Grace wasn't against alcohol, as long as it tasted mild, or was hidden by the taste of something else, but the expensive looking brandy and scotch she was offered smelled too much like something she'd regret in the morning. When she refused the drinks, Chang snapped his fingers and someone quickly provided a bottle of a brand of Kentucky bourbon Grace recognized as the most expensive on the market. "From your homeland," Chang said with a smile. Grace shivered at the knowledge that he must have compiled a dossier about her; in a town where knowledge truly was power, he undoubtedly had dossiers on everyone in the room. He was gracious when she turned the bourbon down.

Chunhua proved to be a more talkative companion than Grace had expected after the chilly meeting, but only after she'd downed several glasses of a liquid Grace could smell even from her own place at the table.

"I've only been in this desolate place for a few weeks," she told Grace. "I was transferred here from Beijing." Grace learned she was a financial secretary with hopes of moving up in the Communist Party. "They told me my future advancement was dependent on my coming here."

Grace had heard that the Chinese government would pay handsomely to any Han Chinese family who was willing to move to the Wild West of the Xinjiang Province. In addition to financial incentives, there was an opportunity to be exempt from China's restrictive One Child policy. It was a campaign built on the idea that sheer numbers could solve the "minority" problem, that if the country's ethnic minorities didn't have places like Kashgar where they were actually a majority, then they would be more likely to assimilate into Chinese culture and less likely to keep demanding independence from China.

The problem with this well-constructed plan was that most Chinese had no desire to live where they might have contact with the minorities. Hence, the only solution was to forcibly transfer officials and families to the region. For Chunhua, this transfer was tantamount to a tragedy. "And what do you do?" she finally asked.

"Grace does admirable work with our underprivileged children," Chang answered, raising his glass to her. "She teaches at a school for Uyghurs owned by that American, Wanderline Andrews. Uyghurs from all over the city send their sons and daughters to her school for its emphasis on Uyghur culture and language. Even the children from the orphanage with the tightroping team go there. Do I say this right?" His smile was saccharinely sweet.

"You teach at a Uyghur school?" Chunhua said, after Chang was called away by a waiter who said he had a telephone call. Her tone was incredulous.

"I do," Grace said proudly. "I teach English there."

"But how can you stand it?"

"I don't understand."

"The children." Chunhua leaned in closer and lowered her voice with a quick glance at Abdulsalam, who was deep in conversation with the man beside him. "They *smell!*"

Grace laughed. "I think all children smell bad at one time or another. You just get used to it."

"No." She was insistent. "The *Uyghur* children. They *smell.*"

Grace finally understood, but she didn't know what to say. She was happy for the return of Chang, who at that moment, announced that the dancing was about to begin. Abdulsalam rose from his chair and made his way over to the wings of the stage. He disappeared behind a curtained-off area.

"See, Chunhua?" Chang's voice was affectionate. "There are good Uyghurs. Just look at Abdulsalam, a Party member if ever there was one."

The musicians took their places in chairs off to the side of the stage. Grace recognized her music teacher, Turghunjun, but he didn't immediately see her. The music began and Grace was transported into the past, as the traditional instruments Uyghurs have played for thousands of years made plaintive sounds. She wished her school children were there to listen; she imagined their faces quiet with delight.

Dancers in brightly colored costumes made their way onto the stage and the music became more raucous and quick. Grace was caught up in the dance, her breathing as fast as the music. It wasn't until she heard Chang speaking to the man beside him that the spell was broken.

"They're a beautiful people, I must admit. The women, in particular, are quite attractive, and a man is tempted to take them to bed. Take that one in yellow up there—I bet she's never had someone touch *her* in the right places. These Uyghurs pretend to be a pure lot, but I know from experience that they squeal just like Chinese women."

Grace felt ill. The girl who had caught Chang's eye couldn't be more than sixteen. She thought of her own experiences with her older cousin. *Let her stay a child.*

One of the dancers stepped to the edge of the stage. "There goes a tale," she said, "of three brothers. They were sent out to the world to seek their fortunes. The first brother found gold, the second brother silver, but the third brother found a musical instrument. When they returned home, their parents were thrilled with the fortunes the first two sons had won, but they called the third son a beggar and sent him away forever. He found a lonely glade and played his sad songs there until the Sun's daughter came to him and asked why he played such a lonely tune.

"'I am sorrowful,' he told her. 'I have spent three years learning to play my instrument, yet I have no way to make a living and my parents say I'm a beggar.'

"The Sun's daughter went away and told her father about the third son. 'Let him play for me,' the Sun said.

"The young man came and played his songs for the Sun. He played happy songs that made the Sun dance across the sky. He played sad tunes that made the Sun droop, lower and lower in the horizon until he disappeared and all was darkness. Finally, the Sun told the young man that He couldn't go on without the music the third son brought to him. Being wise, the Sun said that half the songs should be happy, and half should be sad. But because the sad songs left the people in darkness, he searched the sky until he found the moon to offer light when he was sad.

"This is the story of day and night."

The dancers began to move, telling the story with their bodies. Grace recognized the simple folk tune the musicians were playing as one Turghunjun had taught her. She looked over at Turghunjun and found him looking back at her with a smile. He motioned for her to come to him.

Grace thought for a second about her dress and how out of place she looked. Then, she rose from the table and went to Turghunjun. The musician next to him stood and handed her his khushtar. Grace sat down and began to play. She lost herself in the melody, her body swaying to the music.

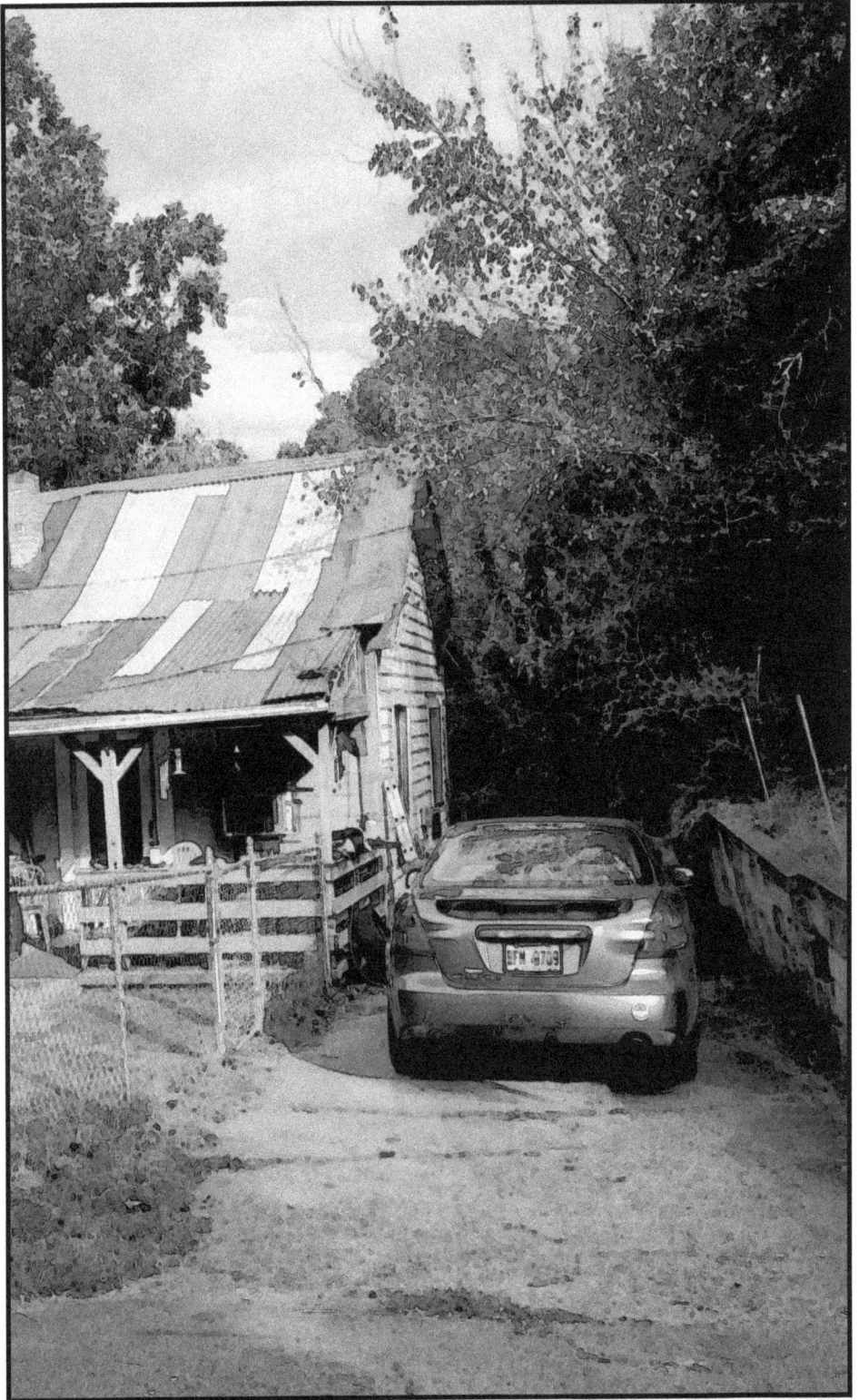

CHARLES D. BROCKETT

APPENDIX: SOCIAL MOBILITY & INEQUALITY

We have always known in the United States that we have had both rich and poor but the essence of the American experience has been the domination of society by our vast middle class. Supposedly this set us apart from the Old World and certainly from the newer countries of the developing world. Each generation could expect to be better off materially than the one before. With more hard work than luck, the enterprising could also climb up the social status ladder, perhaps even up to among the wealthy.

Such social myths take hold because they have roots in reality. Up until recently generational material progress had been the norm. Stories of social mobility are legion, including in this anthology. The U.S. indeed was once more egalitarian than Western Europe.

But as the evidence that follows demonstrates all too clearly, there have been dramatic changes in the United States across the last few decades: inequality has been increasing while social mobility has been in decline. One's chances of climbing the social status ladder are now better throughout much of the rest of the advanced industrial democracies than in the U.S.

As a society we are increasingly aware of serious strain between our myths and our social reality. Out of that strain comes change. We encourage you to not only consider the following evidence but to follow it back to its source materials. Share this information. Let's make some changes, let's make America more egalitarian again.

Increasing U.S. Inequality Since Late 1960s

**Inequality (Gini) in the USA 1929-2009
(gross income across households)**

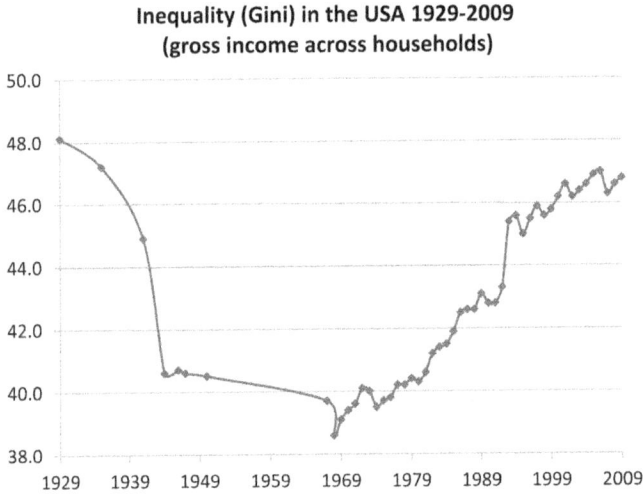

The Gini Index is the standard way to measure inequality: the higher the number, the greater the inequality. So, as this graph shows, inequality among U.S. households fell from its high point in 1929 through the New Deal (FDR) period and again with the Great Society (LBJ) in the late 1960s. Since then inequality has rather steadily increased to where this graph ends with 2009 (and has continued increasing since).

Source: Branko Milanovic, "Trends in global income inequality and their political implications." Autumn 2014. Web. Milanovic, formally the World Bank's lead research economist, is a senior scholar with the Luxembourg Income Study Center.

Making Less Than Our Parents

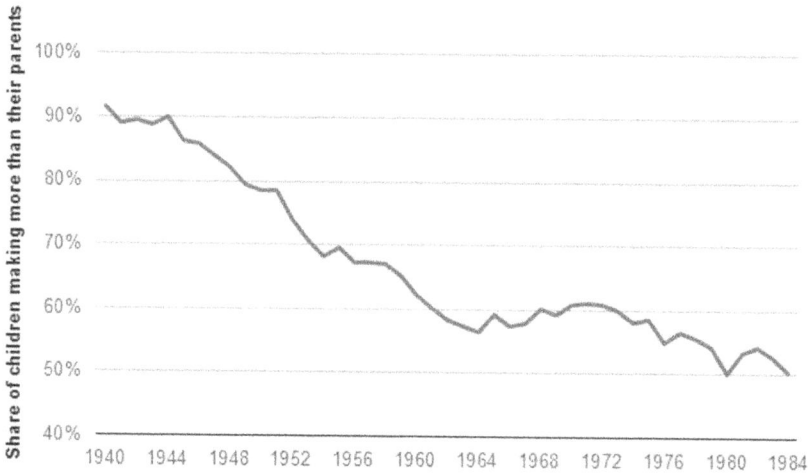

The standard American dream is each generation is better off than that of its parents. For children born in the early 1940s that has been overwhelmingly true: over 90 percent have had incomes greater in real terms (i.e., taking inflation into account) than their parents did at the same age. For those born in the early 1980s, however, only about one half have surpassed their parents income at the same age.

Source: Richard V. Reeves and Eleanor Krause, "Raj Chetty in 14 charts: Big findings on opportunity and mobility we should all know," Brookings. 11 January 2018. Web. A professor of economics at Harvard University, Chetty is a recipient of the Macarthur "Genius" Fellowship and the director of the Equality of Opportunity Project.

The Inheritance of Income Status

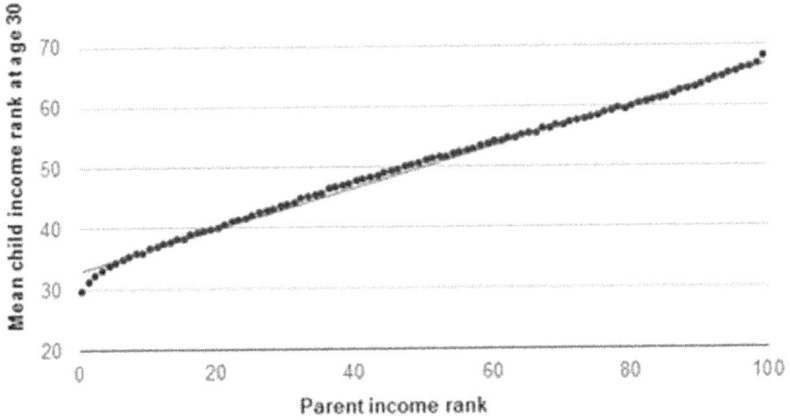

Nonetheless, there remains a strong connection between a child's income status (here measured at age 30) and that of their parents: the higher the parental income compared to that of everyone else (the bottom horizontal axis) the higher the child's income rank (left vertical axis).

Source: Reeves and Krause, "Raj Chetty in 14 charts."

College Attendance Depends on Parental Income

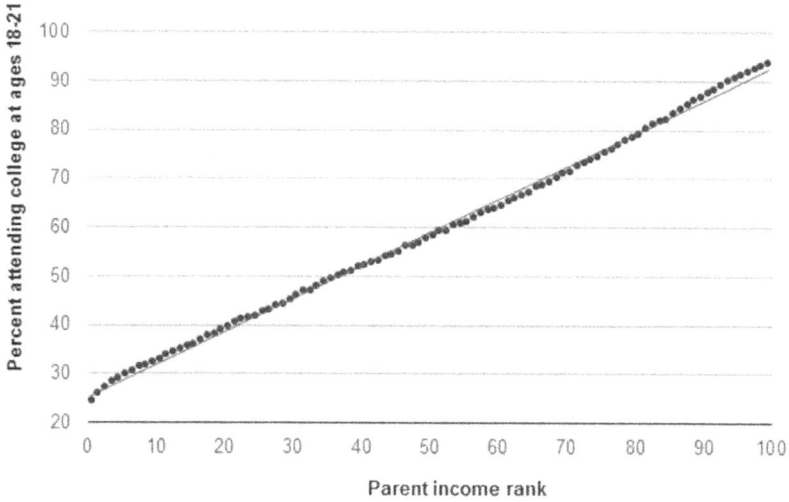

Going to college and especially getting a college degree are among the most important boosts to upward mobility. Unfortunately, the probability of being in college as a young adult (left vertical axis) is tightly tied to parental income, here shown as their income compared to that of everyone else (the bottom horizontal axis).

Source: Reeves and Krause, "Raj Chetty in 14 charts."

How Should Wealth Be Distributed?

Top 20%   2nd 20%   Middle 20%   4th 20%   Bottom 20%

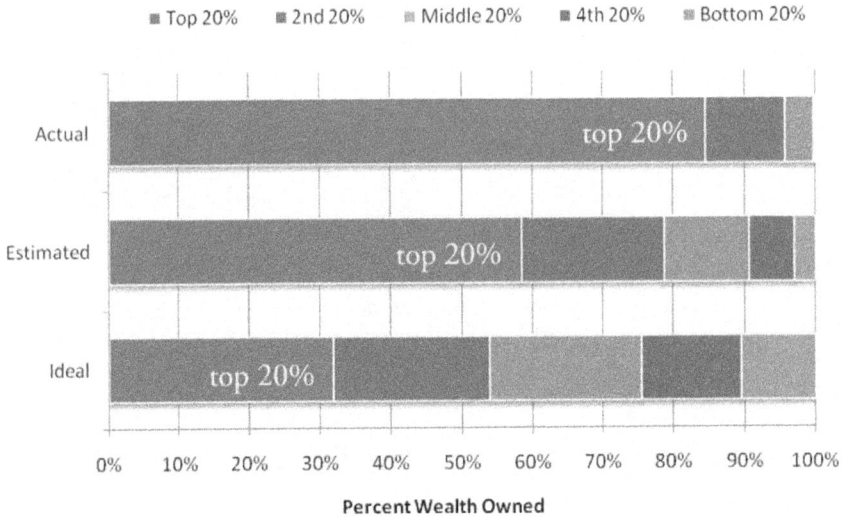

Percent Wealth Owned

A large representative sample of the U.S. public was asked in 2005 how they thought wealth *should* be distributed in the country (the bottom row, labeled "ideal") as well as what they *estimated* the actual distribution to be (the middle row). The top row provides the *actual* distribution. The top 20% actually possess about 85% of all wealth while the average estimate was about 58% and the ideal about 32%. Further analysis (not shown here) found little difference between Bush and Kerry voters concerning their ideal distribution or between those with less than $50,000 income and those with more than $100,000.

Source: Michael I. Norton and Dan Ariely, "Building a Better America—One Wealth Quintile at a Time," *Perspectives on Psychological Science*. 2011. 6: 9. Web. The authors are professors at the business schools of, respectively, Harvard and Duke.

The Geography of Mobility

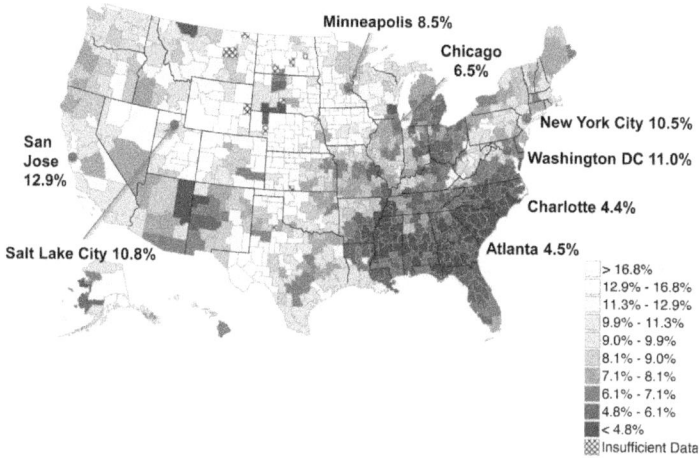

The lighter the color on this map, the greater the probability of upward mobility for some one in that area, more specifically, the probability of someone starting in the bottom 20% of the income distribution reaching the top 20%. Your chances for upward mobility, for example, are much greater in Iowa and Nebraska than in Georgia and South Carolina and almost three times greater in San Jose than in Charlotte.

Source: Raj Chetty, "Course Materials: Introduction and Geography of Upward Mobility." *Using Big Data To Solve Economic and Social Problems.* Stanford Center on Poverty & Inequality. Web.

Mobility Is Lower in the United States

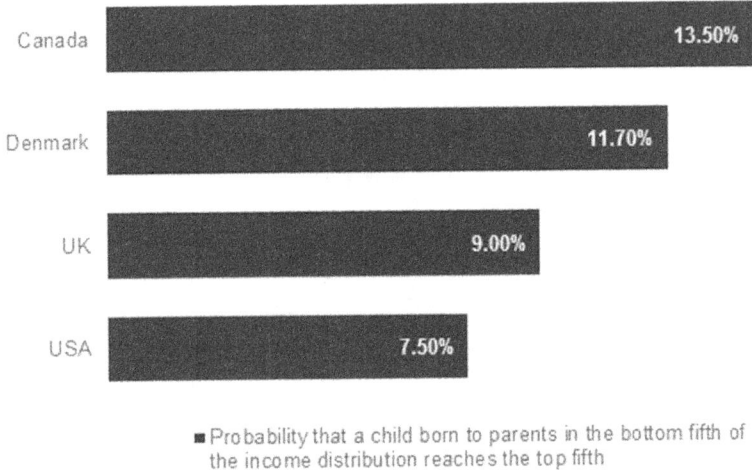

Canada ███████████████████████████████████ **13.50%**

Denmark ██████████████████████████████ **11.70%**

UK ████████████████████████ **9.00%**

USA ███████████████ **7.50%**

■ Probability that a child born to parents in the bottom fifth of
the income distribution reaches the top fifth

Using the same measure of mobility as the previous map, the probability of a person starting life in the bottom 20% of the income distribution reaching the top 20% averages only 7.5% for the United States as a whole (bottom row), about only half that of the probability in neighboring Canada (top row).

Source: Reeves and Krause, "Raj Chetty in 14 charts."

Inequality Is Why U.S. Has Lower Social Mobility

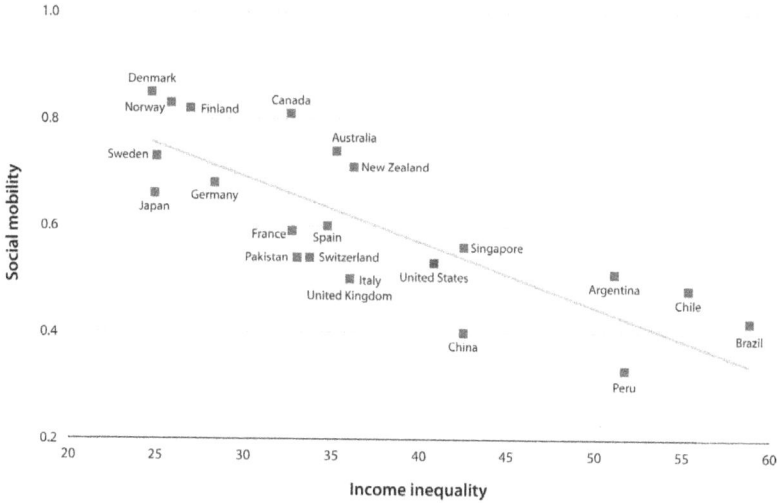

You can find the United States in about the middle of this graph. Social mobility (the vertical axis) is higher in many other countries than in the U.S., which falls at about the same level as not only Italy and the United Kingdom but also Pakistan, Argentina, and Chile. All of the countries with higher social mobility have less income inequality. Notice too that the U.S. has the greatest income inequality of the advanced industrial democracies shown.

Source: Michael Greenstone, et al., "Thirteen Economic Facts about Social Mobility and the Role of Education." Brookings Hamilton Project. Web. Greenstone is the Milton Friedman Professor of Economics at the University of Chicago.

Inequality Gives U.S. More Health & Social Problems

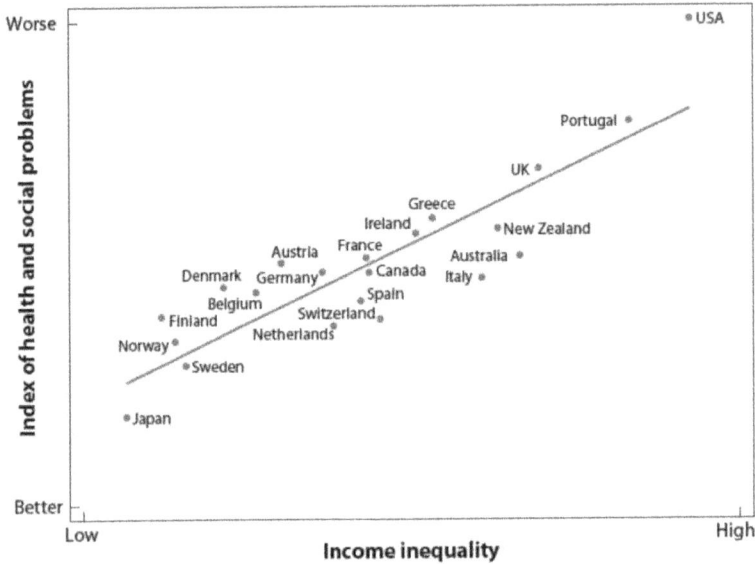

You might miss the USA on this graph—it is by itself in the top right corner with both the greatest income inequality and the most health and social problems of any of the almost two dozen countries included. The problems index combines data on: life expectancy, mental illness, obesity, infant mortality, teenage births, homicides, imprisonment, educational attainment, distrust and social mobility.

Source: Kate E. Pickett and Richard G. Wilkinson, "Income inequality and health: A causal review." *Social Science & Medicine*. 2015. 128: 316-326. Web. Both authors are leading British epidemiologists.

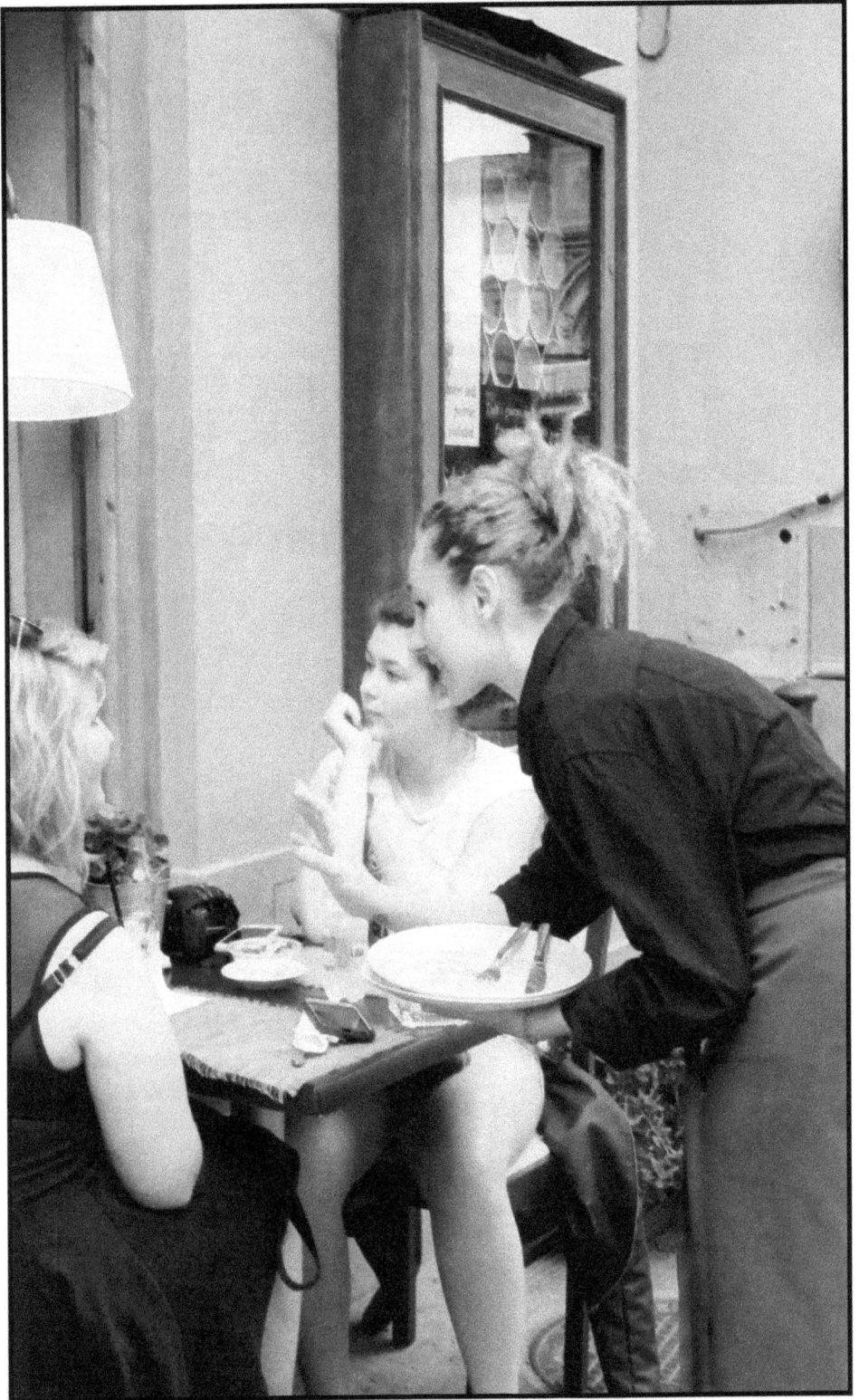

ACKNOWLEDGEMENTS

Danisa Bell's "Princess" was originally published in *Colere* (August 2017).

Maida Berenblett previously published "Looking at Upper Class" in *Making An Appointment With Yourself* (Health Communication, 1994) and *Moving* (Amazon, 2017).

Marian Mathews Clark's "My Study on Stay-Puts" first appeared in *The Sun* (1992).

Gillian Esquiva Cohen's "Our Kind" was previously published in *A-Minor Magazine* (2018).

Susan G. Duncan previously published "Schwinn" in *The GW Review* and *Soundings East.*

Lowell Jaeger's "Carney" and "Sounds Like Bombs" previously appeared in his *Or Maybe I Drift Off Alone* (Shabda Press, 2016).

Daniel Jaffe's "Hide and Seek" previously appeared in *Zone 3* (2006) and his *Jewish Gentle and Other Stories of Gay-Jewish Living* (Lethe Press, 2011).

John Laue's "A Teacher Speaks Out" was published earlier in *The Porter Gulch Review.*

Patricia Smith Ranzoni's "Cultural Guide" was previously published in her *Settling* (Puckerbush Press, 2000).

Mary Kay Rummel previously published "Class for Beginners" and "The Name of Destination" in her *The Illuminations* (Cherry Grove) and "Lilacs & Harley's" in her *Cypher Garden* (Blue Light Press).

Ada Jill Schneider's "Working Class" and "Privilege" were previously published in her *This Once-Only World* (PearTree Press, 2015) while "Views of San Francisco" appeared in her *Behind the Pictures I Hang* (Spinner Publications, 2007).

Heather Tosteson's "Target Fixation" first appeared in *Germs of Truth* (Wising Up Press, 2013). She created the photographs in this book.

Andrena Zawinski's "What They Told Us, What We Believed" first appeared in *Blue Collar Review Journal of Progressive Working Class Literature* (2011), "On the Road, Hijacked by Memory" in *Bloodroot Literary Magazine* (2013), "Women of the Fields" in the Thomas Merton Center's newspaper, the *New People*, and each is also collected in her *Landings* (Kelsay Books, 2017).

A special thanks to Kathleen Housley, Kerry Langan, and Michele Markarian for being such dedicated, generous, able and absolutely indispensable members of the Wising Up Writers Collective. We couldn't do it without you.

CONTRIBUTORS

Danisa Bell's fiction and nonfiction have appeared or are forthcoming in *The Penmen Review, The Diverse Arts Project, Colere, Storgy, daCunha Global,* and *Aji.* Danisa attended the Columbia College Fiction Writing Workshop (2001) and the Tom Bird Writing Workshop (2003). Most recently, she received her Creative Writing Certificate from Emory University.

Maida Berenblatt published a short story collection on Amazon in 2017, *Moving,* in which women move from fear and despair to hope and courage to discover a true sense of self. With her co-author, Alena Joy Berenblatt, *Make an Appointment with Yourself; Simple Steps to Positive Self Esteem* was published in 1994 by Health Communications and highlighted on *Oprah.*

Sarah Bigham writes in Maryland where she lives with her kind chemist wife, three independent cats, an unwieldy herb garden, and several chronic pain conditions. Her work has garnered two Pushcart nominations and appears in a variety of great places for readers, writers, and listeners.

J. Andrew Briseño is assistant professor of English and creative writing at Northwestern State University of Louisiana. His work can be found in *Smokelong Quarterly, Waxwing, Nat. Brut, The Boiler,* and other magazines. He is originally from Fort Worth, TX.

Elizabeth Burton holds an MFA in fiction from Spalding University. She has published short stories in *Roanoke Review, Waypoints,* and *Chautauqua,* and has stories forthcoming in *The Louisville Review, The MacGuffin,* and *Valparaiso Fiction Review.* She lives in Central Kentucky with her husband and two willful dogs.

Marian Mathews Clark graduated from Iowa's Writers' Workshop in 1987, the same year she won the Iowa Art Council's First Place Fiction Award. After retiring from The University of Iowa's Advising Center, she published *Sixty-Something and Flying Solo: A Retiree Sorts it Out in Iowa* (Culicidae Press). She grew up in Oregon but now calls Iowa home.

Gillian Esquivia Cohen has a BA in English and an MA in Bilingual/Bicultural Education. She is an elementary school teacher in Bogotá, Colombia.

Susan G. Duncan's poems have appeared in *Atlanta Review*, *Crack the Spine*, *Light*, *The MacGuffin*, *Soundings East*, *Thema*, and *Yalobusha Review*, as well as anthologies by Red Claw Press and Sixteen Rivers Press. She is a consultant to performing and visual arts clients, capping executive director roles with the Grammy-winning Chanticleer and California Shakespeare Theater, among others.

Katherin Hervey is a writer and filmmaker currently based in Seattle, WA. Her short fiction has been published online. She is also a former Los Angeles public defender and college instructor to people in prison.

Lowell Jaeger (Montana Poet Laureate 2017-2019) is author of eight collections of poems. Jaeger was awarded the Montana Governor's Humanities Award for his work in promoting thoughtful civic discourse.

Daniel M. Jaffe is author of the novels *Yeled Tov* and *The Limits of Pleasure*; the novel-in-stories, *The Genealogy of Understanding*; and the short story collection, *Jewish Gentle and Other Stories of Gay-Jewish Living*.

Murali Kamma is the managing editor of Atlanta-based *Khabar* magazine. His fiction has appeared in *The Apple Valley Review*, *Smoky Blue Literary and Arts Magazine*, *Rosebud*, *Lakeview International Journal*, *Eastlit*, *Asian Pacific American Journal*, *South Asian Review*, *Scarlet Leaf Review*, *The Missing Slate*, *The Wagon Magazine* and elsewhere. He has interviewed Salman Rushdie, Anita Desai, William Dalrymple, Pico Iyer and Amitav Ghosh, among others.

Judith J. Katz is the lead teacher for creative writing at the Cooperative Arts and Humanities Magnet High School in New Haven, CT, where her signature courses focus on writing poetry. Her work has been published in *The Muddy River Poetry Review*, *Edify*, *Of Sun and Sand* and others journals. She recently received an NEH grant to study Emily Dickinson.

John Laue, teacher/counselor, has authored five published books of poetry and one of prose. A former editor of *Transfer* and associate editor of *San Francisco Review*, he coordinates the reading series of The Monterey Bay Poetry Consortium, edits the online magazine *Monterey Poetry Review* and is program director for a local TV series, "Descendants of the Imagination."

Michele Markarian's fiction has been published in the Wising Up anthologies *Families: The Frontline of Pluralism*; *View From the Bed, View from the Bedside; Daring to Repair;* and *Creativity and Constraint*. Michele's plays can be found with Dramatic Publishing, Heuer Publishing, Smith & Kraus and Oxford University Press USA. Her play collection, *The Unborn Children of America and Other Family Procedures* was published by Fomite Press.

Nancy L. Meyer, avid cyclist, end-of-life counselor, and grandmother of five, lives in the San Francisco Bay Area. Journal publications include: *Colorado Review, Tupelo Quarterly, Bitterzoet, Poet's Touchstone, Persimmon Tree, Kind of a Hurricane Press, Indolent Press, The Centrifugal Eye, The Sand Hill Review, Caesura, Snapdragon, Passager.* She is also published in seven anthologies, most recently *Open Hands* (Tupelo Press).

Carl "Papa" Palmer of Old Mill Road in Ridgeway, VA now lives in University Place, WA. He is retired military, retired FAA, now just plain retired enjoying life as Papa to his grand descendants. A hospice volunteer, Carl is a Pushcart Prize and Micro Award nominee. His motto: Long Weekends Forever.

Mark Pawlak is the author of nine poetry collections and the editor of six anthologies. His latest book is *Reconnaissance: New and Selected Poems and Poetic Journals* (Hanging Loose Press). Pawlak's poems have appeared in *The Best American Poetry* and *New American Writing*, among other anthologies and journals. His work has been translated into German, Japanese, Spanish, and Polish. He lives in Cambridge.

Patricia Smith Ranzoni, born up the Penobscot River before the grid, descends from European settlers and indigenous peoples in what became Massachusetts/Maine and Canada. A retired educator, her unschooled poetry appears across the country and abroad, most recently in her twelfth title, *Still Mill: Poems, Stories & Songs of Making Paper in Bucksport, Maine 1930–2014* where she is poet laureate.

Mary Kay Rummel was poet laureate of Ventura County, CA from 2014-2016. Her eighth book of poetry, *Cypher Garden*, was recently released by Blue Light Press. *The Lifeline Trembles* won the 2014 Blue Light Award. New work appears in the anthologies, *Bright Light* (Bright Hill Press) and *Carrying the Branch: Poets in Search of Peace* (Glass Lyre Press).

Ada Jill Schneider, winner of the National Galway Kinnell Poetry Prize, is the author of four volumes of poetry including her most recent, *This Once-Only World* (PearTree Press 2015). She directs "The Pleasure of Poetry," a program she founded, at the Somerset Public Library in Massachusetts. Ada has an MFA in Writing from Vermont College.

Patty Somlo has published four books, including *The First to Disappear* (Spuyten Duyvil), which was a finalist in the International Book Awards, Best Book Awards, and National Indie Excellence Awards; *Even When Trapped Behind Clouds: A Memoir of Quiet Grace* (WiDo Publishing), honorable mention in the Reader Views Literary Awards; and *Hairway to Heaven Stories* (Cherry Castle Publishing).

Jane St. Clair has published over twenty-five short stories in various literary journals and anthologies, including in *SIBLINGS: Our First Macrocosm* from Wising Up Press. Her suspense novel, *Walk Me to Midnight,* was published in 2009. She lives in Tucson, AZ, with her upwardly mobile family.

Robert Stinson is an affiliate scholar at Oberlin College and emeritus professor of history at Moravian College. His novel, *Love and Death on Public Radio* (2014), takes advantage of the years he broadcast classical music on WDIY-FM (Allentown) and will soon be followed by *The Petrushka Problem.*

Donald R. Vogel holds a MA in English from Stony Brook University and has attended the Southampton Writers Conference. Don has published both fiction and nonfiction in several literary journals and is the chief development officer for the YWCA of the City of New York. He lives in Long Island, NY with his wife and son.

Mark D. Walker's *Different Latitudes: My Life in the Peace Corps and Beyond,* was published by the Peace Corps Writers Group. He's worked with CARE, MAP International, Make-A-Wish International and was the CEO of Hagar. His honors include the "Service Above Self" award from Rotary International. His wife and three children were born in Guatemala.

Ken Williams has been published both in America and abroad. He has populated his novels, poems and short stores with the peoples he met, many struggling with mental illness, substance abuse, devastating wounds of war. His novels are: *Shattered Dreams, A Story of the Streets*; *China White, There Must Be Honor,* and *Fractured Angel.*

Andrena Zawinski, born and raised in Pittsburgh, PA, veteran teacher of writing, and feminist activist, is features editor at *PoetryMagazine.com* and founded and runs the San Francisco Bay Area Women's Poetry Salon. Her recent poetry collection is *Landings,* and she has two previous award winning books. Her poems have received accolades for free verse, form, lyricism, spirituality, and social concern.

EDITORS/PUBLISHERS

CHARLES BROCKETT has a PhD from UNC-Chapel Hill and is a recipient of several Fulbright and National Endowment for the Humanities awards. A retired political science professor, he has written two well-received books on Central America and numerous social science journal articles and book chapters. With Heather Tosteson, he is co-founder of Universal Table and Wising Up Press and co-editor of the Wising Up Anthologies.

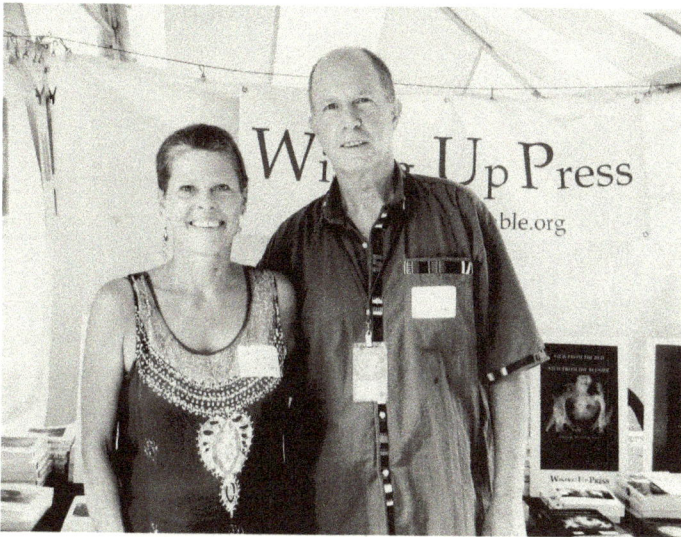

HEATHER TOSTESON is the author of seven books of fiction, poetry and non-fiction, including most recently the novel *The Philosophical Transactions of Maria van Leeuwenhoek, Antoni's Dochter*. She has worked in health communications with a focus on communication across disciplines, racism, social trust, and how belief systems develop and change. She has an MFA (UNC-Greensboro) and PhD in English and Creative Writing (Ohio University).

Visit our website and learn about our other publications, readers guides, and calls for submissions.

www.universaltable.org
wisingup@universaltable.org

P.O. Box 2122
Decatur, GA 30031-2122

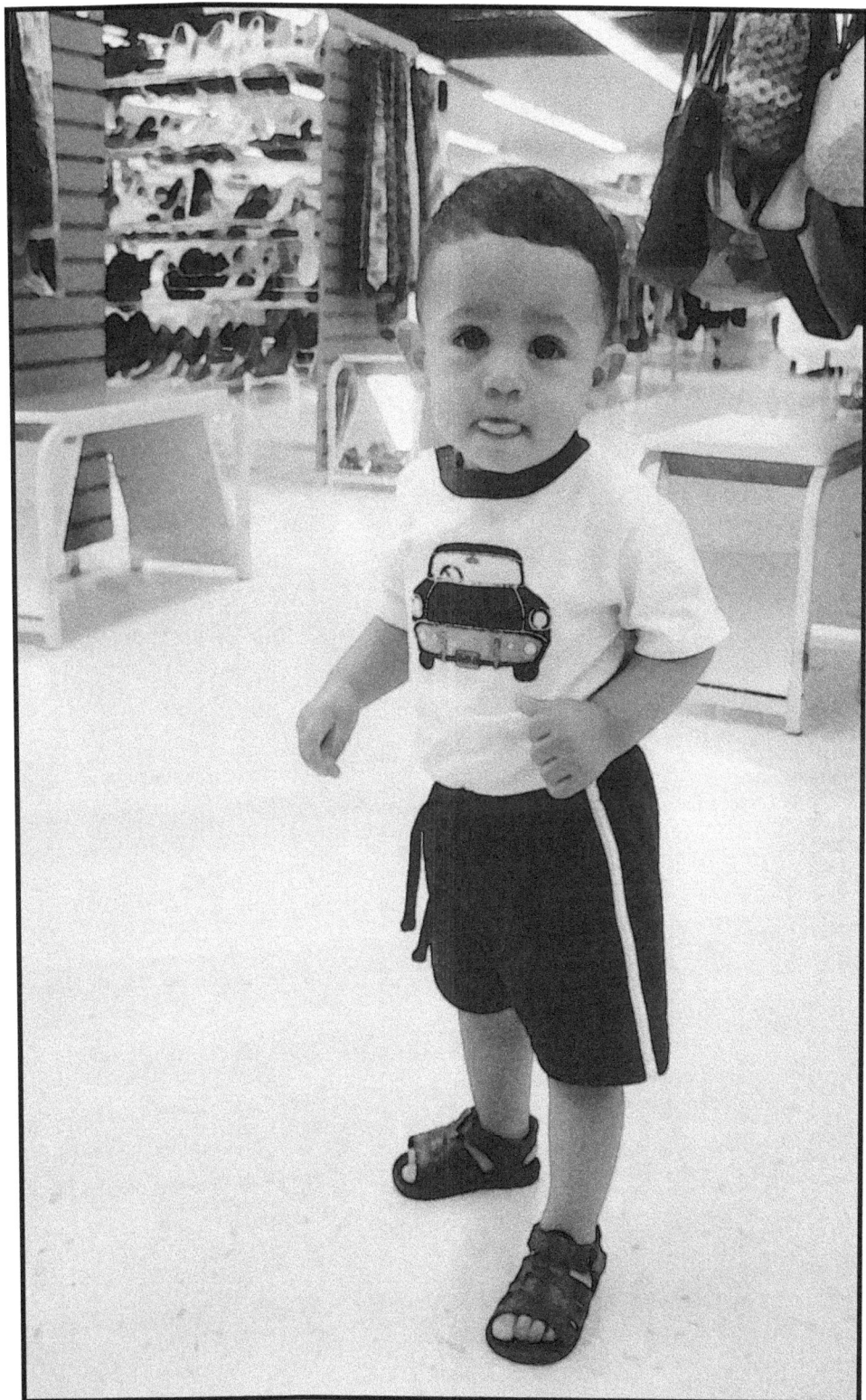

www.ingramcontent.com/pod-product-compliance
Lightning Source LLC
Chambersburg PA
CBHW031427270326
41930CB00007B/602